John Vickers

The Real Jesus

A review of his life, character, and death from a Jewish standpoint: addressed to

members of the theistic church

John Vickers

The Real Jesus
A review of his life, character, and death from a Jewish standpoint: addressed to members of the theistic church

ISBN/EAN: 9783337028565

Printed in Europe, USA, Canada, Australia, Japan

Cover: Foto ©Lupo / pixelio.de

More available books at **www.hansebooks.com**

THE REAL JESUS:

A REVIEW OF

HIS LIFE, CHARACTER, AND DEATH,

FROM A JEWISH STANDPOINT.

ADDRESSED TO MEMBERS OF THE THEISTIC CHURCH.

BY

JOHN VICKERS,

Author of " The New Koran," " The History of Herod," &c. &c.

WILLIAMS & NORGATE,

14, HENRIETTA STREET, COVENT GARDEN, LONDON,

AND

20, SOUTH FREDERICK STREET, EDINBURGH.

1891.

CONTENTS.

INTRODUCTION.

———◦◦◦———

TO MY FELLOW MEMBERS OF THE THEISTIC CHURCH.

IN submitting the following work to your kind
consideration and friendly criticism, it may be
well to report myself briefly, or let you know what
I am doing here, and neglecting to do for the
advancement of the religious reformation which we
have so much at heart. During the eleven years
that I have been perched on this hill overlooking
the ancient city which witnessed the introduction
of monk-worship by St. Augustine, I have endeavoured to instruct in a humble way, and to a
very limited extent, two classes of people—the
Christian population of the country, and those who,
like ourselves and the Jews, are compelled by
conscience to stand outside the pale of Christianity.
It is usual for religious teachers to confine their
attention wholly to people of kindred sentiment,
but the very few that can be found in this
neighbourhood to entertain our views, affords me
an ample justification for acting differently.

Moreover, it has always seemed to me that a person unfettered by sectarian prejudice has a right to instruct any portion of his countrymen, so far as they are willing to receive his instruction. If we go into a school or college, we shall see the pupils regularly grouped in classes according to their ages or gradations of progress, and it is not necessary that every teacher should be strictly confined to one class. He who is now giving lessons to youths or young men may presently do the same to children of tender age, if he only knows how to adapt his instruction properly to their capacity. A nation's religious or sectarian groups are in like manner distinguished, to some extent, by grades of intelligence, and though there cannot be anything like a regular exchange of pulpits maintained, a person who teaches voluntarily in one group may within certain limits very reasonably and conscientiously teach in another.

2. Christian teachers have always been conversionists rather than educationists; they have sought to change people's characters rapidly and entirely by some magical process, instead of trying to improve them gradually according to their growth and development. It is not surprising that some young ardent Theists should have Christian ideas of advancing their cause by proselytism and speedily transforming the face of the world. We cannot do much in this way, but even if we were able to achieve an immense success no great reformation would be effected. All the pupils of a school or college might be suddenly drafted into the higher class, yet such premature advancement would not conduce in any way to their benefit; the mental condition of the lower learners would, in spite of the higher rank conferred upon them, continue just as low as before. So, if persevering proselytism were in the course of a few years to bring the whole English population

into our communion, only a nominal change would thus be effected; there would be as much immorality as ever, as much ignorance, prejudice, and superstition, and the Theistic Church would be speedily broken up into as many discordant sects and divisions as are now seen to exist. In short, we should be imitating the rapid conversion of the Pagan world by the early Christians with very similar results; it would be soon found that we had introduced new names, symbols, and ceremonies, but had made no radical reform in the habits of the people. I never attempt to make converts all round, after the manner of Christian missionaries, and am convinced that what a person honestly believes or disbelieves is to a great extent the result of development. When an imprisoned chick is struggling to burst forth from its cracking shell into a world of light, you may assist it to good purpose, but not at an earlier period while it remains in a state of quiescence. In like manner, people may be properly helped to escape from the dark environment of superstition in which they have been reared, only when they have come to desire liberation, and are resolutely helping themselves. The Christians with whom I come in contact here experience at present no religious difficulties, and are wholly untroubled with doubts. It does not seem to me, therefore, right that these should be rudely thrust upon them so as to cause pain or perplexity: as long as the religious doctrine which they have imbibed suits their mental condition well it cannot be upset or parted from without hurt.

3. It is difficult to teach much when the neighbouring people, by reason of their prejudices, are not prepared to hear you, and those who would listen to you gladly and appreciate your instruction cannot be got at from their being sparsely scattered over the country. The majority of inquiring minds who

need such teaching as the Theistic Church is able
to impart, can only be communed with and helped
to some extent through the medium of literature,
and it is hard to get this diffused so that it
shall fall into precisely the right hands without
giving others offence. A benevolent Christian
gentleman is accustomed to distribute tracts in this
district, hoping that they may be productive of
good, and he occasionally leaves one at my cottage.
I never think of destroying or despising these
little missives, from their being thus unwittingly
misplaced, as some do, but endeavour to distribute
them afresh where they are likely to be treasured
and have a beneficial influence. And if Christians
would only have the kindness to pass on our literature in the same way to those who might be expected to appreciate it, the mutual help would be
profitable to all. Some of them seem determined
to do all in their power to prevent Theistic literature from circulating, under the impression that it
is only published for proselytising purposes, and as
a disturbing influence must necessarily do more
harm than good. So far as I am concerned, its
dissemination has not been directed to unsettle
people's minds, but to assist those already unsettled,
to re-establish themselves on a religious basis of
greater stability. My "New Koran" has never
been introduced to my Christian relatives, nor put
into the hands of any of the neighbouring people,
from the conviction that they are as yet wholly
unprepared for such a work. It would be wrong to
distribute it anywhere, or place it where it is not
wanted, just because most of those whom it would
really benefit are not immediately discoverable.

4. The letters which I send from time to time to
our local journals, as opportunity occurs, go quite
as far as it is safe to go in a rationalistic direction,
without so shocking the orthodox prejudices of the

people as to lose their respect and confidence. When Canon Fremantle was assailed here in 1887, on account of his "New Reformation" article in the *Fortnightly Review,* I wrote as many letters as the most liberal paper would admit in his vindication. More recently I sent a prompt reply to a clerical attack on Mrs. Humphry Ward's "Robert Elsmere," and it was politely returned, with apologies by the editor, who could not venture to give it insertion. The people of this neighbourhood must advance by short and easy steps if they make any progress at all; it would be well if they could only be delivered to some extent from their sabbatarian superstitions. During the wet harvest of 1881 I wrote to the *Canterbury Press* :—" If the disciples were permitted to pluck ears of corn on the sabbath, surely it is lawful for our distressed farmers to save their harvest on the day after the sabbath, yet however favourable the weather, they are, then, for the most part, prevented by superstitious fear from touching a sheaf. The two best harvest days which we have had in this district were the fine Sundays of August 28th and September 4th, both followed by wet Mondays. An abundance of corn was cut and fit to carry, and if the farmers had only set to work vigorously on those exceptional days, they might have had plenty of volunteer help, and would, doubtless, have saved, in a better condition than any that has yet been carried, a fourth of their crops." I further contended that people were as much bound to save their food from water as from fire on a Sunday, and mentioned how Archbishop Cranmer declared the refusal to do necessary harvest work on that day positive sinfulness. If my letters had been seconded by one or two from clergymen to the same purpose, a good effect might have been .produced ; but there was none willing to do this, and a Dissenting minister of

Canterbury wrote strongly in opposition to them, and upholding strict sabbatarianism.

5. The old spirit of sectarian bitterness is happily diminishing, but there is still a great deal of it in this place, and perhaps in most others; the people must acquire broader sympathies, and be made in various ways better Christians, before they can properly become Theists. You may frequently hear throughout the district, Dissenters abused by Churchmen, and Churchmen no less evilly spoken of by Dissenters. I invariably discourage these petty animosities, and endeavour, as far as possible, to get each party of detractors to cultivate a more charitable spirit, and recognise the good which is being done under other forms and rules than their own. It has always been my aim to recommend and help diffuse ~the best Christian literature— publications which are wholly free from bigotry and acerbity—as a means of making the various groups of baptised believers more friendly one with another and tolerant towards the rest of mankind. The opprobrium heaped on the Salvationists of late from so many quarters has been dictated largely by jealousy of their rapid progress, and is mostly undeserved. It must be admitted that their proceedings at Eastbourne, and other places, in defiance of the law, and apparently to seek the glory of martyrdom, are quite inexcusable. But these are very small faults in comparison with the vast amount of good which they have effected in reclaiming the immoral population of our large towns, and in view of their salutary arrangements to relieve the pent-up poverty of such places by migration and emigration.

6. In proportion as sectarian rancour has declined in this country, class hatred seems to have increased, and industrial questions have, unfortunately, risen to drive people into hostile camps

and set them at variance. At one time no right-minded person ever thought of stirring up dis-affection in a workshop and kindling strife between master and man; he would as soon have attempted to cause trouble in families and sow dissension between husbands and wives. It was not till craftsmen, with the introduction of machinery, got to be associated in large bodies that it became worth anybody's while to cultivate grievances systematically among them, and plead as their professional advocate. When an agitator now gets hold of a labour dispute, he has some advantage over the lawyer who foments private quarrels; he can go on humouring his clients, and promising them redress year after year, without having to attend a court and seek in the face of opposition pleading a judicial settlement. He thus obtains a permanent case, and can manage to have things all his own way; they pay him regularly, and are so satisfied with his one-sided advocacy that they do not believe it possible for anything reasonable to be said on the other side. It is just here that many working people especially want enlightening—want bringing educationally up to a higher standing ground so as to obtain the greater breadth of view which will deliver them from their present *ex parte* presumptiveness. The Labour Commission, which has been recently established, will help to accomplish this, and so will local Boards of Con-ciliation, and other attempts which have been made to deal with industrial questions in a judicial spirit; but much more will have to be done in various ways to promote sober discussion throughout the country, and moderate the bitterness of existing class strife. What I have been constantly saying as a peacemaker to intelligent artisans and labourers is this: "In any dispute between em-ployers and employed, the latter must not trust wholly to the impassioned harangues of their paid advocates, and presume, by reason of numerical superiority, to settle the matter by taking the law in their own hands. They are no more competent to judge their own quarrel than any individual disputant is allowed to be, and must bring themselves to listen patiently to the arguments advanced on the other side, and then submit the whole case to the judgment of their impartial countrymen."

7. In 1882 I wrote to several provincial journals —Conservative, Liberal, and Neutral—asking them to insert a series of letters under the heading of "Farmers and Labourers," the object of which was to reconcile to some extent and improve the relations between those two classes whom agitators had set at variance. It was my special wish to obtain in this way an open platform for discussing the objects aimed at by Agricultural Unions, and to receive no shelter from criticism. My letters, to the number of about twenty, were accepted and duly published in the *Hereford Times*, the *Norwich Argus*, the *Kentish Gazette*, and the *Kentish Express*. Some of them also appeared in the *Bucks Herald* and the *Wilts County Mirror*, and a summary of them was published in the *East Anglian Handbook* for 1883. What was advanced in this correspondence encountered some little opposition from Unionist agitators, and a Baptist minister who had taken up the role of an agitator; but the letters, which condemned wrongdoing on both sides, evidently had a beneficial result in clearing away much misapprehension, and helping to reconcile the parties which had been needlessly estranged from each other. In the autumn of 1889, a letter of mine was published in the *Canterbury Press* deploring the prevalent "Strike Mania" and its consequent injury to trade, together with the demoralisation which was being produced in the ranks of industry

by the New Unionism. The Rev. W. Blissard, M.A., Vicar of Seasalter, wrote in reply, defending recent strikes as a justifiable uprising of labour against capitalistic oppression. This gentleman declaimed much against what he considered the tyranny of economic laws, and the too great inequality of human possessions ; and the discussion which thus commenced between us lasted several weeks, when it was finally closed by the editor.

8. In disputing with Christians on any moral or social question where they seem to be at fault, I always endeavour to make the best of Christianity, just as I would make the best of Islamism in disputing with Mohammedans. My clerical opponent said in one of his letters, " Trades unionism in the past has procured justice for working-men where, alas, Christianity had neglected their claim." To this I replied, " It has always seemed to me that Christianity—as expounded and exemplified by its best teachers—enjoins masters and servants, employers and employed, to do their duty towards each other reciprocally, and encourages neither oppression on the one hand nor insubordination on the other. If people who are banded together in a great industrial enterprise would only keep in view the golden rule of doing as they would be done by ; if men would try to see things from the stand-point of their masters, and masters would try to put themselves in the places of their men, while they mutually cherished kindly feelings and a forgiving disposition, there could not well arise between them any serious or prolonged dispute. When a misunderstanding did occur they would be found calm and reasonable, so as to be easily reconciled by the mediation of a friend ; or, if that could not be accomplished, they would in the last resort agree to separate peacefully and form fresh engagements. But trades unionism introduces

another system, and quite contrary principles, for the regulation of those who are associated as profit-earners and wage-earners. I have nothing to say against its good features, its mutual aid and provident arrangements, and only object to it as an organization for industrial war. Those who would see it in its true aggressive character should read the reports of the Government Commission of 1867, and all the details of the terrible barbarities perpetrated at Sheffield and Manchester, where low wages could not be pointed to as a justification. Its unscrupulous leaders, with the view to their own advancement, did their utmost to instil hatred, malice, and revenge, into the minds of the working people, and render anything like a reconciliation with their employers and the establishment of friendly relations impossible. . . . We are now told that this terrible strike and outrage organization has surpassed Christianity in procuring justice for working-men, although industrial freedom has been completely trampled under foot by it, and it would be hard to show where there exists in the modern world a more atrocious system of injustice. Preachers who talk of 'justice for working-men,' should at least have a word to say in behalf of those poor ill-used labourers, who, from no fault of their own, are stigmatized as 'blacklegs,' and not permitted to follow their lawful avocations. We know it is not safe to assume that popularity hunting priests who beg ostentatiously for bands of tumultuous strikers, are all like the priest and the Levite of the Gospel, and indifferent to the wants of the deserving poor, but the latter at any rate suffer from the misdirection of alms, and are doomed in consequence to receive less. I have never hesitated to denounce tyranny of every kind, whether practised by the rich or the poor, the few or the many; also the indulgence in luxury, to say nothing of riotous excess—a moral failing by no means confined to one class—but when your correspondent speaks of working-people having 'felt the grinding pressure of the economic law,' he is, in common with the Socialists, fighting a giant phantom of his imagination. We are all bound to study the economic law, just as much as the law of gravitation, and strictly conform to it, or we must suffer in consequence. The labourer is worthy of his hire, he is worthy of what he bargains for, and the seller of any marketable produce is worthy of his price, and ought not to be at any time defrauded. But if a person seeks to deal commercially with his fellows, where his goods or his services happen to be in little demand, he will of necessity be poorly remunerated, just as the disciples from casting their nets in a wrong direction 'toiled all the night and caught nothing.' A sensible Christian minister, instead of encouraging people, under these circumstances, to murmur at their fortune, and justifying their resort to acts of violence against innocent competitors, would surely give them good counsel and guide and assist them to take, in future, such wiser steps for advancement that their efforts might be reasonably crowned with success."

9. Soon after the close of this newspaper controversy, the Hon. W. H. Fremantle, Canon of Canterbury, wrote inviting me to read a paper at a conference which would be held at his house April 22, 1890, to discuss the subject of "Christian Socialism, or the Labour Question viewed in a Christian light." I respectfully declined the invitation, but he wrote again, and subsequently called upon me, saying that they should be much benefited by having an expression of my views. It became necessary now to announce my religious opinions and ask if they would not disqualify me

from attending a Christian conference. He seemed surprised at my being a Theist, but still thought that I might very properly attend the meeting, and was well fitted on a subject of that kind to confer with Christians. I was induced, therefore, to prepare a paper, and at the time appointed presented myself at the Canon's house, in the Precincts, where a number of clergymen and laymen were collected. Three papers were read at the conference besides my own—the first by the Vicar who had recently disputed with me in the *Canterbury Press*, the second by a Wesleyan minister, and the third by a layman. These gentlemen were apparently in substantial agreement as Christian Socialists, they all seemed from their remarks to go beyond the Maurice and Kingsley school and to be well up in line with the Rev. Stewart Headlam. My own paper disavowed communistic aspirations and the reduction of familyhoods to brotherhoods, and was simply a plea for such practical socialism as would check iniquitous selfishness and bind all classes together in greater friendliness and harmony. In the discussion which followed, two clergymen made some sensible remarks warmly sympathizing with the poorest labouring class and manifesting a disposition to promote social reform rather than to take up with revolutionary socialism. Other speakers denounced capitalism and were led away by the current utopian theories of a reconstructed world; one of them declared that socialism had a scientific basis, so that it was bound to prevail in time, and advised all who were present to procure and read the publications of the Fabian Society. One clerical member of the conference contended that property belonged to the community rather than to individuals, and declared that the great socialistic formula: " From each according to his abilities, to each according to his needs," was in his opinion altogether just. No resolution was passed, but the majority of those present seemed to be decidedly in favour of a communistic form of socialism in agreement with Christ's doctrine and the example of the primitive church.

10. My old opponent, the socialistic vicar of Sea-salter, who was present at this conference, soon afterwards attended the Diocesan Conference of Canterbury at Lambeth Palace, where "The Church's Duty in regard to Labour Disputes" was the principal subject of consideration. He reiterated on this occasion his levelling views, and was, in consequence, severely called to account by one or two lay members present, but did not receive the slightest check from the Primate, who seemed bent on trimming his sails to catch the popular breeze. Very recently Mr. Blissard has published a work entitled " The Socialism of Christianity," the drift of which may be pretty well gathered from the following extracts :—" Taking note of the vast wealth of the country, those whose labour helps to produce it are claiming to receive a larger share as the just reward of their labour ; they want to see a more equitable division of the world's goods." "Thus the foundation principle of all Socialism is co-operation and equity in dividing out the good things wherewith Providence has blessed the world." "This love of riches is thoroughly unsocial. Riches can only be heaped together at somebody else's expense." " What one man has gained another man has first lost. What is added to the rich man's ample store has been taken out of the poor man's empty cupboard." " The man who girds himself to amass a fortune is doing the exact opposite to what Christ commands, for he is making himself rich by making others poor." " A fortune can only be made out of the misfortunes of others.

A

When a man makes money, as it is called, he does not really make it; others have earned it, and he has been enabled by law or by circumstances to appropriate their earnings to his own use. So far the well-known phrase of Proudhon, '*La propriété est le vol*,' expresses a Christian truth. There is robbery in what has been unjustly acquired " (pp. 8–66).

11. This levelling parson, owning besides his benefice two farms in the neighbourhood, could not play the part of a second John Ball if he were disposed to do so, since his practice has always been strangely at variance with his preaching, and he is for various reasons one of the most unpopular ministers in Kent. Even had he been a more consistent Christian Socialist, the working men of this district are for the most part too intelligent and sensible to believe in his doctrine, that fortune-making is a sin, that the accumulation of wealth in business is of the nature of robbery. They know well that in a great community where the majority of people are improvident, incapable of saving when they have the means of doing so, it is well that there should be a few persons of an opposite character able to acquire and store wealth greatly in excess of their individual needs. Funds are thus provided to pay labourers and carry on various works conducive to the general welfare which would otherwise never be accomplished. Here and there a case of churlishness and oppression may be pointed to, but so far from robbing the poor whom they employ in a general way, the provident class give them wise direction and enable them to earn more than it would be possible for them to earn when working independently or in co-operative association. Prohibit the accumulation of large capitals, and there can be no large employers, the rate of wages must in consequence be rapidly reduced throughout the country, and the poor working class, instead of

finding their material condition improved, will only sink into greater poverty. Many labourers at Seasalter, who find it hard to get work throughout the year, would like nothing better for the brightening of their prospects than to see some enterprising millionaire come into the parish.

12. The Vicar of Seasalter does not profess to be a strict communist, but he is constantly declaiming against covetousness, "great inequalities," and what he considers the sin of accumulating much wealth. "We know, as a matter of fact," he says, "that many do amass large fortunes, far beyond what is required for reasonable wants. . . . . They have not been content with enough; they have striven to gain more than enough; in raising themselves they have depressed others" (p. 67). A man who becomes rich by persevering industry and thrift is thus supposed to be akin to the swindler and the thief. Most reflecting labourers know better than this—know that it is impossible for a person to make a large fortune in any useful profession or trade without conferring proportionate benefits on the community. People would soon cease to deal with him or serve him by agreement if the gains effected were entirely or too much on his own side. In the early part of the century there lived here in Canterbury a poor lad, Sidney Cooper, who, being passionately fond of drawing, managed, after awhile, to earn a living as a painter, and has now become a wealthy Royal Academician. Another such talented youth of this place, after acquiring, in a servile position, a good knowledge of medicine, emigrated to Melbourne, where he practised the healing art with so much success, that he has recently bequeathed £10,000 for the purpose of establishing a Working Men's Institute and Free Library in his native city. If these men had been content to

earn less, so as to have just enough to live on, the
public would, by reason of the fewer pictures
painted and the fewer patients healed, have suffered
proportionate loss.   And it matters not whether a
person acquires a fortune by his own skilful hand,
or by organizing and directing the hands of others
as a good industrial captain, he is equally a benefactor of his fellow men; in raising himself, he
does not depress those about him, but helps to
raise them too, and add to his country's prosperity.
Christian Socialists contend that employers, instead
of making fortunes, should regularly share their
profits among their workpeople; but in that case
the losses which they are liable to must also be
shared, and such a regulation would not be advantageous to the wage-earner who wishes to be
secured against risks.   And if all employers were
to allow those working for them to share their
profits without their losses, their capital and the
whole national wealth would be speedily reduced,
the cost of production would be enhanced, every
article of consumption would become dearer, and
the industrial population would soon find that
what they received extra with one hand they would
have to give away with the other.

13. If rich families persistently rob poor families
with whom they have commercial transactions, as
Mr. Blissard makes out, the same charge must of
course be brought against wealthy nations, and
England ought to send a great amount of her
hoarded gains to Ireland, Spain, Turkey, Russia,
and other poorer countries, with whom she is
accustomed to deal, so as to reduce the present
disparity in their circumstances.   Very few English-
men would be got to approve of this " more equitable
division of the world's goods," but that is what
socialising on the communistic principle must come
to if consistently carried out; and the process of

levelling down more and more to get rid of hated
inequalities must soon lead to universal impoverish-
ment. Supposing we determined, by some foolish
legislative measure, to distribute wealth more evenly
only just here at home amongst ourselves, it would
lead to very similar results. The more energetic
and enterprising people, on finding that they must
soon surrender a large portion of their honestly
acquired possessions, would get away to other
countries where they might reap the reward of their
industry, thrift, and good business talent without
disturbance. On the other hand there would flock
in here an immense swarm of poor hungry
continental Socialists eager to share in the general
distribution or communisation of goods, and the
deterioration of character and discouragement of
individual effort thus brought about would soon
reduce the whole country to a condition of beggary.
If the vicar of Seasalter stood alone among the
clergy as the advocate of a demoralising and ruinous
equality, it would not so much matter, but it must
be borne in mind that this gentleman was put into
his present position by the Dean and Chapter of
Canterbury, that the Archbishop has recently
listened to his revolutionary declamation with a
silence which was supposed to imply approval, and
that Bishop Mitchinson has written an introductory letter for the purpose of recommending and
promoting the circulation of his book. Instead of
seeking to enlighten the poor working people who
have been misled by agitators, and directing them in
the true path of social advancement, many prelates
now imitate the agitators in pandering to their
prejudices, and, like unscrupulous politicians, are
constantly bidding against rival parties for the
Labour vote. The Conference at Canon Fremantle's
and the subsequent Diocesan Conference at Lambeth
Palace, have greatly strengthened my conviction

that the errors of Christianity with which we are now called upon especially to deal are not theological, but *social*. Hundreds of popular preachers have almost renounced the former only to take up more strongly with the latter, and the Theistic Church will have to meet them fairly and squarely in this change of front and treat their socialistic illusions as it has treated those of their theology.

14. It must be admitted that I have not been able to do much good in this neighbourhood as a missionary among Christians, trying to mend them a little and lead them on truthwards by easy gradations as far as they would go, but I should have effected still less good by confining myself wholly to the instruction of Theists. To do this it would have been necessary to establish here in some way or other a small congregation, and for such a work I am far from well fitted, having never been a good oral teacher, while being now so near sighted as to be unable to recognise people at a few yards distance. And had I the powers and experience of my younger brother, who is a preacher in the Wesleyan body, little could be done in this quarter for the gathering of people favourable to our religious reformation. Dr. Cyril Greaves, of Blean, formerly a clergyman, tried during the summer of 1887 to establish a Theistic congregation in Canterbury, but with the most discouraging results. He hired a large music-hall for a month, and his religious services were well advertised, but very few persons could be induced to attend them either from sympathy or curiosity. I went to the last meeting to estimate the prospects of the movement, and took the opportunity to distribute some of Mr. Voysey's Sermons among those who were present and likely to appreciate them. No minister could be expected to go on preaching gratuitously, and

paying for the necessary building accommodation to do so, while meeting in the way of attendance such little encouragement.

15. It would be very gratifying if we had a few more such men as Mr. Rowland Hill, of Bedford, to establish Theistic congregations in the largest provincial towns, where there is a reasonable prospect of their being well sustained; for many scattered Theists at present greatly need instruction, together with the sympathy and encouragement which are derived from association with kindred minds. But it seems to me neither practicable nor desirable that we should go on forming groups of rational religionists throughout the country to the same extent as has been done by the Unitarians. The Theistic Church would thus become in a little while nothing better than a sect, and what we ought rather to labour for is the utter breaking down of the barriers of sectarianism. For a Church to be of real service to the country in which it has arisen, it must not merely draw apart a few intelligent and moral people so as to constitute a respectable club, but must to some extent lay hold of and help to lift the unenlightened masses. I once heard an Independent minister denounce the Unitarians as a useless body: he said they did nothing whatever towards reclaiming and elevating the heathen population of the country, and only got their congregations by enticing good people away from other churches. He seemed to me to be under the influence of strong prejudice; but there is still a certain amount of truth in the reproach uttered, and it is likely to be directed for the same reason against congregations of Theists. Unitarians are in general very philanthropic and well disposed to instruct the poor and ignorant, but these cannot be got to come up to their level, or led to appreciate the superiority of a rational form of

Christianity over those which are emotional or sensational. Some of them have on this account been induced to condescend to lower orthodox levels that they might thus find listening crowds and acquire as teachers a greater sphere of usefulness. Mr. J. Goulden, of Blackfriars, Canterbury, told me some time ago that although a sincere Unitarian he no longer attended the neighbouring chapel of that communion, but went in preference to a Church where he could engage in Sunday School work and help to improve the rising generation. Probably several others who once went to the chapel have been induced to leave it in the same way without forsaking its principles, and this would account for the congregation's decline. The sectarian spirit which brings kindred minds together in close fellowship is everywhere getting weaker, and people of generous feelings are disposed to go not where they can get the most sympathy, but where they can do the most good. The Rev. J. Moden, a minister of decided talent, who preached in this chapel a few years ago, is now, for the sake of exercising more influence on his countrymen, a clergyman of the Established Church, and I have reason to believe that he retains as strongly as ever his Unitarian convictions.

16. Where people, who love to climb as reformers, thus lower themselves in an orthodox direction from no selfish consideration, but solely with a view to have a larger educational field and raise more effectively their ignorant and erring countrymen, no blame can be attached to them. It has often seemed to me, however, that they might take with advantage a very different course for the purpose of reaching and elevating a portion of the masses who are suffering from neglect. There are large numbers of working people in this country who attend no place of worship, not because they are

sceptical, but because they are in a Christian sense
rather irreligious and the usual church and chapel
services are to their minds very unattractive. They
believe in God, but not in theology, and much
preaching, praying, and praising is a weariness to
them—it fails to interest them or produce on them
a permanent salutary influence; and as they are
not of an excitable temperament nor greatly troubled
with superstitious fears, the Salvation Army entirely
fails to make any impression on them. Yet this class
of working people need instruction in the economy
of life as much as any other class, and they are
willing to be instructed by those who study their
mental constitution and are reasonably accommo-
dating to their tastes and their intelligence. In
the course of a Sunday walk I am accustomed to
meet occasionally with solitary labourers and small
groups who want no one to preach to them and seek
their conversion, but are glad to be spoken to in a
friendly manner and to get information on any
subject that interests them or is clearly connected
with their well-being. Now and then their minds
are burdened with some special trouble, and a
little timely sympathy, together with advice as to
what course should be taken with the view to mend
matters, is sure to be very thankfully received.

17. These poor men, who regularly absent themselves from religious services and have not much
of the devotional spirit, would readily accept good
moral and social teaching on a Theistic basis. I
have had serious thoughts occasionally of inviting
a number of them to assemble at an old barn so as
to hold a Sunday meeting, and should have done so
ere now if sufficient time could have been spared
for the purpose. A meeting of that kind might be
very properly opened with a short prayer and a
hymn. As news is always well relished, I would
then recount to the audience not the crimes and

horrors of the past week, but some of the most
commendable deeds which had been done and
improvements which had been effected, whether
in their own district or elsewhere. Instead of
giving them a *sermon* for their edification they
should have an authentic *tale*, showing how worthily
some people have acted in resisting temptations
and overcoming difficulties in circumstances similar
to their own. Tales of this description are not at
present sufficiently numerous; it is much to be
desired that Mr. Smiles and some others equally
competent should add to our biographical literature
" The Lives of Labourers." Many estimable men
in this humble rank, to whom attention should be
directed and who ought to be held up as permanent
patterns of great worth, are continually suffered to
pass away into oblivion. At the close of the meeting I would endeavour as far as possible to give
any special information that might be required, to
heal any dissensions that might exist among the
audience, and to soothe and help those who were
suffering from trouble. Possibly some kind of free
labour agency might be established as an adjunct
for the benefit of those who might be wanting employment or seeking re-engagements. It is not to be
expected that all Sunday meetings should take
precisely this shape which I am suggesting; they
might be varied in many ways according to circumstances and still be productive of good, and it may
reasonably be assumed that they would be attended
by one-third of those who find no attraction or
profit in the present religious services. Unless,
after a reasonable period of preparation, we of
the Theistic Church can thus manage to reach and
beneficially influence a portion of the working
population that is entirely lost to other churches,
we shall have no solid ground to stand upon, and
all the arguments and theories which we may choose

to advance will be very naturally treated with contempt.

18. We who are engaged in helping on the work of religious reformation in this country have need of great patience, for we must necessarily encounter a good deal of hostility and make slow progress. Not only in religion but in all other conventional systems which have been long established it is hard to get unreflecting people to entertain the idea of making any change for the better. Many of our country roads are laid out with no more judgment and regularity than the rabbit tracks which wind hither and thither in a wood. In years gone by, when tramping wearily from place to place in search of employment, I often felt disposed to murmur at the waste of land and waste of labour resulting from the crookedness of roads, and to wish for some authoritative power to effect their improvement. I now look out from my window every morning on roads that could be made straighter and better at comparatively little cost, but the majority of the neighbouring people have become so accustomed to their defects and inconveniences that they scarcely deem them such, and cannot be got to consider seriously any proposals for their correction. Then, again, the anomalies which exist in our language and in all languages have come from blind unreasoning imitation and not from design, and, if people could only be brought to take united action, might be reformed away with immense advantage. But these irregularities, however awkward and troublesome to the learner, are pretty sure to be looked upon with favour and respect when once they are learned. The generality of people get so much attached to their old familiar word-forms that any suggestion to alter them with the view to securing greater regularity and economy in the expression of our

thoughts they resent as an uncalled-for innovation. A religion gets established in much the same manner as a language; the theologians, like the grammarians, insist on the most prevalent usage being taught authoritatively as right and orthodox, no matter how unreasonable. And the more completely a people are thus drilled into the same crooked uniformity of practice the stronger is their attachment to it, the greater is their confidence in its soundness, and the more difficult becomes the task of those who see defects in it, and try to introduce beneficial reforms. Resistance to religious progress is further strengthened by superstitious fear; it is supposed to be not only strange, eccentric, presumptuous, but positively sinful to depart in the slightest degree as truth-seekers from the conventionally established belief. The position of orthodoxy is secure enough on its basis of educational prejudice without this further support, nor is there any need that it should be continually fortified afresh by the writers of apologetics. Let us hope the time will soon come when orthodox theologians will be content to say with grammarians, " We teach this doctrine not as divinely inspired and intrinsically true, but because it is popularly established," and not go on as now bolstering up ancient errors with " Evidences," and defending with sophistical arguments what is altogether indefensible.

Certain portions of the following chapters have appeared before as articles which I have contributed at various times to the *Jewish Chronicle* and the *Jewish World*.

JOHN VICKERS.

St. Thomas's Hill, Canterbury,
   November, 1891.

THE REAL JESUS.

CHAPTER I.

HIS MODERN EULOGISTS.

Human judgment biassed by relationship. 2. The magnified personality acquired by kings. 5. Attempts to modernize the character of Jesus. 6. Professor Huxley's view of him. 8. Idealistic and realistic biographies. 9. Matthew Arnold's lofty conception of Jesus considered. 12. The mythical theory of Strauss examined. 18. His estimate of Jesus well criticized by Professor Fisher. 20. The veneration of origins tending to idolatry. 22. Carlyle's estimate of the character and influence of Mohammed considered. 23. The personal influence of Mohammed compared with that of Jesus. 24. Jewish opinions of Jesus. 25. Messiah-worship leading to worse idolatry. 27. Jew-Christian friendliness. 29. The justification of criticism.

IN order to form a tolerably correct estimate of a person's character and life, or a sound judgment of his conduct on any particular occasion, it is desirable that we should have no biassing relationship with him, but should be able to regard him from an entirely independent and disinterested position. This has been universally insisted upon by all those who have concerned themselves with the impartial administration of justice. If the father of a family has a dispute with some neighbour or is charged with committing a fraud or an assault, no one would consider his children com-

B

petent to intervene in the case and pronounce anything like an equitable decision. Neither can they
be expected to draw a perfectly fair and accurate
sketch of his character, for if he only discharges
his parental duties towards them satisfactorily, they
are pretty sure to behold him only on the side of
his virtues and to imagine that his vices are non-
existent. By the outside world with whom he
comes in contact in his business transactions he
may be generally looked upon as an ignoramus, a
knave, a curmudgeon, an idler, a slanderer, a
coward, or a fop; but it is impossible that he
should be so regarded by the little family group
who are dependent on his care and are constantly
being instructed by him in some way or other, and
receiving at his hands benefactions; to them he
will appear in comparison with other human beings
a distinct paragon. "We thought there was but
one wise man in the world, and that was our
father," writes William Cobbett, recalling the
simplicity of his early days in a Surrey farm-
house. The majority of children have an equally
high opinion of their parents, to whom they are
indebted above all others for protection, instruction, and the common enjoyments of life, and wiser
people do not think it worth while to try to
undeceive them, believing that when they grow up
to maturity and mix in the world's crowd they will
soon enough become disillusioned.

2. The superior man who acquires a position of
headship over a larger community, whether as a
ruler or as a teacher, generally wins in a moderated
degree such homage and respect from his dependent people as a father receives from his children.
He is the common friend who always studies their
welfare, gives them counsel and direction, sym-
pathizes with their troubles, champions their
grievances, and binds them together in harmony

and peace. From being thus especially favoured and led by him, they cannot well estimate his relative importance among leaders, nor the merit of any contention in which he may happen to be involved : so far as his paternal influence extends, his personality will be magnified, and he is sure to be partially judged. The greater the social body, the greater and more imposing in appearance becomes its recognized head; but it is only in the case of newly-founded communities that one with the other is usually well proportioned. Men inhabiting the same region and subject to the same climatic and political influences are so nearly on a level in respect to physical and moral endowments that no one among them is able by his own intrinsic excellence to obtain a very large following. A moderately gifted individual may succeed in bringing together a few hundreds who have hitherto been strangers to each other to form the beginning of a sect or a nation ; a leader of greater ability may in like manner, with prolonged exertions, attract and organize several thousands; but there was never yet known on earth a genius towering so high above his fellows and commanding so much respect and admiration, that he could establish a new community of millions. For a social structure to be formed of this magnitude the work of the founder must go on after his death; there will be required the added labours and continued developments of several generations, and his revered figure is thus sure to increase in appearance from age to age till it comes to have something like colossal dimensions.

3. It is no easy matter for a great expansive nation of many centuries' growth to form a correct opinion of their hereditary ruler when only a very few of their number ever come into his presence or have any direct communion with him. He may be

a person of real ability admirably fitted for his
high position, or he may be incapable and hold it
only by the fortune of birth, yet even in the latter
case his defects, if well covered by wise ministers,
will hardly be perceptible to the mass of his loyal
people. So long as the government goes on
satisfactorily and peace and order are maintained,
he is pretty sure to be credited with most of the
good work and recognized as his subjects ever-
watchful guardian and benefactor. Moreover, a
great deal is done systematically to cultivate loyal
sentiment and exalt a sovereign's reputation in the
eyes of the multitude; prayers are constantly said
in his behalf; songs and anthems are sung in his
praise; demonstrations are got up to do him honour
in every part of his dominions, and those few who
happen to take an unfavourable view of him and
refuse to join in the general chorus of laudation
may deem it politic to keep their discordant
sentiments to their own breasts. The gifted statesmen who stand behind a constitutional monarch to
assist him, or rather use him as a puppet in governing the country, will, by falling in with the popular
homage, treat him as their superior, although
conscious that he is both intellectually and morally
their inferior. Thus he shines with a borrowed
lustre; the people believe that he alone has royal
attributes—the qualities and virtues of a true predestined king, and consequently the strength and
excellence of the nation gather about him as it
would not gather about anyone else to turn to
good account their illusion. With all the artificial
surroundings calculated to favourably impress the
people and attach them to the throne in the interest
of public order, and with all the mythical stories
both of good and bad import which get circulated
among the credulous, it is next to impossible that
a living monarch should be judged fairly and

accurately within the limits of his realm as we are accustomed to judge an ordinary man. His character may perhaps be depicted with some approach to truthfulness by a shrewd unbiassed foreigner, otherwise we must wait for his correct portraiture till some historian diligently collects evidence respecting him after his death, when the glamour which surrounded him has been completely transferred to another.

4. Religions spread further and last longer than nations, and a spiritual monarch who has reigned for a thousand years and more over many distinct peoples can hardly fail to be proportionately magnified. Christ, as an ancient religious founder, has grown great in the imagination of his countless disciples in precisely the same way as Buddha and Mohammed have grown, nay, has become still more exalted, and rendered mysterious from his supposed divine relationship. Enlightened Christian teachers, even if they were not themselves more or less subject to the prevalent illusion respecting his moral pre-eminence and absolute perfection, would have to pander to it in order to maintain their influence. Some of the more thoughtful may now and then in their closets feel assured that the modern Church has produced men greatly superior in every way to the rude Galilean preacher who serves as its figure-head, but they would on no account venture to hint this to the idolatrous multitude. They know well that within certain wide geographical limits there is no other name to conjure with like that of Christ, that people believe in him as they would believe in no one else, that the prestige attached to him as a universal Saviour is unbounded, and therefore they proceed to make the best of him as a moral exemplar by ascribing to him their own virtues and every other excellence that has yet been recognized in Christendom. It

would be unreasonable to blame them for doing what they are thus constrained to do under the pressure of the popular current, just as it would be wrong to censure the statesmen who gather about the hereditary occupant of a throne and humour the multitude in their political idolatry. But it must be clearly understood that their action, however justifiable as a means of uniting, harmonizing, and influencing for their good the many who cannot be guided by reason, is directly opposed to the interests of historical truth. The judgment of those Christian writers, who profess to set the prophet of Nazareth clearly and correctly before the world, is tremendously biassed by relationship; they cannot possibly estimate his character with any approximation to fairness so long as they treat him differently from all other prophets—that is, will not hear one word whispered in his disparagement, and vie with each other as to who shall best describe his virtues and accord him the highest praise.

5. From a Christian standpoint much may be said in favour of the many recent biographical attempts to modernize the character of Jesus so as to make him appear somewhat less of a world-renouncing saint and more of an enlightened philanthropist. They undoubtedly serve a good educational purpose by introducing to the advanced intelligence of the Church an improved ideal, but they have not the slightest claim to historical truthfulness or authenticity. If we examine the representations of Christ's physical features which have been given us by Raphael, Correggio, Delaroche, Holman Hunt and other eminent artists, we shall find a great deal of variety in their conceptions, but each seems to have done his utmost to depict a model man, to surpass all preceding portraits in sweetness and dignity of expression. And so it is with the "Life" pictures

which Christian biographers continue to draw of their venerated Master, and with the hymns of praise which Christian poets from time to time present to the world. They improve one upon another; they show us in these works of art their own surpassing ideas; they reveal in each case something of their own mental peculiarities, but tell us very little of the original mind of Christ. As long as one who lived in barbarous times is firmly believed in, and held aloft as a supreme moral pattern, it is desirable that his character, to accord with the progress of his followers, should thus receive continual embellishment. In short, whatever advanced thoughts may be developed in the mind of a modern Christian, there is no way in which he can so effectively teach them or obtain a wide recognition for them as by ingeniously ascribing them to the Church's authoritative head. This is what was done by many primitive Christian writers in a more unscrupulous fashion; they were accustomed to forge and interpolate gospels in order to put into the Master's mouth their own successive doctrinal developments. All who seek historical truth must be well on their guard against such tendencies. The following remarks of Professor Huxley on the idealistic portraits of Christ are deserving of attention :

6. "In the course of other inquiries I have had to do with fossil remains which looked quite plain at a distance and became more and more indistinct as I tried to define their outline by close inspection. There was something there—something which, if I could win assurance about it, might mark a new epoch in the history of the earth; but, study as long as I might, certainly eluded my grasp. So has it been with me in my efforts to define the grand figure of Jesus as it lies in the primitive strata of Christian literature. Is he the kindly

peaceful Christ depicted in the Catacombs? Or is
he the stern judge who frowns above the altar of
SS. Cosmas and Damianus? Or can he be rightly
represented in the bleeding ascetic broken down
by physical pain of too many mediæval pictures?
Are we to accept the Jesus of the second or the
Jesus of the fourth gospel as the true Jesus?
What did he really say and do; and how much
that is attributed to him in speech and action is
the embroidery of the various parties into which
his followers tended to split themselves within
twenty years of his death when even the threefold
tradition was only nascent? . . . . . If
a man can find a friend, the hypostasis of all his
hopes, the mirror of his ethical ideal, in the Jesus
of any or all of the gospels, let him live by faith
in that ideal. Who shall or can forbid him?
But let him not delude himself that his faith
is evidence of the objective reality of that in which
he trusts. Such evidence is to be obtained only
by the use of the methods of science as applied to
history and to literature, and it amounts at present
to very little " (*Nineteenth Century*, No. 144, pp.
178-186).

7. Professor Huxley well contends that Christians
have no moral right to thrust their idealistic portraits
of Jesus on the unbiassed scientific world whose
business it is to study realities and separate fiction
from fact. But he would probably himself admit that
he is scarcely justified in representing that historical investigators have at present not sufficient evidence to pronounce either favourably or unfavour-
ably of the character of the prophet of Nazareth.
Indecision and doubt constitute a favourite mental
attitude of some inquirers, and it is often a commendable one, but they may carry their equipoise too far;
it now and then happens that they do not merely
avoid rash judgments, but so hesitate to commit

themselves as to be ill qualified for assuming a judicial position. Notwithstanding all the myths of the first and second centuries, and the successive developments and numerous discrepancies of the Gospel narrative, the true outline of the character of Jesus—the substance of what he said and did—stands out as clearly revealed to an unprejudiced inquirer as the moral features of Mohammed or St. Paul. The Apocalyptic doctrines which originated in Judea during the Maccabean period were unquestionably entertained by Jesus ; those who formed with him the Nazarene community believed in vaticination, were influenced in no small degree by such spurious writings as the Book of Daniel and the Book of Enoch. He had what might be called a representative sectarian character: it is seen not only in his predecessors and contemporaries the Essenes, but in his genuine followers the Ebionite Christians and in all the world-renouncing saints and martyrs of the primitive church. Where a man takes a prominent part in some well-known religious movement and organizes a new society which rapidly extends itself after his death and undergoes changes from continued proselytism, however meagre and inadequate the record of his biographers, and however much the popular imagination may invest him with myths, the nature of the original impulse which he communicated to those around him can never be so entirely obscured as to become a matter of conjecture.

8. There are many venerated teachers besides Jesus of whom it is desirable that two distinct biographical portraits, or classes of portraits, should be produced—one idealistic, for the contemplation of his affectionate adherents ; and the other realistic, for the study of the outside world. Those who endeavour to hold a man up to admiration as a hero, a reformer, or a moral exemplar, are

naturally desirous that the most should be made of his virtues, and that anything tending to lower him in the public estimation or detract from his influence should as far as possible be overlooked or explained away. On the other hand, people who have felt a considerable interest in his teaching and the extent of his influence in the world, without being themselves particularly attracted towards him, would like to know equally well both sides of his character and every striking detail of his life, whether creditable or the reverse. When Mr. Froude wrote the biography of his friend Carlyle he seems to have entertained some hope of producing a work which should satisfy at once disciples who want eulogy and non-disciples who want truth, but of course failed to do so, and in consequence of mentioning certain matters which were not likely to call forth admiration, incurred a great deal of obloquy from ardent Carlyleans. Any similar attempt to take a medium course in exhibiting the character of Jesus, so as to afford satisfaction to Christians and non-Christians, must evidently be still more of a failure. The biographers, who wrote of him in the first instance, were not merely sympathetic friends but enthusiastic followers, and their aim was altogether eulogistic; they wrote especially for the faithful, the Christian brotherhood, and would not be likely, on the score of truthfulness, to mention disparaging facts, as an independent narrator might have done. In their simplicity, however, they recorded many things which a modern eulogist, placed in the same position, would have doubtless thought it best to leave out; what did not strike them as being in any way faulty or reprehensible has got to seem very much so in an age of greater enlightenment. Hence they have been blamed, like Mr. Froude, for painting blemishes on a noble countenance that ought to have been free from the slightest disfigurement; a cry has been raised that they were dull of comprehension, that they did not in the least understand their perfect Master, and that instead of doing justice to his character, they ascribed to him their own failings and prejudices.

9. The attempts of modern Christian scholars to put the Gospels through a process of sifting and refining criticism, so as to derive from them an improved portrait of Christ, are commendable enough as tending to break the bonds of literalism and encourage a spirit of progress. But when the same fanciful reconstructive work is taken up by writers outside the Christian pale, who are supposed to be independent investigators delivering an unbiased judgment before the world, it is much less entitled to respect. The reputation of Matthew Arnold as a philosophical critic deservedly stands high in this country: he is more clear-sighted, impartial, and free from rancour, than the majority of distinguished writers. In a review of Professor Dowden's "Life of Shelley" he contends that the biographer, trusting to the partial judgment of Mrs. Shelley, has in some instances taken a too favourable view of the poet's character. What Mrs. Shelley has said may be natural enough from her point of view as an affectionate and appreciative wife, but her statements should not have been adopted fully without question by an independent writer desirous of setting before the world the plain unvarnished truth. The soundness of this criticism in its general application is indisputable; in order to estimate people correctly we must not be too much influenced by the praises accorded them by warm-hearted relatives and friends. So when Christians exalt and magnify their founder, it is all very proper from their standpoint, and quite to be expected, but they must not be trust-

fully followed by a philosopher who undertakes to
deliver impartial judgments.   Yet Mr. Arnold
(who could hardly be expected to detach himself
from Christian sympathies) has done so, in short,
has fallen elsewhere into just such mistaken
guidance as that for which he corrects Professor
Dowden.   This is what he writes of the New
Testament and Jesus in a spirit of super-lucidity
more worthy of Swedenborg than of any cool
investigator of historical truth.

10. " The book contains all that we know of
a wonderful spirit far above the heads of his
reporters, still further above the heads of the
popular theology which has added to its own
misunderstanding of the reporters to the reporters
misunderstanding of Jesus.   And it was quite
inevitable that anything so superior and so profound should be imperfectly understood by those
among whom it first appeared and for a very long
time afterwards, and that it should come at last to
stand out clearer only by *Time*, as the Greek maxim
says, *the wisest of all things for he is the unfail-
ing discoverer*.   Yet however much is discovered,
the object of our scrutiny must still be beyond us,
must still transcend our adequate knowledge, if for
no other reason, because of the character of the
first and only records of him.   But in the view now
taken we have—even at the point to which we
have already come—at least a wonderful figure
transcending his disciples, attaching them but
transcending them in very much that he uttered
going far above their heads, treating Scripture
and prophecy like a master while they treated it
like children, resting his doctrine on internal
evidence while they rested it on miracles, and yet
by his incomparable lucidity and penetrativeness
planting his profound veins of thought in their
memory along with their own notions and pre-

possessions to come out all mixed up together but still distinguishable one day and separable—and leaving his word thus to bear fruit for the future. Sure, to follow and extract these veins of ore is a wise man's business, not to let them lie neglected and unused " ("Literature and Dogma," p. 164).

11. Mr. Arnold professes, like Strauss, to reject the miraculous in Christian history, and yet proceeds to set before us in Jesus of Nazareth a prodigy of exceptional development transcending natural limits quite as much as the wonderful works ascribed to him or any that have since obtained credit in the Christian community. He believes the Galilean prophet to have been a genius who towered so high above the heads of his contemporaries that he was as good as lost among them, and is only now, after the lapse of eighteen centuries, beginning to be understood and rightly appreciated by a few of the most enlightened investigators of the present age. To ordinary students of ancient history—men who have no cabalistic secret for interpreting the gospel's hidden wisdom nor gift of literary clairvoyance—Jesus seems to have been quite as well understood by his immediate followers and others who had communion with him as John the Baptist, St. Paul, St. Dominic, or any other ascetic teacher that ever lived. He and his disciples were evidently men of congenial mind, entertaining certain notions then widely prevalent; they had the same belief as he in charming away diseases and casting out devils, the same disposition to renounce industrial pursuits and roam about the country as mendicant preachers preparing for the end of the world. There was certainly no material difference between them in their interpretation of Scripture and prophecy; it cannot be made out that he was less deceived than they by the forged Apocalyptic writings of the Maccabean period,

and neither did he any more than they anticipate
the discoveries of modern scholars in reference to
the composition of the Psalms and the Pentateuch.
It was not till several years after his death and
supposed resurrection that Jesus began to be
misunderstood by newly-converted disciples, who
exercised their imagination freely about him from
having never heard his discourses or been in his
company.   From the time of Paul's divergent
teaching and the importation of Alexandrian ideas,
the majority of professing Christians wandered
further and further from the founder's views, while
they rendered him increased homage, and, with the
help of mythical stories, made him actually divine.
The theologians have disputed one with another
and variously magnified him for many centuries,
and now at length there are nurtured in the bosom
of the Church learned critics who clear away the
misconceptions of his orthodox worshippers only
to metamorphose him still further, and convert
him into a reforming philosopher.   Mr. Arnold
writes more truthfully in one of his beautiful
poems where he tells us that Christ is just that
grand benevolent being that the idealizing faith of
Christendom has made him—a being who, having
no objective basis for his claims, must change more
and more with the change of human thought and
aspiration.

12. Many English thinkers besides Matthew
Arnold have been too much influenced by the
"Leben Jesu," the great exegetical work of Dr.
Strauss, in reference to the Evangelical narratives.
This eminent German scholar, like his predecessor
Paulus of Heidelberg, undertook the task of
explaining away the Gospel miracles as illusions
without involving those who produced them in the
slightest moral obliquity.   In the eyes of modern
rationalizing Christians this is the especial merit

of his criticism; the miracles, which have been a stumbling-block to so many inquiring minds, he reduces to unconscious myths. He wrote his first "Life of Jesus" not as a philosopher of the Lessing or Gibbon school, but as a Christian reformer continuing the work of Luther, and he naturally felt chagrined that the orthodox clergy should attack him with so much virulence and so little appreciate his motives. Notwithstanding his later sceptical developments which carried him far beyond the pale of the church, the mythical theory which he propounded is highly esteemed at the present day by many thoughtful progressive ministers both here and in Germany. They give him credit for having introduced a masterly method of obviating the difficulties which continually present themselves to educated readers of the New Testament. The work supposed to have been accomplished by him is, indeed, little short of giving to the world a Fifth Gospel for the purpose of clearing away the clouds of myth which it is alleged half hide and blemish the grand figure of Jesus in the canonical Four. If objection is made to any of the outrageous precepts there ascribed to him, the ready answer of those who profit by the labours of Strauss is, "These are not the genuine doctrines of Jesus, but simply the notions which were imputed to him by ignorant and mistaken Christians of the second century." Then if any of the Gospel miracles are criticized, they reply, "Jesus was no thaumaturgist; he started a great religious reformation by the force of his superior character and genius, and was invested with a halo of miracles by the imagination of his followers in a subsequent age."

13. That there were a certain number of fabulous miracles attached to Jesus by the legendary writers of the primitive church as well as those of a later

period is quite indisputable. Such was the wonderful portrait which, according to Damascenus, he impressed upon his mantle, and which, being sent as a present to Abgarus, King of Edessa, was in after years carried around that city when attacked by the army of Chosroes, so as to save it from the besiegers' flames. Such also are the fanciful wonders recorded in the Gospel of the Infancy and other apocryphal writings of the second and third centuries. And to the same class belong the undoubted mythical stories of the birth and childhood of Jesus prefixed to the Gospels of Matthew and Luke. But we are not warranted from all this to infer that the whole of the wonders recorded by the Evangelists are unhistorical, and that Jesus never professed to work miracles. Faith-healings and exorcisms were greatly practised by the religious teachers of that age, and that he should acquire a reputation for performing such works without ever attempting anything of the kind is wholly inexplicable. The miracles ascribed to Catholic saints are generally considered illusory by Protestant investigators from three different causes. They commenced from pure enthusiasm; the saint laid his hands on the sick and prayed for their cure, when they fancied themselves bettered, and in some instances actually were so through the efficacy of a powerful faith. This success led others to feign sickness for the purpose of exhibiting apparently more wonderful cures, and so increasing the excitement and adding to the saint's reputation. Then after the dramatic came the mythical : when the holy man had terminated his career, and it was desirable that an account of his life should be written, some of the performances ascribed to him were considerably embellished, while there were added signs and wonders which were altogether legendary.

14. Instead of studying carefully the "Lives of the Saints" and the history of the new sects and religious orders which at various times have sprung out of Christianity, for the purpose of forming a correct opinion of its own origin, Dr. Strauss wandered away to a religion of quite another genius, and expected to find for his instruction analogous features in the Grecian mythology. Paulus, in assuming the Gospels to be historical throughout, was something like a traveller who mistakes the distant cloud configurations on the horizon for solid land; while Strauss with his theory was as one who falls into the opposite error of supposing a large tract of hazy hill-tops to be wholly a collection of mist. Both in the realm of nature and in that of art it is often easy to be thus deceived by things which happen to be associated or brought into juxtaposition. In a narrative, as well as in a picture, the real may be so mixed up and blended with the fictitious that no one unacquainted with the secret of its production shall be able clearly to distinguish one from the other. We have sent to us the photograph of some intimate friend, who is represented as standing on the sea-shore in the midst of rugged and romantic scenery. As the picture tells its story our friend must have recently visited some part of the coast, and we may perhaps be disposed to believe it, but it turns out on inquiry that he has not been there at all: his likeness was really taken in some London studio, with a sea-painting put behind to produce an artistic illusion. With similar ingenuity people have been photographed occasionally in the presence of well got-up spectres, so as to afford strong confirmation to the popular belief in the visitation of ghosts. So also thousands of real characters have come down to us in the pictures of history, with legendary surroundings and em-

C

bellishments, and if the true and the false are
made to blend well, it may be impossible to draw
any sharp clear line of distinction between them,
unless we have some clue to the manner in which
the work was produced.   It very frequently
happens, however, both in photographic representations and in narrative sketches, that the real
and the fictitious have not been well blended, and
there is such a want of harmony and proportion
between them that an experienced critic, if he
cannot draw a distinguishing line with any great
exactness, may yet point out without difficulty
all their more prominent and decided marks of
difference.

15. In the "Lives of the Saints" and other
similar records it is generally very easy to say of
the marvels introduced, which were produced by
dramatic art, and which must be considered undoubtedly mythical.   Dramatic miracles are as a
rule less extravagant than those generated by a
poetic imagination, and it will be seen, especially
in the case of apparitions, that they move people
very strongly, that they produce an immediate and
powerful impression on the minds of believers.   A
consciousness of being in the presence of the supernatural, of seeing mysterious shapes and hearing
voices presumably divine, has often roused simple
credulous people as nothing else could rouse them,
has kindled in a little while an infectious enthusiasm among them almost amounting to madness.
Well-known modern instances of such dramatic
excitement may be pointed to in the occasional
apparitions of the Virgin Mary in out-of-the-way
places causing in a little while new churches to be
erected, and bringing about religious revivals,
numerous faith healings, and a regular succession
of crowded pilgrimages.   But no corresponding
stir has ever been caused immediately by preaching

alone or by legendary stories of wonders occurring at an earlier period. Such stories, if they happen to take well, are propagated very slowly, and it generally requires centuries to get them sufficiently established in the popular belief to give rise to commemorative festivals and awaken some feeling of enthusiasm. For primitive Christianity in all its fervour to have originated from the unassisted labours of preachers and poets, as the advocates of the Mythical Theory endeavour to make out, is clearly impossible. Even if there were no record of Jesus and those connected with him having worked miracles, such as the Christian Church has since occasionally exhibited, we should be forced to believe that something of that kind must have been done, for in no other way but by appealing dramatically to the supernatural could have been kindled the disciples' world - renouncing enthusiasm.

16. If the prophet of Nazareth had been, as Dr. Strauss has represented, an eminent moral philosopher and not a thaumaturgist, he would have gathered about him, like every other ancient sage, a band of cultivated and thoughtful disciples, and his religion would have had no attraction whatever for the ignorant multitude. Nor would miracle-working, if repudiated by him, have been introduced into the church after his .death and more or less practised in every succeeding age for the kindling and revival of religious enthusiasm. Mohammed presented himself to his countrymen as a prophet and revelator, but he made no appeal to miracles for the attesting of his mission, and it is well known that his followers have never since craved for that kind of stimulant, being content with their one miracle, the Koran. It is true that Arabian poets have created many myth wonders, but we do not hear of ingenious contrivances in

mosques to suggest supernatural intervention, or
of new pilgrimages being got up in any Mussul-
man country through the instrumentality of apparitions and other dramatic illusions. And any other
religion may be expected to exhibit the same
amount of continuity or correspondence between
its primitive character and that of its mature
development. If Jesus had been simply a mystic
like Mohammed, or a sage of the type of Socrates,
the community originating from him would have
borne the permanent impress of his mind; the
instruction which he delivered would have been
quietly read and expounded in the churches, and
Christendom would not have been overrun and
agitated for many centuries by wonder-working
monks and other revivalists.

17. Dr. Strauss writes as follows of the Galilean
prophet whose life he professes to present to the
world free from mythical embellishment: "Few
great men have existed of whose history we have such
an unsatisfactory knowledge as we have of that of
Jesus. How much more clear and distinct beyond
all comparison is the figure of Socrates, which
is four hundred years earlier. . . . . . The
Roman conceived of man as he ought to be differently from the Greek, the Jew differently from
both, the Greek after Socrates differently from and
unquestionably more perfectly than before. Every
man of moral pre-eminence, every great thinker
who has made the active nature of man the object
of his investigation, has contributed in narrower
or wider circles towards correcting that idea,
perfecting and improving it. And among these
improvers of the ideal of humanity Jesus stands at
all events in the first place. He introduced
features in it which were wanting in it before, or
had continued undeveloped, reduced the dimensions of others which prevented its universal

application, imparted into it by the religious aspect which he gave it a more lofty consecration, and bestowed upon it by embodying it in his own person the most vital warmth; while the religious society which took its rise from him provided for this ideal the widest acceptance among mankind " (" New Life of Jesus," Book xi. § 99, 100).

18. It is evident that a strained and hollow eulogium of this sort will neither conciliate the hostility of orthodox Christians who believe in the divinity of Jesus nor yet satisfy independent inquirers who are desirous, in his case as in that of Mohammed, to get at the unvarnished truth. Professor Fisher, of Yale College, one of the ablest of the Christian opponents of Strauss, makes the following pertinent reply to him : "Let us suppose that Socrates had claimed to be invested with all power in heaven and on earth, had required the acceptance of his doctrine on his mere authority, had demanded of all men an implicit obedience to his will and styled himself the lord and master of his disciples, had assumed to pardon impiety and transgression, had professed an ability to allot to men their everlasting destinies, besides delivering them from the hands of death, and had declared himself to be the constituted judge in the future world of the entire race of men. The question we put is, whether assumptions of this character, notwithstanding the acknowledged virtues of Socrates, would not exhibit a demented understanding, or an ingrained monstrous self-love, and self-exaggeration only to be explained on the supposition of a deep moral perversion ? Should we not be driven to conclude that claims so extravagant and presumptuous in a sane mind imply that the character is off its true foundations ? How else could self-deception and self-exaltation reach this height ? And would not complacency for certain traits and actions of

Socrates be lost in the repugnance we should feel
for this arrogance of pretension ? An enthusiast
is ordinarily looked upon with compassion by sober
minds.   But when enthusiasm leaps so high and
leads to the usurping of a rank far beyond the
allowance of truth and the moral law, it inspires a
feeling of moral aversion.

19. " Had Jesus stood forth simply in the character of the promulgator of some high and perhaps
forgotten truth in theology or morals with which
his whole being is penetrated, we might look upon
the mistaken belief in a supernatural mission with
a less unfavourable judgment.   It is conceivable
that the light which flashes on the intelligence
should be wrongly attributed to a supernatural
source, that the intuition should be taken for
miraculous revelation, and that a glowing absorbing
conviction should be held to come from above in a
supernatural way.   Such we should be willing to
grant was the principal source of Mohammed's
original faith in his own inspiration.   The feebly
recognised truth of the sovereign control of one
almighty will came home to his soul with a vivid-
ness which nothing in his view but preternatural
influences could account for.   In this or some
similar way a man comes to recognise himself as
the chosen repository of a great vital truth and the
chosen instrument for its propagation.   And such
a conviction is even consistent with humility so
long as the truth is kept uppermost and the function
of the prophet is felt by himself to be merely subordinate and ministerial.   Nay, the very contrast
between the sublimity of the truth of which he has
been made the recipient and his own poor merits may
intensify the feeling of personal unworthiness.   It
is true that pride ever stands near and self-flattery
and arrogance gain easy admission.   The humility
is apt to be retained only in semblance while it is

really supplanted by a principle wholly antagonistic. Still more important is it to remember that even this sort of self-deception belongs to men who, whatever may be thought of their earnestness and relative excellence, partake of the sinfulness of humanity. If they fall into the error of supposing that they are specially chosen agents of heaven when they are not, this is among the illusions which are due to the darkening influence of the sin which is common to mankind. Apart from this consideration, there was in fact no one idea of religion to which the mind of Jesus was surrendered and in which he was swallowed up. . . . His exalted claims then, in case they are not allowed, must be credited to the self-seeking which corrupts the simplicity of the enthusiast and moves him to put himself before the truth. Pride and ambition, however hidden and subtle, are at the root of this gross and unwarranted self-elevation" ("Essays," p. 533).

20. To say that the prophet of Nazareth had no substantial ground for the supernatural claims which he advanced, and yet to place him before the world as a pattern man, as many gifted writers have done in the present century, is clearly to take up a position which is wholly untenable. The fact is Jesus has more than any other ecclesiastical figurehead an artificial character; he is judged not by his intrinsic merits, but by the commanding place which he holds in the church by the fortune of priority. It is the old superstitious worship of origins that has contributed beyond anything else to magnify and mystify his personality. People of poetic temperament have always been prone to imagine that whatever attains greatness by long growth must have a corresponding high parentage or such a beginning as should seem to fitly foretoken its maturity. The Nile and the Ganges were once

supposed to flow from a celestial source by the
inhabitants of those countries which are nourished
by their vast confluence of fertilizing floods. Some
of the most famous Oriental dynasties were believed
in the kingdoms subject to their sway to have a
genealogy that could be traced back to the Sun
and the Moon or a descent from the national
divinities. So every distinguished warrior, philosopher, and saint, when the story of his life came
to be written, invariably had his birth accompanied
by supernatural manifestations indicative of his
future eminent career. And if any historical
inquirer had endeavoured to show from very clear
evidence that the nativity of the famous individual
was an ordinary one, or that the ancestors of the
renowned dynasty were people of humble rank, the
notion of greatness having been developed from
such a poor and low beginning would have been
scouted as preposterous. In like manner investigators of the present day who venture to trace
back the wonderful growth of the Christian Church
to any other than a divine source are sure to be
very generally discredited. The apologists who
uphold its supernatural claims are constantly
arguing to this effect: "Is it possible that the
whole fabric of Christianity with its humanizing
and civilizing forces, its moral and social triumphs,
its renovation of a dead Pagan world, its spiritual
supremacy, its identification with all the noblest
thoughts, feelings, and aims of mankind—that all
this is built on no more solid foundation than the
dreams and illusions of a few Galilean peasants?"

21. Some of the finest cathedrals in this country
are said to have been at their first erection scarcely
better than thatched barns, and there is nothing in
the present grand development of Christianity from
rude beginnings in the least inconsistent with what
we know to be the general order of human progress.

We occasionally meet with some eminent divine whose extensive learning, good sense, amiability, and unremitting exertions to promote human welfare make a profound impression on us. But if we prosecute inquiries and trace back his history far enough, it will be found that he was not formerly such an exemplary character, that there was much less in him to charm and command respect when he was passing as a young man through his collegiate course. And if we can only get reliable information respecting his childhood it will probably be told us that he was then ignorant, selfish, untruthful, extremely credulous, and subject to all sorts of illusions. The same upward progress, the same increase of wisdom and virtue with advancing years which is thus seen in the individual Christian may also be witnessed in the Christian community. The standard of morality and intelligence is generally admitted to have gradually risen in the Wesleyan body, as well as in that of the Baptists, the Quakers, and every other Evangelical sect since it started years ago under the excitement generated by miracle belief. And it would be strange indeed if there were not a corresponding betterment in the great body of the Christian Church during its long growth of nineteen centuries. It is well to show a proper respect for our religious ancestors, to honour those who acted up to their convictions and did their duty as far as they understood it in a less enlightened age; but when people look back reverently on the past, and imagine their spiritual forefathers to have been more holy and perfect than themselves, they fall into an idolatry which restrains their freedom and renders it more than ever difficult to look ahead and make the progress that is required by the times. Chaucer is deservedly honoured in this country as the Father of English Poetry; it would not, however, conduce to the advancement of our literature if his verses were constantly thrust before us as models for imitation, and every critical remark made in reference to them were resented as a graceless profanity.

22. The illusion which so many writers are under at the present day with respect to what they consider the grand and lofty moral figure of Jesus cannot be better shown than in the language with which an orthodox Christian points out in the *Wesleyan Magazine* the corresponding error of Carlyle in estimating the character and influence of Mohammed. "Now let it be assumed," says this writer, "that Mohammed has often been misrepresented and maligned; that he had certain commanding moral qualities as well as intellectual gifts, that he was not in the vulgar sense of the word an impostor, since it may be held that no man ever imposed a new creed on mankind till he had first imposed it on himself; and hypocrisy is but a subordinate—we had almost said unconscious—element in the forces of fanaticism. But we submit that the spread of his tenets is out of all proportion to his individual powers. We must look for the secret of his success rather in the character and circumstances of the Arabian people than in the personal greatness of their Prophet. Indeed it is a common error of Mr. Carlyle and his fellow-worshippers to magnify individual human agency till it is something godlike, and then to render it an undue homage. They forget 'what great effects from trivial causes spring.' They know it is certain that mighty consequences must spring from *adequate* causes, but the river rolling through the plain is not all due to the rill escaping through a cleft of the mountains. It is fed by neighbouring rivulets and augmented by the winter rains, the higher table-land is secretly but surely drained for its increase,

and a thousand independent springs find glad fellowship and a swifter course in its community of waves. And such is the history of Islamism in relation to the influence of its Prophet."

23. Exactly so; and such, too, is evidently the history of Christianity in its relation to Jesus of Nazareth. But the personal influence of the Arabian prophet was really much greater in his lifetime than that of the Galilean, and is seen to extend much further in moulding the character of the religion called after his name. Jesus simply headed a little band of Jewish communists who had imbibed the Essene doctrines, and were bent on establishing the predicted "kingdom of saints" (Dan. ii. 44) in anticipation of the approaching end of the world. What he and others attempted to bring about on the strength of predictions was an entire failure, and would have been speedily forgotten after his death only for the successful miracle drama of his resurrection. The young mystic, Paul of Cilicia, gave a completely new turn to the religion of Jesus, and holding him aloft as the risen Christ and Saviour of those who believed, commenced a vigorous missionary campaign to effect the conversion of the Gentile world. Christianity thus modified, after vainly endeavouring for three centuries to extirpate Paganism, eventually compromised matters, formed a give-and-take alliance with it, and thus became the established religion of the Roman Empire. This wonderful *dénouement* was not in the remotest degree foreseen by the suffering Messiah of Nazareth and his circumcised apostles who were to sit on twelve thrones judging the twelve tribes of Israel (Matt. xix. 28). But it cannot be said that Islamism has so changed its front from time to time and entirely run away from its founder's directions and designs; the

modern religion which we see flourishing at Cairo, Damascus, and Agra still retains the features which were impressed on it by Mohammed, and his written instructions are as strictly obeyed now as when he went forth at the head of his first followers and overthrew the Arabian idolatry.

24. Modern Jewish scholars have in general been too much taken up with Talmudic studies to give any great attention to the Gospel narrative so as to be able to throw additional light on the personality of Jesus. Orthodox rabbis in their sermons occasionally deal rather severely with the Nazarene as a noted heresiarch and misleader of the people now become an object of Gentile idolatry, but they seldom do more in the way of criticising his claims than to show how he clearly broke the Law and misinterpreted the Prophets. Rationalizing Jews, who reject the supernatural in history, have fallen a great deal under the influence of Strauss and Renan, and are disposed to take their favourable and highly-coloured views of the prophet of Nazareth. Professor Graetz, in his " History of the Jews," says, " The merits of Jesus consisted principally in his efforts to import great force to the precepts of Judaism, in the enthusiasm with which he followed them out himself, in his ardour to make the Judeans turn to God with filial love as children to their father, in his fervent upholding the brotherhood of men." He considers him, however, decidedly inferior as a teacher to his learned contemporary Philo of Alexandria, and says rightly enough that " his death was more effective than his life." Dr. Felix Adler, of New York, president of the Ethical Society (Jewish by birth but not by faith) has in his published lectures entitled " Creed and Deed " drawn a very pleasing portrait of Jesus, which as a work of art might vie with the sketch of

Ernest Renan. "There is," says he, "a rare and gracious quality in the personality of Jesus which has exercised its charm on the most heterogeneous nations and periods of history wide in the order of time and culture. To grasp the subtle essence of that charm, and thereby to understand what it was that has given Christianity so powerful a hold on the affections of mankind were a task well worthy the attention of thoughtful minds," &c., &c. But the writings of Jewish reformers, such as the late Dr. Benisch, who, while cultivating friendly relations with Christians, hold on firmly to the faith of Israel and point out those portions of the Gospel teaching which they feel conscientiously bound to reject, are far more worthy of being studied by investigators who are desirous of getting at honest Hebrew opinion.

25. There are some few modern Jewish teachers, such as Rabbi Gottheil of New York, who hold the prophet of Nazareth in high estimation, and might, perhaps, without renouncing Judaism, be almost persuaded to take the view of him suggested by Canon Fremantle in his *Contemporary Review* article on "The Future of Judaism." But the majority of thoughtful Jews at the present day, while lightening their ritualistic yoke, are further removed than ever from the position of Unitarian Christianity, since they no longer contemplate the reconstruction of their nation in Palestine and reject Messianism altogether as a superstition of their forefathers inevitably tending to idolatry. When we say that God from time to time raises up an able man to accomplish some great and beneficial work, we affirm nothing that is inconsistent with the fundamental principles of the Jewish religion or contrary to the universal experience of mankind. But it is quite another thing to get hold of the notion that one

who renders an important service to his people,
or is expected to do so, was marked out and
designed for that particular mission long before he
was born, and even from the beginning of the
world.   When Palestine was under Roman domination, any wise observer of what was going on
among the Jews might have anticipated that the
continual looking for a long-predicted Prince to
gather the tribes of Israel would lead to Messiah-
worship when once an individual should present
himself in that character and obtain a certain
amount of recognition.   As it was represented by
learned interpreters of Scripture that the coming
of this mysterious personage was foreshown to the
patriarchs and hinted at from the time of the creation,
the notion of his pre-existence very naturally
arose : it was thought that one who had been in
people's minds for so many generations must be
something more than man, must be really the
companion of the Eternal.   The Jewish mystics,
who in the seventeenth century gathered about
Sabbathai Sevi with enthusiastic homage, went
quite as far in suggesting a divine character and
relationship for that fulfiller of Messianic predictions as the early Christians did in the case of
Jesus.   He was supposed to have a soul purified
from original sin, he was believed to be the incar-
nate primitive man (Adam Kadmon), and thus to
be a constituent of the creating Deity.   And if
Abraham Yachni, Samuel Primo, and other of
his more influential adherents could only have kept
him out of the hands of the Turks awhile longer,
and then brought him into collision with them in
such a way that they could have exalted him as a
martyred Messiah and created a belief in his resurrection, he would have been certain, so far as his
sect extended, to become a permanent object of
idolatry.

26. The Jews in the first century were asked to acknowledge simply the Messiahship of Jesus, for very few at that period entertained the idea of proclaiming his divinity. In the second century he was magnified by theologians and raised to a position higher than that of man but considered not quite the equal of God. A hundred years later the idolatrous homage of the Church had gone so far as to make him the Second Person in the Trinity, and there was ˙eventually launched upon the world the monstrous·and bewildering Athanasian Creed. At the present day it is the well-known policy of orthodox Christians, who aim at converting the Jews, to take.up in their presence a strictly Unitarian position and keep their Athanasian doctrines carefully in the background. The missionaries at first ply those on whom they have designs with the teaching of the New Testament and refrain from making the slightest allusion to the Church's subsequent theological developments. By simply confessing that Jesus was the promised Messiah and submitting to the initiatory rite of baptism, an unsuspecting Jew is received as a convert, and it is not doubted that a regular church attendance with the customary singing of hymns and repetition of formularies will make him eventually a good Trinitarian. Thus every individual Jew now won over to Christ is expected to make, in about three years, the same amount of declension from the pure faith of his fathers, the same amount of downward corrupt progress in idolatrous worship that the collective church made originally in three centuries. Enlightened Israelites, therefore, knowing well what lies before them in the old beaten track of Messianism, will not be enticed into it at all; they see plainly that they are expected as converts to take up an insecure position at the head of a

dangerous world-drift, and they hold back and
resolve to keep their feet firmly planted on the
hard rock of truth.

27. Though Jewish reformers are thus compelled
to reject the claims of Christianity on much stronger
grounds than those advanced by their orthodox
brethren, they are well disposed to cultivate friendly
relations with the great rival religion which is so
widely established in the world, and even to assist
its educational progress. In England and other
countries Jews have occasionally contributed sums
of money towards the erection of Christian schools
and churches in a spirit of liberality and broad
religious sympathy worthy of the great Herod and
king Solomon.   From America we have reports of
Christian congregations while their chapels were
rebuilding or undergoing repair being kindly
allowed to assemble and conduct their worship in
the neighbouring Jewish synagogue.   Such commendable acts as these will do far more to reconcile the divided communities than any accommo-
dating bridge that Canon Fremantle may contrive
to build between their discordant theologies.
Thoughtful and progressive Jews are also fully
prepared to approximate more to their Christian
neighbours in emancipating themselves from the
old pernicious race prejudice and in lightening the
burdens of the ceremonial law.   They believe that,
circumstanced as they are now, it would be conducive both to their material and spiritual interests
to alter their ancient time-table to some extent
and synchronize with their Christian neighbours in
sabbath-keeping.   They are further well disposed
to follow the lead of the churches in substituting
the vernacular for the ecclesiastical tongue in their
public worship, so as to bring religious instruction
more effectively home to the common people.

28. The *Jewish Chronicle* said some time ago in

a leading article, "There is much that we Jews could learn from the practice of Christians." This opinion will be endorsed not only by every enlightened and conscientious Israelite, but equally by members of the Theistic Church. It must be admitted on all hands that a great deal of moral excellence which deserves respect may be found in the various Christian communities. When we come to cast our eyes around on those who are marshalled under the banner of the cross, it is possible to point to hundreds of most estimable characters, notwithstanding their prejudices and superstitions. If we may consider ourselves superior to them in some things, they will be found to surpass us in others, and we may watch them to good purpose and derive from their example profitable instruction. One meritorious Christian may be taken as a pattern for his courage and patriotism, another for his industry and perseverance, a third for his commercial probity, a fourth for his high sense of honour, a fifth for his affability, a sixth for his unostentatious generosity, a seventh for his forbearance under provocation, an eighth for his patience and fortitude under prolonged adversity, a ninth for his efforts to allay strife, a tenth for his unceasing endeavours to mitigate human suffering —and we shall be pretty sure in this way to mend our own defects all round and make a greater approach to moral symmetry. Distinguished modern Jews may be copied in like manner with advantage by Christians just as they study for edification those of old time and are able to see in Abraham, Joseph, Moses, David, Solomon, Job, and other great Scripture characters some special virtue calculated to impress their minds and conduce to their own improvement.

29. But when our Christian neighbours hold up for universal imitation and regard a miraculous

man—one who is said to combine in his person not merely certain eminent virtues, but all the moral excellences that ever blossomed under heaven without a single counterbalancing defect— we are compelled to question the truthfulness of their representations and to doubt whether they are really taking a right course for the promotion of morality, especially as we are told that this model of perfect manhood is the one religious exemplar who must be taken on trust, and on no account tested by adverse views or subjected to the slightest breath of criticism. Pass a free judgment on all the other prophets and wise men who ever lived; show where they were strong and where they were weak; separate that which is good in their characters from whatever appears unworthy; but beware of treating in such a manner the life and conduct of Jesus of Nazareth. If you consider him not wholly free from human fallibility; if you whisper against him one disparaging word; if you venture to hint that in any little thing that is recorded of him, he fell short of absolute perfection, you blaspheme at your peril, and will not only be marked out as an object of universal reprobation in the present life, but will suffer everlastingly in hell-fire. Why, under such conditions as these —if judgment is to be paralyzed by profound reverence; if people are to look on overawed and dumb by the systematic working of ecclesiastical terrors—the Mikado, the Grand Lama, or any other human being invested with a garb of sanctity and enveloped in incense, may be made to appear a supreme moral character abounding in all virtues and entirely without spot or blemish. If Jesus is not an imposing artificial figure, if the transcendent merits claimed for him are altogether native and genuine, the thousands of eulogists who are constantly vying with each other as to who shall

exalt him most, instead of deprecating criticism,
ought to earnestly invite it just to make it quite
clear that the worship which they minister to will
stand any testing and is in no way allied to idolatry.
Equality before the law is a universally respected
principle; the eminence or sanctity of a person
will not obtain for him exceptional treatment at
any of our courts of justice, and there is no reason
why one prophet should be favoured more than all
others at the great bar of public opinion ; to claim
that this or that holy man shall be exempted
from all cross-examination is to offer a very cogent
argument for his being subjected to the more
severe scrutiny.

30. Instead of helping to praise one who has
been extravagantly overpraised and made to appear
the equal of God, a conscientious Israelite should
mete out commendation to some of the many
unpretending reformers and patterns of virtue
whom an idolatrous world has greatly neglected or
altogether consigned to oblivion. He should
especially endeavour to do justice to the memory
of those who have long been misjudged by popular
prejudice and blackened and disfigured by outrageous calumny. If he accepts the Gospel's one-
sided sectarian story, as he is invited to do, he
must not only soon come to believe that the
Nazarene leader was divine, but must admit that
those who did not follow him—all the most
cultivated and influential portion of his countrymen—were diabolical. The criticism, which tends
to bring down to a human level one ancient Judean
who has long been worshipped, and raise to a
human level many others who have been unjustly
execrated, is not a work of malignity but of charity.
It is besides absolutely necessary to advance from
time to time on ancient religious types and improve
authoritative moral standards. Not very long

since certain Protestant writers were severely
denounced for venturing to see moral features
which were not wholly beautiful, and acts which
were not altogether commendable and wise in
Tertullian, Cyprian, Augustine, and other eminent
Fathers of the Church. It was considered the
greatest presumption and even impiety for obscure
modern investigators to think of detracting from
the reputation of these eminent saints, and gloomy
anticipations were expressed with regard to the
probable consequences of weakening the veneration
for ancient authorities; but it is now generally
admitted that their criticism has healthfully
stimulated religious inquiry and proved altogether
beneficial in its results. The Jewish teachers and
Mr. Voysey, who have gone a step further in their
sermons and dared with clearer light to remove
from the heads of the Founders of the Church their
miraculous aureola, however much reprobated at
present by orthodox worshippers, will be recognized
in a while as genuine religious reformers who have
done a good service for mankind. There are
indeed already a considerable number of progressive
Christian ministers in thorough accord with them,
and quite prepared to preach the same mist-
dispelling doctrine, only that a majority of their
congregants are as yet too prejudiced to grasp it
effectively or hear it with appreciation and profit.

CHAPTER II.

HIS MESSIANIC CLAIMS.

The modern Jewish dispersion voluntary and not a divine
judgment on the race. 2. It did not commence at the
death of Jesus, and neither was foretold by the prophets.
5. The Jews' reasons for not accepting Jesus as Messiah.
6. He failed to advertise himself or make his claims
generally known. 7. One who aspired to rule the nation
should have first been its deliverer. 9. He failed to
reconcile the divisions of his countrymen, and prepare
them for self-government but rather embittered their
strifes. 12. His anarchical doctrines wholly unfitted him
to be at the head of the nation.

THERE is a very prevalent Christian belief that
the Jewish race are dispersed throughout the
world at the present day as a punishment for their
rejection and crucifixion of Jesus of Nazareth, who
claimed to be their anointed king. But every
unprejudiced Christian scholar knows well that
this belief has no support from Scripture, and no
foundation in fact. It is evident, in the first place,
that the Jews for a very long period have not
been strictly exiled from the land of their fathers
and forbidden to return there or prevented from so
doing, but have voluntarily dispersed themselves
in the pursuit of commerce in much the same way
as we now see scattered very widely the modern
Armenians and Greeks. During the last half
century a considerable number of Russian, Polish,
and Roumanian Jews have actually returned and
settled in Palestine, yet so far from thereby bettering their fortunes, they have generally, from bad
leadership and the want of a proper agricultural

training, been greatly impoverished, so as to become more or less dependent on the charity of their dispersed brethren. The attempts at restoring the nation that were made in former times, under Persian, Greek, and Roman domination, if they had a greater measure of success, or led in various ways to greater results, proved in the end still more calamitous to that portion of the community who, on the strength of predictions, were so ill advised as to commit themselves to that retrograde course. All the more intelligent and prosperous Jews of Western Europe and America have long since renounced nationalist dreams, and would only return to settle in Palestine if taken and conveyed there by force, and even then they would seek the first favourable opportunity to escape from the country and re-disperse themselves. They desire freedom to wander into all countries where they may find good openings for trade, and so long as they are permitted in this way to follow their bent, they cannot be considered a doomed race subjected to a terrible divine judgment. Moreover, unless people can be brought to know and feel that they are suffering judicially for certain past misdeeds, it is clear that the correction administered will be vain and purposeless, and will not in the slightest degree conduce to their amendment.

2. If great calamities had fallen on the Jews immediately after the crucifixion of Jesus, and their general dispersion from Palestine had commenced at that period, there would have been a much better ground afforded for the present popular Christian belief. But from all that we can learn, the chief priests, rulers, and scribes—those who are said to have been the principal opponents of Jesus—went peacefully to their graves, and it was not till a new generation had grown up that the country was

much troubled with war and Jerusalem was at
length besieged and laid in ruins by Titus. A
large number of captive Jews were then sold and
dispersed as a punishment for the determined
resistance which they had offered to the Romans,
while those who fought on the Roman side or had
taken no part in the war were permitted to remain
undisturbed in Palestine. This was no new experience to the people; they had been treated in precisely the same way before when their city was
taken by foreign conquerors, as indeed they were
at a subsequent period in the great rebellion that
was subdued by Adrian and Severus. It was the
policy alike of the Romans, and of the Greek and
Assyrian rulers who preceded them, to banish from
the country as much as possible all Hebrews who were
likely to cause trouble, and to encourage the more
peaceable and industrious to persevere in the
cultivation of their native soil. But owing to what
they suffered from the attacks of freebooters and
the general disturbed state of the country, a large
proportion of the peaceable class became dis-
heartened at their prospects, and were induced to
migrate to foreign lands where they could enjoy
greater security. They went by preference to
Babylon, Alexandria, Antioch, Rome, Carthage,
Spain, and other places of commercial importance,
so that when Christianity was first preached, there
are said to have visited Jerusalem on the feast of
Pentecost, "Jews, devout men, out of every nation
under heaven" (Acts ii. 5).

3. The modern dispersion of the Jews as a divine
judgment on them is said to be very clearly foretold
in their own Scriptures, especially in Lev. xxvi.,
Deut. xxviii., and Jer. xxix. But this can only be
apparent to very fanciful and prejudiced minds, for
we find no hint there of the general abandonment
of agriculture by the Jewish community and of

their adopting by preference commercial pursuits. Nothing is said there of their suffering ill-treatment at the hands of Gentile nations who at the same time would bow down and reverence one of their brethren and acknowledge the excellence of their law. The author of Deuteronomy simply depicts in prophetic language the sorrowful condition of the Jews forcibly dispersed in Chaldea, where they subsisted by the cultivation of the soil and suffered from plagues incidental to a dry climate. It is expressly declared that the people together with their king should be subjected to heathen idolaters, should become so impoverished as to borrow from their Gentile neighbours and not be able to lend, and should experience such miseries as then usually befel a recently vanquished and subjugated people—all of which is a true picture of the condition of the exiles in Chaldea, but does not in the least apply to the modern community dispersed on commercial business thoughout the civilized world. Certainly Jeremiah threatens some of the Babylonian Jews with a wider dispersion into all kingdoms of the earth in consequence of their listening to opposition prophets, but it is clear that he no more predicts or has in view the present general distribution of the race than he foresees the Arabian conquest of Palestine, and the erection of the Mosque of Omar in the place of the Temple at Jerusalem.

4. This belief that the Jews, on account of the treatment that the prophet of Nazareth received from some of their race long ago, have been thus set in the pillory, as it were, throughout the world, to be hooted and pelted by Gentiles who claim to know the meaning of their ancient Scriptures better than they do themselves, is altogether a very serious delusion. However much they may have suffered from many centuries of calumny and per-

secution, they have not been all this time under a terrible divine curse, and it is manifest that their accusers have formed a very exaggerated estimate of the measure of their guilt. The indictment which we hear continually brought against them is of a twofold nature: they are charged with wickedly refusing to acknowledge Jesus as their king, and with still more wickedly putting him to an ignominious death. On both these counts, when a hearing is only granted them, they are able to offer a very complete defence. But Jewish scholars have seldom spoken out with freedom as apologists for their nonconforming position, even when permitted to do so, because it is impossible to defend effectively the memory of their aspersed forefathers without impugning the credit and lowering to some extent the pretensions of primitive Christianity. And whatever injustice may have been done by the Christian Church in earlier and ruder times, they sincerely respect the enlightened and charitable spirit which it now generally manifests, and they especially wish to forgive past wrongs and live on terms of friendliness with their Christian fellow-countrymen.

5. It must be apparent to every impartial observer of the world's political strifes, that the culpability of the Jews in refusing to accept Jesus as their king was not nearly so great nor their blindness so palpable as that of many rebellious and disloyal communities. A nation has occasionally been well ruled for a number of years by some able and upright monarch, one who has defended it from external enemies, encouraged its industrial development, extended its commerce, and given it a long period of prosperous tranquillity. Yet a selfish faction, unmindful of all these benefits, have for the attainment of their own ends contrived his assassination, or have conspired against him, fought

against him, and eventually effected his overthrow. We can imagine Jesus being treated in such a manner by a rebellious faction of Jews when he had ruled their country admirably for some ten or twenty years and in various ways bettered the condition of the people. In that case the conduct of the guilty party would well deserve to be held up to the reprobation of posterity, although it would still be very unjust to involve the entire Jewish community in their condemnation. But the rejection of Jesus—that is, the failure of a large majority of his countrymen to rally to him and acknowledge his claims—if it is to be considered wrong, was at the worst an error of judgment, a want of appreciation on their parts, and was not an act of rebellion at all. For he was not actually a king of Judea and able to point to a long course of successful government, nor even the son of such a monarch, but simply one of many humble aspirants for the long vacant Jewish throne, and those who held aloof from him had no evidence whatever of his kingly capacity. They might know him to be an earnest preacher, a very successful exorcist and faith-healer, and one quite able to control a small band of communistic followers, yet might reasonably doubt whether he would succeed equally well in reconciling their factions, suppressing their robber-bands, maintaining friendly relations with other countries, and giving them at once the inestimable blessings of freedom and peace.

6. Jesus was wholly without experience of government affairs, and he did not even do that which is invariably expected and required of every candidate for leadership, however poorly qualified; he continued nearly the whole of his life-time in strict provincial seclusion and failed to bring his claims fully before the people. A true Messianic aspirant should have placed himself conspicuously

in the midst of the nation, and at the same time sent messengers and manifestoes to all the families of Israel that were dispersed throughout the world. Jesus, instead of thus declaring himself and making all necessary preparations for ruling the people, was in the prime of manhood, that is, from the age of twenty to thirty, hiding his light under a bushel in a carpenter's shop at Nazareth and rendering his country apparently no higher service than what could be performed by any ordinary Galilean peasant. The inhabitants of Jerusalem evidently knew little or nothing of him till a short time before his self-sought martyrdom, when he entered the city at the head of a band of excited followers and caused some disturbance. Even at the period of his spectacular death it is highly probable that nine-tenths of the Jews of Palestine—to say nothing of the still larger community dispersed in other countries—had never so much as heard of his existence. The fact that not the slightest allusion is made to him by Philo and other contemporary writers, while the disputed passage in Josephus is now admitted by all the best critics to be a Christian interpolation, renders it quite evident that he must have been in lifetime a very obscure personage. There is then, really, no foundation for the common belief that the majority of his countrymen rejected him, for they could not possibly reject a person claiming to be the Messiah of whom they were as entirely ignorant as though he had never been born.

7. When a people are brought under a foreign yoke and longing to be free, the first duty of a prince or ruler who rises up among them must surely be to effect their deliverance; he can have no claim whatever to rule them till he has shown in an unmistakable manner that he is able to defend them and save them from their foes. David would

never have been accepted as king by the tribes of
Israel, if he had merely gone from place to place
as a preacher and faith-healer and done nothing to
free their land from the Philistines. Moses, Gideon,
and Judas Maccabeus, preach and prophesy as
they might, would not have been trusted to act as
national rulers if they had not first very completely
demonstrated their power as valiant deliverers.
And all oppressed or subjugated nations have
been in this respect very much alike in their expec-
tations and demands of those aspiring to a position
of authority. Would the great Alfred of England
have gained the confidence of his people by lingering during the chief part of his lifetime in the Isle
of Athelney or by wandering about with a few
peasants in other provinces as a preaching and
miracle-working monk? Such an unworthy line of
conduct in a young and valiant prince would have
completely discredited him and made him an object
of derision. The first great reform of that eminent
ruler and the foundation of all his other reforms
was the expulsion of the Danes from the country.

8. It has been affirmed that the waging of war,
even for a good purpose, was altogether incompatible with the pure and lofty mission of Jesus.
He made war in a certain fashion, however, and
put a combative spirit into his followers ; it cannot
be said that his mission was one of conciliation and
peace. When supported by a mob of partisans
he did not hesitate to drive some of his countrymen
from the Temple court by physical force even when
they were there pursuing lawful occupations ; how
then could he, as a "Son of David," have the
slightest objection to clear by such means the land
of Israel from its heathen oppressors? Moreover,
he was credited by his followers with possessing
supernatural powers, and in that case he could have
easily fed any number of hungry soldiers, healed

those that were sick and wounded, and even
resuscitated the slain so as to render his army
irresistible and their work of deliverance comparatively light. Nay, he might have dispensed with
military forces; it was only necessary that he
should go to Rome, obtain an audience of Cæsar
and the Senate, and make his powers pointedly
felt in their presence, and the liberation of the
country would have been speedily effected without
shedding a drop of blood. The Jews did not want
war if freedom could have been obtained in any
other way; but they were fully assured, from the
teaching of their past history, that no man could
be a true Messiah and rightly sit on the throne
of David, unless he by some means or other removed the foreign yoke and gave his country
complete independence.

9. It has been further said that Jesus did not
attempt to deliver his countrymen from the Roman
domination because they were in a very unsettled
state at that period and wholly unfitted for the
responsibilities of a free people. They certainly
were in a condition unfavourable for the attainment of national independence; but then it was
his duty as Messiah to thoroughly reform them in
this respect and prepare them for self-government.
He should have done everything in his power to
heal the terrible divisions and strifes that prevailed
throughout Palestine and gather about him an
orderly and united people. When the Greeks, the
Bulgarians, or any other modern nation happen to be
in want of a king, they generally invite some foreign
prince to come and settle among them, under the
conviction that he will be free from their local and
sectional prejudices, and therefore well qualified to
mediate in their disputes as a chief magistrate and
bind them together in harmony. The governors or
viceroys whom England sends to occupy a regal

position in her colonies are supposed to be qualified
in like manner better than any native politician to
hold the balance fairly between conflicting parties
and interests and take into consideration the welfare of the whole community. A native-born chief
magistrate may in some cases succeed as well and
command the respect of all his countrymen, that
is, if he understands his position properly and what
is required of him, if he studiously avoids identifying
himself with this or that party and maintains an
attitude of strict impartiality. And a good religious
ruler ought to be similarly endowed for moderating
extreme tendencies, reconciling discordant views
and promoting general harmony. Every clergyman who is sent into an English parish to be its
minister should be above all things a man of broad
sympathies and a peacemaker—not one who will
gather about him a little party or sect, but a
mediator between parties and a healer of sectarian
strifes.

10. The Jews of Palestine had many bitter dissensions when Christianity was first preached among
them; probably no troubled and divided nation
ever stood in greater need of a reconciling head.
If then Jesus had been in any degree qualified to
undertake the duties of a prince of peace, there can
be no manner of doubt as to what would have been
his attitude and the general direction of his efforts.
He would have earnestly entreated his countrymen
to sink their petty differences and regard each
other in a more tolerant and charitable spirit.
Instead of calling themselves Pharisees, Sadducees,
Essenes, and what not, and bitterly denouncing
those who held other views or followed other ritual
practices, he would have exhorted them to study
rather how they might do their duty to God and
their fellow-men and become one and all good
Israelites. The sects that had long opposed one

another with fruitless strife he would have endeavoured to reconcile and band together in close
moral union that they might present a strong front
to contend with the lawlessness and wickedness
which then greatly discredited the country. An
efficient voluntary police would have been organized,
and the robbers, that infested every province to
the terror of the agricultural population, would have
been compelled to renounce their evil habits and
live industriously and honestly as other men. And
when all this was accomplished, when the cities
were tranquillized, the shepherds were keeping
their flocks safely, and the husbandmen cultivating
their fields in peace, he would have written and
assured Cæsar that the Jews were at length well
able to maintain law and order without the assistance of the Roman legions, which should therefore
be withdrawn for their mutual advantage and good-
will and directed against turbulent populations elsewhere.

11. So far, however, from proceeding wisely in
this way to reform the people and fit them for self-
government, Jesus took the very opposite course :
he was not a uniter but a divider of his countrymen, making their already confused condition still
worse. There cannot be a doubt that he was
conscientious and determined to do what seemed
right, like many another zealot, but he acted all
along as though it was his chief business to aggravate sectarian rancour and intensify the bitterness of
class strife. The Pharisees, the Sadducees, and
other religious Jews, who should have been mildly
reconciled and encouraged to persevere as good
citizens in keeping the commandments on which
social order is based, he fiercely denounced as vipers
and hypocrites deserving the damnation of hell.
On the other hand his forbidding all judicial and
repressive measures afforded encouragement to the

predatory class, and he spoke words of commendation to the ignorant and immoral populace who
were unable to dispute with him and easily induced
to acknowledge his claims. He was far more
solicitous to have a number of credulous idlers
crowded together and making demonstrations in his
honour than to see sober men go forth in all directions quietly discharging their social duties, and thus
manifesting true loyalty to God. Instead of seeking
to strengthen the bonds of society and improve the
relationship of the classes, he rather laboured to
produce separation and division : the poor were
prompted by his communistic discourses to abhor
the rich, and the illiterate to despise their learned
brethren. The dissemination of his doctrine was
not only expected to raise a great ferment and
divide the nation, but he looked hopefully to its even
breaking up families and producing universal sectarian discord. " Think not," said he, " that I came to
bring peace, I came not to bring peace, but a sword.
For I am come to set a man at variance against
his father, and the daughter against her mother, and
the daughter-in-law against her mother-in-law.
And a man's foes shall be they of his own household" (Matt. x. 34–36).

12. The Messiah was expected to rule the people
justly as a true king of Israel, but Jesus did what
he could to diffuse throughout the community a
spirit of sanctified anarchism and make such rule
utterly impossible. "Resist not evil" and "Call
no man master" are precepts which strike at all
governing power and authority. It should be the
aim of every genuine Israelite to resist first the evil
within himself and afterwards that which breaks
out in aggressive acts among his ruder and less
enlightened brethren. So long as mankind are not
equally intelligent, virtuous, and law-abiding, and
cannot by educational efforts be made so, it is just

as necessary to establish, as Moses did, a magistracy for the settlement of disputes and the repression of disorders that arise among them as for parents to rule over their children. No greater troubles can afflict society than those which come from the want of good government, or from the temporary suspension of the administration of justice, so that evil is for awhile permitted to go unresisted. The Gospel, instead of showing how such calamities are to be averted, how a just and harmonious social system is to be established, requires a communistic segregation of believing saints who are to have nothing to do with the political arrangements of the outside world (Mark x. 42, 43). Whatever may be said against Mohammed in these days, he at least puts the virtuous man in his true place as the ruler and treasurer of his weaker brethren, bids him judge equitably even if it should be against his own family and friends, and dispose of his property fairly at death : he also enjoins righteous dealing between nation and nation, and the settling of their disputes by arbitration in preference to war. (Koran vi. xlix., &c.) But Jesus, looking for the future reversal of human fortunes, requires the saint to become the slave of the sinner, and the believing master to renounce his mastership, and he who has been a good storekeeper of society to deliver up his possessions at once, and distribute the means which he has of rewarding many labourers among the idle and improvident multitude (Matt. v. 39; vi. 20; xix. 21). In fact he legislates not for ordinary men, but for monks; he provides no code for settled society, but is always contemplating society in a state of dissolution; he teaches his countrymen how to leave the world with much hurry and apprehension in view of its predicted doom, and not how to live in it and care for its continual improvement.

E

CHAPTER III.

HIS APPEAL TO MIRACLES.

Thaumaturgy no proof of kingly capacity. 2. The poor results of supposed supernatural powers. 3. The uniformity of nature conducive to human welfare. 6. Miracle-belief has bad moral effects. 7. The perversion of the Greek Mysteries to evil purposes. 8. Judicial miracles have not promoted justice. 9. Beneficent miracles morally injurious. 10. Modern missionaries rightly exhibit as vouchers mechanical inventions. 11. Miracles astonish and intimidate, but fail to enlighten. 12. Christian miracles worthless for attesting doctrine. 13. Cures effected by enthusiasm and pretension. 14. Works of Wesley and Irving. 17. Scenes produced by sham demoniacs. 18. Worthless apologetic assumptions. 19. The resurrection miracles dramatic. 20. The acting of Ananias and Sapphira. 21. Weak position of the early Christian apologists.

WE sometimes hear it said that the Jews ought to have accepted Jesus as their Messiah without the slightest hesitation on account of the unequivocal vouchers which he presented to them in the way of miracles. Supposing that he really had the great preternatural gifts which have been ascribed to him, they would have been of no avail for demonstrating his fitness to govern the people. At that period there were in Palestine and throughout the East hundreds of thaumaturgists whose feats were believed to transcend natural human powers; yet, because they exhibited wonders before ignorant crowds, they were not considered capable of ruling nations. If some of the Jewish rulers in earlier times were credited with working miracles, it was their superior natural abilities and performances that really won for them the respect of their countrymen. The Witch of Endor was evidently a woman of very little account in Israel although she was reputed to be able to raise the dead. On the other hand David and Solomon were not considered miracle-workers but simply wise and valiant men, and they are said to have ruled the nation and defended it with consummate ability. In ancient times tradition often ascribed miracles to distinguished men on account of their great natural achievements—what they did in the way of constructing bridges, canals, ships, cities, temples, and other public works. But where a person could point to no performances but those of a thaumaturgic character calculated to afford a little temporary excitement, he was suspected by wise observers of pretentiousness, and he invariably failed to command any wide and general respect.

2. It is said, however, that Jesus was incomparably superior to all his miraculously gifted contemporaries; he is even alleged to have been a divine man, so that to him nothing could have been impossible or too hard to accomplish. In such case the work which he set about to do ought to have been proportionately great; he might have easily transformed the whole face of the earth and regenerated every nation, while living in obscurity at Nazareth; and he must be considered of all the idle and negligent men that ever breathed the one who made the poorest use of his opportunities and powers. Only consider how much permanent benefit a wise and good man, able to do whatever was suggested to him, might have speedily conferred on his compatriots, and indeed on the whole human race. If Jesus had, as we are told, legions of angels at his beck and call, he could not only have delivered Palestine from a foreign yoke, but might have speedily broken up and disbanded all

other armies and put an end to the curse of war.
He, who could make the winds and the sea obey
him, might just as readily have set rocks, reefs,
and sandbanks in motion, and thus removed the
numerous natural obstructions to navigation and
human intercourse. One who could foresee the
end of the world—the final wreck of the sun, moon,
and stars—ought to have revealed the solar system,
foretold the return of comets and eclipses, and
anticipated every important discovery that has
since been made by the progressive intelligence of
scientific men. But, with all the unlimited powers
ascribed to him, he did just as little for the advancement of civilization and the enlargement of the
field of accurate human knowledge as Buddha or
Zoroaster. He was thought to be able to move
mountains, but did not turn a stone in the way of
useful engineering; he failed to suppress with his
angel armies a single freebooter or deliver his
friend John the Baptist from prison; all the
miracle cures which he effected were not sufficient
to bring to him such patients of rank and intelligence as visited a good Greek physician, and while
supposed to have a knowledge of everything in
heaven and earth, he really invented and discovered
nothing.

3. The fact that miracles are not wrought on a
large scale to gratify human wishes and convert
the world into a paradise, that every step in the
way of progress and improvement has to be
accomplished by our own patient exertions, has
often been adduced as an argument against Theism,
but it is only against the old superstitious form of
Theism that it really has any force. Modern
Theists are not accustomed to consider the Most
High an omnipotent magician sitting apart from
the world as from a piece of mechanism, and from
time to time arbitrarily interrupting its established

course. They believe God to be the good overruling Spirit immanent in nature and man, and
regularly helping on in the right path those who
help themselves. This view is now getting to be
more and more adopted both by reforming
Christians and by Jews, as they perceive clearly
that the constancy of the order of nature is conducive to human welfare. "Physical science,"
says Canon Fremantle, "cannot advance a step
without the assumption of the uniformity of nature.
This uniformity is tested at every stage and never
fails. The idea that it can fail becomes almost
inconceivable. When the student turns to experience he finds that violations of natural order
which were supposed to take place in old times
now take place no more; that no such violations
can be found in times and places where they can
be verified. Even in the sphere of Christian
apologetics this is admitted more and more. The
position of miracles has completely changed. They
are no longer the basis of the argument, but are
themselves the subject of apology. One accepted
writer puts them in the fifth rank of evidence.
Bishop Temple in his ' Bampton Lectures' shows by
his treatment of them that they have lost
their power. It is only the fact that they are
supposed to be bound up with the moral and
spiritual forces of Christianity which prevents
their being treated wholly as indifferent"
(*Fortnightly Review*, No. 243, p. 445).

4. We are accustomed to admire the regularity
of a well-managed railway, where the trains are
observed to run pretty true to their time and
accidents are carefully guarded against and prevented. Many thousands of people who travel and
despatch goods trust to this regularity and learn to
conform to it, that is, to make their arrangements
accordingly. And any unexpected departure from

the order thus established would be certain to produce much confusion. If a train were now and then delayed for half-an-hour to accommodate some negligent passenger, or diverted from its track to avoid hurting some foolish person happening to stray there, although it might afford satisfaction to those erring individuals, it would be sure to cause harm and inconvenience to others, and would by no means conduce to the general welfare. The confidence reposed in railway regularity would inevitably be weakened by such interruptions; uncertainty would begin to manifest itself, and those who had cultivated habits of carefulness and punctuality would be less careful and punctual in future. Therefore when we have proof that a train has actually been delayed or thrown off its track we regard it as an unfortunate occurrence; we ascribe it not to any design on the part of the managers, but deem it a rare accident which all their wisdom, watchfulness, and foresight have been unable to prevent.

5. In the regularity of the constitution of nature as understood by the man of science, the navigator, the agriculturist, the engineer and the artisan, we have what is far more admirable and of incalculable advantage to the whole human race. On this fundamental rule all other rules—all our industrial operations, laws, institutions, social customs, and domestic arrangements—are systematically founded; and, were it to fail so as not to be relied upon, we should be thrown into utter confusion. Those who still write in defence of miracles contend that although the stability of the natural laws which operate throughout the world is conducive to human welfare, occasions may now and then arise to make their suspension desirable and even necessary precisely as in the case of human ordinances. But if this were so, the parallel must

hold good throughout; it would be indispensable that people should be well advertised of the interruption, so that they might not be thrown into any uncertainty. When the English Government determines on suspending the Habeas Corpus Act on account of sedition prevailing in a certain province, or on closing the cattle-markets in consequence of an epidemic, people are duly warned as to the precise limits to which the departure from the ordinary course of things shall extend, and there is thus caused as little inconvenience as possible and no room afforded for disputation, doubt, or surprise. The same conditions are invariably observed when any alteration is made in railway or post-office regulations, or in the ordinances of the churches. It is conceivable that natural laws might occasionally be suspended in the same way so as to cause no perplexity and very little inconvenience to mankind. But it cannot be shown in the whole history of the supernatural that this has ever been the case; the worst thing to be said of the miracles reported in past times and those still believed to occur is, not that they have been departures from the order of nature, but that they have been capricious and unlooked-for departures, so as to confound and astonish people and render it impossible for anyone to point out between the natural and the alleged supernatural a clear dividing line.

6. It is quite indisputable that supernatural wonders, whether real or imaginary, have had to a large extent a bad moral effect where they have been said to occur; miracle-belief, for one thing, will be generally found more or less conducive to madness. Any derangement of external nature, or what is thought to be such, must necessarily tend in some degree to derange the mind. There are many

instances on record of people having been astonished by miraculous appearances, and made suddenly and permanently insane. And those who have disordered minds are constantly beholding spectres and other marvellous phenomena which they conjure up around them; they may be said to live in a world of illusions. Many poets and mystics who turn their thoughts strongly and continuously in one direction become thereby partially mad, and are led to believe in the pictures created by their own imagination. An outburst of fanaticism or strong enthusiasm is a kind of epidemic madness affecting a large number of people, and marvellous appearances regarded as spiritual interventions have generally been its exciting cause. Credulous zealots so influenced may renounce some of their old habits, take to a new course of life, and exert themselves strenuously to advance the movement with which they are connected, and yet not be by any means in a healthy moral condition. Their minds are so ill-balanced that, however well disposed to live blamelessly and walk in the path of rectitude, they are pretty sure, when carried along by blind impulse, to overstep the mark somewhere and fall into pitiable excesses. Instead of going about their duty quietly as good law-abiding citizens, their desire is rather to encounter trouble and adversity, to throw aside discretion and risk every danger, and even selfishly rush upon death as the surest means of attaining speedily a happier existence.

7. Such miracles as apparitions would, from a moral point of view, be unobjectionable under certain conditions, that is, if they only came to all people openly and above board and we had unequivocal proof of their reality. It is quite conceivable that they might thus as celestial messengers convey

regularly such good instruction to mankind as
should render all other teaching superfluous. But
the apparitions, which we hear of, favour some
persons and neglect others, appear stealthily in
out-of-the-way places and under cover of the night,
or become visible in buildings where facilities exist
for getting up theatrical illusions. Good moral
results are not likely to come from intercourse with
supposed spiritual beings in this way when their
form is altogether manlike and there is no
guarantee against deception. Apparitions in the
character of celestial messengers were regularly
witnessed at the Greek Mysteries, and they are
said to have produced a great impression on young
people by discoursing of future rewards and punishments, and exhorting them to lead virtuous lives.
Epictetus and other eminent Pagan teachers commended them for this reason as being likely to
have a wholesome influence. But it is clear that
the good moral lessons would have been better
imparted without the miracles, because simple
people, from what they then saw, became thoroughly
convinced of the reality of spectres, and were prepared to be gulled by all sorts of designing
impostors in a spiritual disguise. Robberies were
perpetrated by such plotters, and the young soldier
who had learnt to be sober, honest, and truthful at
the Mysteries, was liable soon after to be frightened
from his post by some night prowler in a white robe
whom he ought to have captured or speedily put to
rout. Moreover, the Mysteries themselves were in
time perverted from their original purpose to serve
bad ends ; simple women were occasionally seduced
in the temples by spectres who pretended to be
their departed husbands, or gods who had come
down upon earth in the likeness of men. Josephus
gives an account of a pious Roman lady being
debauched under a stratagem of this kind practised

by Decius Mundus in the temple of Isis, which, on the scandal being discovered, led to the punishment of the guilty parties and the temple's destruction (Ant. xviii. iii. 4). Rich profligate men, such as Mundus, and corrupt priests knew well how to turn dramatic representations of the spirit world to immoral ends, and thus at many places the nocturnal assemblies to witness the Mysteries became scenes of lewdness and depravity. Religious apparitions to influence people for good could have been perverted in Judea as well as in any Gentile country; although they would not have been allowed there to minister to obscenity, they could have been turned by crafty schemers in various ways to dishonest purposes. The apparitions which served as vouchers for the doctrine of Jesus were in every way as objectionable as those which commanded the approval of Epictetus, because they could be readily imitated, and so long as people were guided by external appearances rather than by the inward monitor of their conscience, they could never be sure whether the attesting miracles presented to them as Divine were not after all Satanic.

8. If the world were really governed to a great extent by supernatural messengers, as is often assumed, it is quite conceivable that the administration of justice, as we now see it carried on in all countries, might by such means be vastly improved. There might, for instance, be posted at every law court and assize an angel of justice to watch the proceedings carefully and thus prevent the perpetration of judicial wrong. And where disputes unhappily arise between nation and nation, and there is no earthly tribunal to which they can make an appeal for judgment, the timely arrival of an arbitrating angel might prevent them from resorting to hostilities. It is hard to see how superior beings, to whom good men are supposed to approxi-

mate, could be more worthily occupied than in thus
systematically aiding the administration of justice
on earth and helping estranged nations to terminate
their disputes equitably and settle down in concord
and peace. But universal interventions of this
kind, which would undeniably conduce to human
welfare, have never formed any portion of the
world's judicial economy. On the other hand, the
special miracles reported as occurring on various
occasions for the furtherance of the ends of justice,
have, by their very limitation, been favours conferred
in here and there a case, or works of partiality, if
not of a worse character. In former times, when
apparitions were universally believed, it was easy
by such means to incriminate a hated or suspected
individual when no positive proof could be adduced
of his guilt. And it is well known that hundreds
of innocent people were condemned to death on
spirit testimony or on other evidence which was
regarded as miraculous during the terrible witchcraft
persecutions. A witness of good character, who
should now appear in any of our courts and testify
on oath of strange preternatural phenomena which
had come under his observation or of what he had
been privately told by spirits, would not obtain
credit for a moment. It is in thus adhering
strictly to the natural and the reasonable, and rejecting everything which is not in thorough agreement
with the established order of the universe, that our
modern administration of justice owes its immense
superiority over that of bygone times.

9. It is claimed for the miracles ascribed to Jesus
that they were for the most part of a decidedly
beneficent character, such for instance as the healing of the sick, the raising of the dead, the rendering of poisons innoxious, the turning of water into
wine, and the multiplication of loaves and fishes.
But performances of this kind are at the best

a capricious distribution of favours, a mere flinging of supernatural presents among the multitude, and likely to create a false trust in their repetition on future occasions, so as to be more hurtful than profitable in the end. Had Jesus discovered a universal antidote to poisons, he would have rendered life more secure from fatal accidents and conferred a great boon on mankind, but to render poisons innoxious to believers in his doctrine for an indefinite period would only have been to introduce confusion on earth and probably make people less guarded and discriminating than before, so as to lead to an increase of suffering. The feeding of the multitude by supernatural means would make the recipients of the largess less disposed than ever to apply themselves diligently to raising food from the soil by agricultural industry. By introducing better sanitary regulations, as Moses did in his day, he might have effected far more than he ever accomplished by miraculous charms and exorcisms towards improving the general health of the community. The healing of diseases by miracles, however complete, would be sure to make people less disposed to investigation, less capable of tracing effects to causes, and thus discovering the true natural remedy for their infirmities. They would also be rendered more than ever credulous in regard to extravagant stories of the supernatural, and, from not being able to distinguish genuine from spurious wonders, would listen to impostors and become an easy prey to all kinds of magical illusions.

10. Modern Christian as well as Mohammedan missionaries, who go forth to preach to rude African tribes and reclaim them from barbarism, never think of exhibiting miracles in confirmation of their doctrine, but they produce vouchers of a far superior character. They present to the

inspection of the wondering native people car-
penters' tools, agricultural implements, watches,
telescopes, sewing-machines, and other useful
mechanical inventions. They instruct them in
gardening and building operations, in wood-work,
metal-work, brick-making, pottery, surgery, and
medicine. The savages are thus convinced by these
outward credentials of the missionaries' superior
wisdom, and are willing to repose some confidence
in their religious and moral discourses.   They
believe that men who excel them so much in the
useful arts, and are so kindly disposed and evidently
desirous to promote their welfare, are likely to be
right in the impeachment of their heathen customs
and in the new rules of conduct which they prescribe.   Had Jesus really towered above the heads
of his countrymen in intelligence, as a civilized
missionary does above savages, he would doubtless have put before them the same kind of evidential works. He would have made it clear that
he had a far better knowledge than they of the
abstruse operations of nature, and would have
introduced useful arts and contrivances of various
kinds greatly in advance of all that had yet been
invented in that age.   He would thus have become
a great centre of attraction for all thoughtful and
inquiring minds not only in Palestine but throughout the world. Enthusiastic learners would have
flocked to him from every quarter to seek his wise
counsel and imitate his superior workmanship, just
as they now gather to an industrial exhibition or to
a university. And they would have been so favourably impressed with the many proofs of his
transcendent ability as to give a calm and patient
hearing to whatever he might have said in opposition to their religious prejudices or in reproof of
their superstitions and moral errors.

11. Where religious teachers have attempted to

accredit their doctrine by the exhibition of miracles the bulk of the converts won over by such means have not been really reformed but only intimidated. A man believed to be endowed with supernatural power is often feared by ignorant people just as a despotic ruler is feared, for it is thought that if any offence is given, he will probably inflict on them some terrible punishment. He does not bring his followers to love right conduct for its own sake; he entirely fails to educate their moral perceptions and cause them to feel the happiness which invariably results from leading a virtuous life. Any precepts of a wholesome character which he gives may be exceedingly distasteful to them, so that, if they outwardly obey him, it will only be from fear of otherwise incurring evil consequences. It is not therefore a high morality which he teaches, but a very low morality; his adherents feel no genuine delight in living worthily and treading the path of rectitude, and are always liable under pressure of strong temptation to relapse into an immoral course. Moreover, the history of several modern religious sects shows that when miraculous powers are ascribed to a teacher by some of the least sober and least truthful of his disciples, it is pretty sure to have a prejudicial influence on his own mind and carry him far in the direction of fanaticism. He was perhaps at one time a pure, gentle, humble-minded reformer intent only on promoting religious earnestness and improving the conduct of his fellow-men; but, deceived by the undue homage and exaggerations of ignorant people and believing in the wondrous gifts imputed to him, he becomes filled at length with a conceit of extraordinary sanctity and imagines himself to be in a special manner the chosen messenger of Heaven. Pride and arrogance begin to have dominion over him, he feels as one in high authority entitled to receive from every quarter the utmost deference and respect; and instead of reasoning calmly with opponents as in former years, upbraids them severely and deals in denunciations and threats. The more intelligent and thoughtful people, who were accustomed to hear his discourses, now fall away from him, while the ruder followers who continue to magnify and applaud him will tolerate no opposition nor questioning of his claims, and if the circumstances of the time are only sufficiently favourable, will go on to establish by force a complete spiritual despotism.

12. The miracles of Jesus were clearly of no more worth for the purpose of attesting doctrinal truth to an erring world than those of a similar character which were wrought at that period by other religious teachers. Had the supernatural gifts, which he is said to have transmitted to his followers, been of any real efficacy in guiding them to a right decision in religious matters, they would have been distinguished from all other communities by their perfect agreement, by their having no serious and prolonged dispute. It is well known, however, that the Apostles, and afterwards the Fathers of the Church, engaged in controversy like ordinary men, and had to meet in council and come to a decision by vote; in no instance did they get a decision by miracle, unless, in common with other superstitious people of that time, they resorted to some kind of divination. All the primitive Christian sects professed to have their miraculous gifts, and it was only through superior natural powers and a more commanding position that one of them at length prevailed over the rest and became the Roman Catholic Church. This church has always laid claim to supernatural powers as the sure proof of her infallibility, but the articles of her creed have been established from time to time by

the decision of ecclesiastical councils. For several centuries the doctrine of the Immaculate Conception was treated as an open question among Catholics; it was advocated with enthusiasm by the Franciscans and as strongly opposed by the Dominicans, and in support of their different views both of these great religious fraternities appealed to miracles. It was only in quite recent years that an Ecumenical Council was convened at Rome by Pius IX., and the Franciscan opinion, which had been steadily gaining ground, was determined at length by a majority of representative voices to be an established doctrine of the Church.

13. Very similar miracles to those wrought by Jesus and his apostles have been occasionally exhibited among Christians in each succeeding century, but they have never been of such a character as to produce universal conviction in the churches. A Roman Catholic miracle is only believed by the more credulous portion of that community, and is invariably rejected by the rest of the religious world. So far from helping to unite Christians, every supernatural manifestation witnessed among them is a subject for wrangling and tends to increase their divisions. Dr. Douglas, Bishop of Salisbury, produced a controversial work in the last century, the aim of which was to discriminate between genuine and spurious miracles, as the Rev. Joseph Glanvil at an earlier period had tried to do in cases of witchcraft. The bishop's criticism is directed chiefly against modern Roman Catholic wonders, although some of these, which he rejects, are supported by much stronger testimony than any of those recorded in the Gospels to which he attaches implicit credit. After showing that a large proportion of Romanist miracle cures can be satisfactorily explained as the effects of strong faith or enthusiasm, he proceeds to notice other

cases which no hypothesis of mental excitement will suffice to account for, and these he thinks must be ascribed to imposture. A powerful emotion might occasionally remove or alleviate palsies, fevers, and other ailments due to obstruction or derangement of the nervous system, but would not enable a confirmed cripple to suddenly recover the use of his limbs or a totally blind man to see. Yet it is evidently possible for a person to feign lameness, blindness, or any other incurable ailment, and then proceed to astonish people by exhibiting on a fitting occasion an apparent cure by miracle. Such dramatic artifices have been more or less practised at every period in connection with faith-healing. The enthusiasm that is excited in the first place can hardly fail to lead on to imposture, since wonderful curative results are intensely relished by ignorant minds, and they are generally disposed to heighten and exaggerate them so as to make them appear more wonderful still.

14. It was from enthusiasm being supplemented by conscious deception that the celebrated Edward Irving was imposed upon by a number of his imaginative followers. He had excited by his preaching much religious fervour and a belief in the revival of the miraculous gifts which are said to have been exercised by the apostolic church, and at length they began to fancy that they could speak with other tongues as the spirit gave them utterance. And one went a little further than another in exhibiting the volubility of his newly-acquired speech, till that which was at first simple fanaticism ended with cases of downright imposture. Irving, being thoroughly honest and pure-minded himself, was not in the least inclined to suspect deception on the part of any who entertained his religious views. He believed that the unintelligible jargon that he heard around him was really miraculous—

an inspired utterance which only needed interpretation to edify the church—and was thus completely deluded and carried away by the wonder-working artifices evoked by his own preaching.

15. Another revivalist, John Wesley, was deceived in exactly the same way by the pretences of a number of ignorant and fanatical people who were brought together by his ministrations. A recent writer commenting on Southey's "Life of Wesley," says : "The effects which he produced both on body and mind appeared to himself and to his followers miraculous. Diseases were arrested or subdued by the faith which he inspired, madness was appeased, and in the sound and sane paroxysms were excited which were new to pathology, and which he believed to be supernatural interpositions vouchsafed to him in furtherance of his efforts by the spirit of God or worked in opposition to them by the exasperated spirit of evil. . . . . Imposture in all degrees, from the first natural exaggeration to downright fraud, kept pace with enthusiasm. Some of his followers began to get up exhibitions of demoniacal possessions and heavenly trances. The violent convulsions which these people had the art of bringing on themselves, Wesley was clearly convinced were owing to the malice of Satan or to the work of the spirit of God according to the nature of the case. Even children were principal actors in these exhibitions. A girl at Bristol being questioned judiciously concerning her frequent fits and trances, confessed that what she did was for the purpose of making Mr. Wesley take notice of her. . . . He had not discerned that when occasion is afforded for imposture of this kind, the propensity is a vice to which children and young persons are especially addicted. If there be any natural obliquity of mind in the parties, sufficient motives are found in the pride of deceiving their elders, and the pleasure

they feel in exercising the monkey-like instinct of imitation" (Barker's " Review," vol. iii. p. 86).

16. The ignorant people who followed Jesus and on whom his miracles of healing were wrought, had such bodily and mental infirmities as are experienced by persons of a corresponding class in our own country. Not only had they the same palsies, fevers, epilepsies, and manias as those which were cured or relieved by Wesley, but they had the same passion for exaggeration, the same love of excitement, the same unscrupulous zeal to further a religious cause. What, then, could prevent them from resorting to the same artifice of counterfeiting diseases of an irremediable character in order to astonish people by exhibiting their apparently supernatural cure ? It will be said by some Christian controversialists that any attempt of the followers of Jesus to prac- tise deception in this way would have been instantly detected and rebuked by him. But there is no record of his ever having detected and exposed either sham cases of sickness, forged scriptures, or any of the other numerous impostures which abounded in his lifetime. Those who admit that Jesus was a natural-born man subject to the common errors of humanity (and we care not to argue with others) must surely allow that he was more likely to be deceived by supernatural appearances than either John Wesley or Edward Irving. For he did not belong, as they, to the educated class; he had not seen, as they, the illusions of zealots repeatedly exposed in the pages of ecclesiastical history, and he lived before the dawn of scientific investigation when even educated people were for the most part extremely credulous and superstitious with regard to mysterious phenomena.

17. In every age and country where exorcism has been practised, the counterfeiting of madness for the exhibition of a supposed supernatural cure

has to some extent accompanied it. Bishop Douglas, in his "Criterion of Miracles," mentions an instance of this kind occurring in Poland in 1564, when the object of the pretended demoniac was to exalt the virtue and spread the fame of certain curative relics; but, as his imposture happened to be suspected, Prince Radzívil expelled the devil from him by the vigorous application of a whip. In the *Millennial Star* for August 1st, 1847, there is an interesting account of the expulsion of devils in the Mormon community. "The scene of the 20th of June," says the writer, "will long be remembered by us as a day of rejoicing in the glorious manifestation of the power of God confirming the faith of the Saints and spreading the Gospel further than we could have done in a long time. . . . . The sight was awful, but it has done us all good. I may as well say the devils told us, they were sent some by Cain, some by Kite, Judas, Kilo, Kelo, Kalmonia, and Lucifer. Some of these they informed us were presidents over seventies in Hell." There may be embellishment in this Mormon report, as well as in some of the Gospel stories of casting out devils, but it evidently originated in the stratagems of pretended demoniacs. To get up a sham opposition from devils, and so obtain their adverse testimony to the truth of the Mormon doctrine, would be well calculated to confirm the faith of the ignorant saints and obtain new conversions to the cause. Such a spiritual drama could have been just as well contrived eighteen hundred years ago by some of the more astute world-renouncing saints of Palestine, and it would have been equally effective in winning popular support for a religious movement like that of the Nazarenes.

18. Dr. Paley, in the introduction to his "Evidences of Christianity," makes the extrava-

gant assumption in behalf of his twelve hypo-
thetical witnesses—the apostles—"it was impossible
that they should be deceived." Was there ever
known in any age of the world human beings who
were thus absolutely undeceivable ? Wesley, in a
letter to the Bishop of Gloucester, says of the
witnesses of Methodist miracles, "they could
neither deceive nor be deceived." Orson Pratt says
also in his "Authenticity" of the witnesses of
Mormon miracles, "The nature of their evidence
is such that it precludes all possibility of their being
deceived. . . . . If they were deceived there
is no certainty in anything." This postulating
that poor fallible human creatures can in no way
.be deceived as a ground for believing their testimony to the supernatural is a mere begging of the
question ; it is the introducing of one miracle to
form evidential support for another. We know
that shrewd intelligent observers of phenomena
are sometimes mistaken in very ordinary appearances of nature, how much more are simple
untrained witnesses in a fever of religious excitement liable to deviate from accuracy in viewing
and reporting what to them is extraordinary. An
inferior rule cannot prove the incorrectness of a
superior rule ; however honest and veracious people
may be, they can no more as witnesses make it
certain that the laws of nature have failed in
constancy than a trusty clock or watch by being at
variance with solar time can demonstrate that there
has been any irregularity in the sun's course.

19. Those who view the Gospel scenes from one
standpoint, as a drama is commonly viewed by
spectators, are apt to imagine that Jesus had no
higher human assistance than that of his twelve
chief disciples, who always appear in the front-
ground wandering about the country with him and
subsisting on alms. But we may discover moving

mysteriously in the back-ground a more intelligent class of partisans who were possessors of property, and who, without following Jesus, freely entertained him occasionally, and as far as possible rendered him assistance. There can be little doubt that such religious friends as Jairus, Lazarus of Bethany, and Joseph of Arimathea contrived to attach to him dramatically the superior miracles which confirmed his Zoroastrian doctrines and powerfully worked on the imagination of the multitude. The successful feigning of diseases as a basis of miracle-cures would be likely to suggest to them, as well as to others, the possibility of counterfeiting death itself, so as to excite a still greater amount of wonder and faith by the exhibi-. tion of an apparently miraculous resurrection. It is not necessary to discuss here, whether Jesus was taken down from the cross alive and borne to the tomb in a state of coma so as to be able in a little while to present himself again to his disciples, or whether he really died, and, on his body being conveyed from the tomb secretly, a personator with crucifixion wounds appeared in his place. Investiga-tors are likely to differ on this question for some time to come, but his resurrection was clearly a dramatic miracle and not a myth, as Strauss has suggested, or it could never have produced the strong impression which it did and given such a great impetus to primitive Christianity.

20. The story of Ananias and Sapphira being struck dead for mendacity (Acts v. 5–11) is generally accepted by unbiassed critics as having an historical basis. It is reasonable to suppose that they were actors in a religious drama, and that their retributive deaths were feigned for the purpose of impressing new converts strongly and deterring them from understating the value of their possessions. The idea of the chief apostle

taking part in such a stratagem is naturally enough repugnant to modern Christian sentiment; but venerable prelates of the Roman Catholic Church have often enough stooped to similar expedients for the purpose of frightening simple people from an evil course. If the man and his wife assumed death in the manner of tragedians, submitted to a form of burial and presently arose and left the neighbourhood secretly or reappeared in another guise, the worst that can be said of Peter is that he had a very objectionable priestcraft method of inculcating truthfulness. But on the supposition commonly believed, that he really struck two converts dead by supernatural power for failing to give a correct account of what they had obtained by the sale of their property, his proceeding was simply atrocious. It was not to be expected that Ananias and Sapphira, on first joining the Church and seeking instruction in righteousness, should have freed themselves at once from their old worldliness and vicious propensities, and it would have been very harsh treatment if there had only been pronounced for their offence a sentence of expulsion. To put them to death suddenly, however, and not allow them a moment's time for repentance, would have been capping their breach of the moral law by one of much greater magnitude; it looks as if the Church slew them to appropriate the whole of their goods. It would have been especially scandalous on the part of Peter to punish with so much severity a want of truthfulness in newly-converted people, when he had himself recently been in this respect a more flagrant transgressor, had lied passionately with oaths and curses. That the members of the infant Church did not view the matter in this light only shows, as many other cases have done, that the superstitious fear generated by miracle-working is not favourable to reflection and can hardly fail to paralyze to some extent the moral perceptions.

21. Dr. Paley, in his "Evidences," makes the following references to Justin Martyr and other early apologists of Christianity : "Justin expressly assigns the reason for his having recourse to he argument from prophecy rather than alleging the miracles of the Christian history, which reason was, that the persons with whom he contended would ascribe these miracles to magic, 'lest any of our opponents should say, What hinders but that he who is called Christ by us, being a man sprung from men, performed the miracles which we attribute to him by magical art ?' The suggestion of this reason meets, as I apprehend, the very point of the present objection, more especially when we find Justin followed in it by other writers of that age. Irenæus, who came about forty years after him, notices the same evasion in the adversaries of Christianity and replies to it by the same argument: 'But if they shall say that the Lord performed these things by an illusory appearance, leading these objectors to the prophecies, we will show from them that all things were thus predicted concerning him and strictly came to pass' (Iren. I. ii. c. 57). Lactantius, who lived a century later, delivers the same sentiment upon the same occasion : 'He performed miracles—we might have supposed him to be a magician as ye say, and as the Jews then supposed, if all the prophets had not with one spirit foretold that Christ should perform these very things' (Lactaut. v. 3)." ("Evidences," Part III. ch. v.).

22. It is thus seen from the early Christian apologists whom Paley has quoted, that their Pagan opponents acknowledged that Jesus might have performed many wonderful works, but contended that these works did not prove him to be divine,

because they resembled well-known wonders of a magical or illusory character and were plainly within the reach of human contrivance. Paley calls this very sound argument which they advanced an "evasion:" it was really nothing of the kind, but just such an objection as Protestants have always been accustomed to urge against Roman Catholic miracles. They thought it quite possible, from their knowledge of human nature, that the madness and sickness which Jesus worked upon were counterfeited, and that those whom he was supposed to restore to life were only dead in appearance. How did the early apologists meet these objections? Not by taking the high moral ground that Paley and other modern divines would have done. They did not declare indignantly that any attempt to convince people by such artifices had never been sanctioned in the Church and was altogether inconsistent with the principles of Christianity. It did not occur to them as being easy to show that the miracles of Jesus were so immensely superior to those of ordinary thaumaturgists as to place them wholly beyond suspicion of any resemblance or relationship. They candidly admitted that his performances were similar in appearance to magical illusions, and might indeed be mistaken for such by any one ignorant of the Jewish scriptures, but declared that what in their estimation proved them to be divine miracles was the circumstance of it being expressly foretold by the prophets that Christ should do these things. This is a very poor argument; because, even if it had been predicted by all the prophets that the Messiah, who was expected to deliver Israel, should turn water into wine, multiply loaves and fishes, heal the sick, and raise the dead, the works of Jesus might only have been fictitious fulfilments. There is, however, not a single prediction to this effect

in the Old Testament, and those passages of
Scripture, which are said to point clearly to him, are
very far from dispelling all suspicion of unscru-
pulousness on the part of his early followers
in respect to imposing on the world with evidential
deceits or propping their faith with false appearances.

CHAPTER IV.

HIS PROPHETIC EVIDENCE.

Prophetic evidence more readily tested than that of miracles. 3. Forged predictions of the early Christians. 5. Mythical and dramatic fulfilment of Scriptures. 6. Application to Jesus of texts referring to others. 7. The Christian enthusiasts saw what was in their own minds. 8. The personifications of suffering Israel. 9. The afflicted servant in Isaiah's Restoration poem. 10. Exposition of the fifty-third chapter. 12. The predictions of the pseudo-Daniel in reference to the "kingdom of saints" and the successive attempts to prepare for its fulfilment. 14. The Scriptures misquoted and misinterpreted by the New Testament writers.

THE prophetic testimony adduced in support of the claims of Jesus is generally considered stronger than that furnished by his miracles. Its value is certainly subjected more readily to critical proof. In the case of his healing the sick, casting out devils, raising the dead, and multiplying loaves and fishes, we cannot now see what the disciples saw; for the phenomena which produced a miraculous impression on their minds soon disappeared. The same may be said of the apparitions or visions that were occasionally presented to them; had a photographer been there to fix the marvellous appearances permanently and hand them down for the observance of posterity, they would perhaps not have made a corresponding impression on us, and we should have reason to deem the reports of them highly coloured. But his fulfilments of Scripture, which were thought by the early Christians still more marvellous, have really been transmitted to us faithfully by literary art, so that what especially wrought conviction on them we can now examine for ourselves. Like the Rainbow, the Volcano, the Rocking-stone, the Voice of Memnon and other ancient prodigies, they may be looked upon as permanent miracles, yet they fail to impress people now and fill them with wonder as they did in a rude and unenlightened age.

2. In order that fulfilments of prophecy should be of any worth as evidence of a divine mission, the agreement between what is spoken of as being in the future and what actually comes to pass, must be clearly beyond the reach of human contrivance. When, for instance, a monarch dies suddenly, and some imaginative person shortly after writes a prediction of the event or professes to discover one, however exactly the writing may point to the occurrence, it will afford no proof of supernatural foresight. In like manner if the death of a ruler is honestly foretold, and some one in consequence proceeds at the given date to assassinate him, the fulfilment of what was spoken, which he thus endeavours to establish as the design of Heaven, will be equally worthless. All the prophecies which the early Christian apologists appealed to as furnishing the strongest evidence of the divine claims of Jesus will be found in one way or other of this defective character—either the prediction was written after the event, or the event was made by dramatic or poetic art to square with the prediction. In not a single instance can it be shown that the agreement between the prophetic word and the recorded deed was of supernatural ordering and what could not possibly have been brought about by human design.

3. The Apocryphal book called "Esdras" contains the following striking prediction and one or two others equally clear: "For my son Jesus

shall be revealed with those that be with him, and they that remain shall rejoice within four-hundred years. After these years shall my son Christ die and all men that have life ". (2 Esd. vii. 28, 29). But this book of Esdras was not actually written by Esdras or Esra, who took a leading part in the restoration of the Captivity; it is the work of some unknown forger of Scripture who lived at a later period. And even his spurious production has been subsequently corrupted: as the above texts cannot be found in the earlier versions of the book, they are so manifestly open to the suspicion of being interpolated by some primitive Christian writer that no one now ever thinks of appealing to them as Christian evidence. A book greatly esteemed in the early Church called "The Testimony of the Twelve Patriarchs," fortells the coming of Jesus as the Messiah and the principal events of his life with as much clearness as could be desired, and it imposed on many learned defenders of the faith, from Origen to Dr. Whiston. Its spurious character, however, has been established beyond doubt, and it is now universally acknowledged to be a Christian production of the second century. Dr. Lardner says, "It appears to me very evident that these ' Testaments ' are not the real last words of the Twelve Patriarchs. The clear knowledge of Christian affairs and principles shows this book to have been written, or else very much interpolated, after the publication of the Christian religion " (" Credibility," ii. 348).

4. The famous " Sibylline Books," a series of forged predictions commenced by Aristobulus, an Alexandrian Jew, about 150 years before the Christian era, had a wide circulation and obtained immense credit; and when copies were at length got hold of and interpolated by Christians, they proved of very great service in convincing Pagans

that Jesus was the world's Messiah. "The Sibyl," says Justin Martyr, "not only expressly and clearly foretells the coming of our Saviour Jesus Christ, but also all things that should be done by him" (Ibid. ii. 335). Tertullian, Origen, Augustine, and several other Christian Fathers, appealed with equal confidence to these prophecies so clear and un-mistakable in referring to events of the Gospel narrative. And when it began to be shown by learned opponents that they were "blasphemous interpolations," they contended in reply that this charge was only trumped up by unbelievers in order to evade the force of the evidence. "Confuted by these testimonies," says Lactantius, "some are wont to shelter themselves by saying that these are not Sibylline oracles, but verses forged and composed by our people" (Ibid. ii. 345). Proof of this being actually the case got to be so strong at last, however, that few ventured to deny it, and the famous Sibyl gradually fell into discredit. The appeal that had been made to prophecies of this character to show that Christian miracles were not deceptions was only calculated to increase the distrust of such works ; for a people, who did not hesitate to pervert Scripture for the establishment of their claims, would be thought just as likely for the same purpose to falsify nature.

5. The early Christians not only forged pro-phecies and historical testimonies, such as that inserted in Josephus (Ant. xviii. iii. 3), to fit the generally received record of the life of Jesus, but they also forged biographies of him to a certain extent which could just as readily be made to agree with the Jewish Scriptures. A considerable number of spurious Gospels are known to have existed in the second century, some of which have come down to our own times, and no one would now think of attaching the slightest credit to any

prophetic evidence that they might exhibit independently.   But certain portions of the canonical
Gospels are of the same character, are admitted
by the most competent .critics to be unhistorical,
notably the marvellous and discordant birth stories
which are prefixed to the narratives of Matthew and
Luke.   In the first of these introductory legends
we have presented to us a number of Scripture texts as being wonderfully fulfilled, such as,
" Behold, a virgin shall be with child," &c.   " And
thou Bethlehem, in the land of Juda," &c.   " Out
of Egypt have I called my son " ;   and " In Rama
was a voice heard, lamentation, and weeping," &c.
(Matt. i. 23; ii. 6, 15, 18).   These prophetic
texts are not forgeries like those interpolated into
Esdras and other books, but the fulfilments, or
events made to accord with them, are invented so
as to render the connection which the writer seeks
to establish equally worthless as evidence.   For
many learned Christians as well as Jews now freely
admit that Jesus was not born of a virgin, that the
place of his nativity was not Bethlehem, that he
was not taken by his parents into Egypt, and that
the alleged Massacre of the Innocents never
occurred.   There is good reason to believe the
proper Gospel narrative dealing with the public
ministry of Jesus and its tragical close to be
mainly historical, notwithstanding numerous discrepancies, but this does not render in any degree
less worthless the appeals which are there made
to prophetic testimony.

6. When Jesus, in the character of the suffering
Messiah, went about with his partisans as actors in
a religious drama studiously doing certain things
" that the Scriptures might be fulfilled," they were
scarcely better employed in the way of getting up
evidence than if they had been forging Scriptures.
The agreement of some of his actions with what the

Hebrew prophets and psalmists said was just as much a work of human contrivance as the accordance between portions of the Gospel narrative and verses of the Sibylline books. A genuine Messiah might have been expected to fulfil Scripture unconsciously and on a much grander scale; he should have performed such commanding feats to regenerate and save the nation as were impossible to all the rest of his countrymen. Any pretender could ride into the city on a young ass to suggest thereby the fulfilment of a text of Zechariah, referring to the leader of the restored captives whom the King of Persia had sent long ago to build up its ruins. Thoughtful Jews were not to be imposed upon by such cheap devices, and led to imagine that they had got in their midst a great national deliverer when they knew that he had not even been able to deliver his friend John out of prison. The greater part of the prophetic evidence which has been adduced in support of his claims is the work of an enthusiastic imagination, and cannot be considered in any sense a fulfilment of prophecy; it is simply the application of poetry. Verses from Shakspeare, Byron, Scott, and other well-known poets are occasionally placed at the head of chapters of modern history or biography, not to pretend that thus it came to pass as was spoken by the prophet Shakspeare, &c., but to show that what he wrote long ago may be applied to other persons than those to whom he immediately referred. And this is all that can be reasonably said of those texts of Scripture which were originally written of Joshua, David, Hezekiah, Zerubbabel, and others, and have been applied with good or bad judgment to Jesus so as to array him as it were in borrowed robes.

7. St. Francis of Assisi has been called a Pan-Christian, because in all his rural rambles he is said to have beheld in external nature types and

emblems of Christ. Many saints of the primitive church greatly resembled him in this respect, and were perhaps even more fanciful and visionary; they frequently saw the form of their risen Lord in the clouds, on the mountain tops, in the shadows of the forest, and by the sea-shore, when to the eyes of ordinary observers nothing in the least suggestive of him appeared. And the same highly-coloured mystic spectacles that brought their Messiah before them in the features of external nature, enabled them to see his form delineated with equal clearness in the pages of Scripture. The Emperor Constantine, who beheld in the heavens the wonderful apparition of a cross which foretokened his victory, saw no less distinctly that Christ and Christianity were spoken of prophetically in the fourth eclogue of Virgil. So, many of the primitive saints, to whom Jesus appeared in frequent visions, were convinced that he was portrayed or pointed to in every chapter of the Old Testament from the beginning of Genesis to the end of Malachi. Modern Christians are much more sober and reflective students of Scripture; they accept but a limited number of texts as having genuine reference to Jesus, and some of these are built on incorrect or doubtful translations, such as Gen. xlix. 10; Isaiah vii. 14; Jer. xxiii. 6; and Psalm xxii. 16. Several other instances might be pointed to where advantage has been taken of a little ambiguity in the Hebrew text to put a construction on it which will serve to turn it into Christian evidence, rather than one which a knowledge of the genius of the language and a careful and unbiassed study of the context would indicate as the writer's probable meaning.

8. The Hebrew prophets personified their afflicted nation in various ways—as a barren woman, a sucking child, a son, and a servant—and one passage

in which the latter similitude is strongly set forth was believed by Jesus and his partisans to refer to himself as the suffering Messiah (Isaiah lii. 13,–liii.). It was therefore conformed to dramatically in the closing acts of his life, and in the arrangement that was made for his burial. Modern evidence-writers still defend it as a Messianic prediction as vigorously as Justin Martyr, Tertullian, and others defended the old Sibylline forgeries. It will be easy to show, with the help of a few cognate texts from Isaiah and other books, that the meaning of the passage is perfectly clear in its proper connection, and that there is not the slightest warrant for detaching it from the rest of the discourse and applying it prophetically to Jesus or any other suffering individual. What has been done by those who have appropriated it to the service of Christianity is very much like cutting a figure out of an old picture, slightly recolouring and labelling it, and then pasting it into another very different picture so as to give it a meaning which the painter never in the remotest degree contemplated.

9. The subject-matter of the poem of the pseudo-Isaiah, commonly called Isaiah of Babylon, is the Restoration of the Captivity. The captive and redeemed Israel is spoken of as a servant (xli. 8), as a servant whom God upholds (xlii. 1), as a blind and erring servant (19). Because of transgression this servant Jacob is given to the curse and reproaches, but on repentance will be pardoned and restored (xliii. 28 ; xliv. 1-21). "Go ye forth from Babylon ; flee ye from the Chaldeans. With a voice of singing declare ye, tell this, utter it even to the ends of the earth. Say ye the Lord hath redeemed his servant Jacob" (xlviii. 20). Then in the next chapter captive Israel takes up the song, "Listen, O isles, unto me, and hearken ye people from far," &c. And the prophet afterwards

gives good counsel and encouragement to the redeemed people. "Depart ye, depart ye, go ye out from thence, touch not the unclean thing," &c. At length we reach the passage which has been eagerly fastened on and made to do duty as Christian evidence. " Behold my servant shall deal prudently " (lii. 11-13), that is, the servant Israel shall deal prudently in departing from Babylon as admonished by the prophet. We now proceed to the fifty-third chapter.

10. " *Who hath believed our report and to whom is the arm of the Lord revealed?* " " The Lord hath comforted his people, he hath redeemed Jerusalem. The Lord hath made bare his holy arm." (lii. 9). " *For he shall grow up before him as a tender plant and as a root out of dry ground.*" " The men of Israel his pleasant plant " (v. 7). " I will pour floods on the dry ground " (xliv. 8). " She is planted in the wilderness in a dry and thirsty ground " (Ezek. xix. 13). " *There is no beauty that we should desire him.*" " From Zion all her beauty is departed " (Lam. i. 6). " Thou hast made thy beauty to be abhorred " (Ezek. xvii. 25). " *He is despised and rejected of men.*" " And they that despise thee shall bow themselves down at the soles of thy feet " (lx. 14). " Thus have they despised my people " (Jer. xxxiii. 24). " *Surely he hath borne our griefs and carried our sorrows.*" " Our fathers have sinned and are not, and we have borne their iniquities" (Lam. v. 7). "*He is brought as a lamb to the slaughter.*" " I will feed the flock of slaughter, even ye, O poor of the flock " (Zech. xi. 7). "*He was taken from prison and from judgment.*" " Bring out the prisoners from the prison, and them that sit in darkness out of the prison house (xlii. 7). " Say to the prisoners, go forth " (xlix. 9). " *Who shall declare his generation?* " " And they shall repair the waste cities, the desola-

tion of many generations" (lxi. 4). *"Through the transgression of my people came affliction upon them"* (Jewish translation). "For our transgressions are multiplied before us and our sins testify against us" (lix. 12). *"And he made his grave with the wicked and with the rich in his death."* "Babylon hath been a golden cup in the Lord's hand . . . . . . O thou that dwelleth on many waters abundant in treasure, thine end is come and the measure of thy covetousness" (Ezek. li. 7–13). *"He shall see his seed, he shall prolong his days."* "And I will bring forth a seed out of Jacob, and out of Judah an inheritor of my mountains" (lxv. 9). *"Therefore will I divide him a portion with the great, and he shall divide the spoil with the trong."* "And they that spoil thee shall be a spoil" (Jer. xxx. 15).

11. In acting the part of a suffering Messiah Jesus did not fulfil in every particular what was supposed to be prophesied in this figurative representation of suffering Israel. He might have conformed more closely to what was written than he appears to have done; he might, for instance, have got himself imprisoned for a time as another Messiah, Sabbathai Sevi, managed to do, but the evidence so fabricated would still have been utterly worthless. It is easy for any religious enthusiast to imagine that a certain passage of Scripture points prophetically to himself and to take such a course of action as is calculated to lend support to the belief. And even if he is not under any such illusion, some of the more fanciful of his followers may discover texts which seem to have a marvellous application to him after his death. The Mohammedans point to several portions of Old Testament scripture as having special reference to their Prophet and the wonderful spread of their faith. Equally ready have been the Mormons in

discovering texts that may be made to serve their purpose. "Take," says Orson Pratt,"the testimony of Isaiah xxix. 11, 12, 18, and Ezekiel xxxvii. 16, in connection with the testimony of Moses concerning the " precious things of heaven " which should be given to the land of Joseph (Gen. xlix. 25), and join this with the testimony of John concerning the restoration of the Gospel by an angel (Rev. x. 2) and the testimony of Daniel concerning the stone cut from the mountain without hands representing the latter-day kingdom of God (Dan. ii. 34, 45), and we have by a combination of all these testimonies prophetic evidence of the divine authenticity of the Book of Mormon which should convince the most incredulous " ("Authenticity," p. 98).

12. It is now generally admitted by the best Biblical critics that the unknown author of the Book of Daniel lived in the Maccabean period, and wrote B.C. 168–164. His prophetic visions of the composite Image and of the four beasts were intended to represent four Eastern monarchies, and the Little Horn spoken of in the seventh and eighth chapters has always been identified with Antiochus Epiphanes, who is also probably meant by the " prince that shall come " and the " desolator " (ix. 26, 27). Up to the time of this monarch the prophecy, like all forged predictions up to the date of their origin, is very clear in its reference to a succession of historical events, but afterwards becomes vague, cloudy, and obscure. The writer could show plainly in figurative language what had already happened, but not that which was yet to come. So far as he did hazard any forecast of events his vision was speedily falsified, for the Syrian dominion, instead of being followed by the General Resurrection and the establishment of the Kingdom of Saints, was destined to be succeeded

by the Roman, Saracen, and Turkish dominions : in fact the Gentile world, instead of being destroyed, was to endure, and Israel, instead of being translated to Heaven, was to suffer further oppression and dispersion. But although the prophecy had thus manifestly failed when the Græco-Syrian kingdom came to an end (for in the angel's interpretation no succeeding earthly kingdom is hinted at), that portion of the Jewish people on whom it imposed did not lose confidence in it or doubt of its eventual fulfilment. When the Grecian power gave way to the Roman the interpreters extended the aim of the prediction to the latter empire, and after the conversion of Pagan Rome its scope was by Christian interpreters still further extended. Indeed the failure of this Maccabean forged prediction in the first instance led to three subsequent attempts at different periods to bring about or prepare for its fulfilment by the organization of the "kingdom of saints." The primitive Christians from the first to the third century aimed at establishing this kingdom to succeed what appeared to them the doomed Roman empire. The Anabaptists, Fifth Monarchy men, and other Protestant sects, attempted to establish it in the seventeenth century to follow the overthrow of prelacy and popery. The Mormons are now professing to set it up in the nineteenth century to supersede all other religious communions or take the place of what they call "Apostate Christendom."

13. Pratt, the Mormon apologist, says : "The kingdom of God set up in the first century of the Christian era was not the fulfilment of Daniel's prophecy. His prediction reached forward to a much later period of the world—namely, to the time when the angel should bring the Gospel to the time when the great image representing all the kingdoms

of the world should be complete, from the head of
gold to the feet of iron and clay. The kingdom or
church established eighteen centuries ago does not
by any means correspond with the time for the feet
and toes of the great image; it was not till many
centuries after that the Roman empire, represented
by the legs of iron, became divided into feet and
toes. But Daniel says to Nebuchadnezzar, ' Thou
sawest till a stone was cut out without hands, which
smote the image upon his feet that were of iron
and clay, and brake them to pieces'. . . . .
The nations of modern Europe, including England
and the Gentile nations of America, compose the
legs and feet and toes of the image, while the other
portions will be found mostly among the Asiatic
nations. The geographical position of the image
is from east to west; its head is found in Asia, its
toes in Europe and America. When the kingdom
of God is set up, it must be somewhere near the
western extremity of this great image, for the toes
and feet are first broken by it, and afterwards the
other portions, from which we learn that its advancement is from west to east. The progress of the
kingdoms of the world has been from east to west,
the progress of the kingdom of God is in a retrograde direction " (" Authenticity," p. 85).

14. The early Christians were not able to corrupt
the canonical Hebrew Scriptures with interpolations
as they did the Apocryphal Book of Esdras and
other writings, but they took the greatest liberty
in misquoting them and misinterpreting their
meaning. Several passages cited as Scripture by
the New Testament writers, such as, " He shall be
called a Nazarene " (Matt. ii. 23), " Out of his belly
there shall flow rivers of living water " (John vii. 38),
" And let all the angels of God worship him "
(Heb. i. 6) are nowhere to be found in the genuine
Hebrew Bible, so that they must be errors of the

Septuagint version then in use, or misquotations.
Many other texts are given inaccurately, and in some
places we find what appear to be broken sentences
from two or more writers pieced together to serve
the occasion, and presented as the distinct utterance
of one. For instance, the text, "Tell ye the daughter
of Sion, Behold, thy king cometh unto thee,
meek, and sitting on an ass, and a colt the foal of an
ass" (Matt. xxi. 5) is compounded from Isaiah lxii.
11 and Zech. ix. 8. The text, "I have found David
the son of Jesse, a man after mine own heart, which
shall fulfil all my will" (Acts xiii. 22) is from
1 Sam. xiii. 14, and Psalm lxxxix. 20. Another text,
"God hath given them the spirit of slumber, eyes
that they should not see, and ears that they should
not hear unto this day" (Rom. xi. 8) is from
Isaiah xxix. 10, and Deut. xxix. 4.

15. In the interpretation of Scripture texts the
early Christians were bound by no fixed rule; they
simply seized on everything that could by straining
or twisting be made to serve their purpose. To
some clearly literal passages they unwarrantably
gave a figurative meaning, while other texts whose
figurative signification cannot be mistaken by any
unbiassed mind they insisted on rendering literally.
Thus in the texts, " When Israel was a child then
I loved him, and called my son out of Egypt "
(Hosea ix. 9), and " Yet have I set my king upon
my holy hill of Zion . . . . Thou art my son, this
day have I begotten thee " (Psalm ii. 6, 7), it is
clear that the word *son* is in the former instance a
figurative expression for God's people, and in the
latter for the king that he had set over them. The
Christian interpreters, however, decided that a
literally begotten son was in each case intended,
that is, the virgin-born Jesus. Very little was
known in his time of the construction of the various
books which composed the canon of Scripture.

Neither he nor his followers had the least idea that
Psalm cx. was written _of_ a Jewish ruler and not
by him.   Dr. Benisch renders the introduction,
"Unto David a Psalm, Declaration of the Eternal
unto my lord, Sit thou on my right hand until I
make thine enemies thy footstool."   Some modern
Biblical critics believe this Psalm to have been
one of those written in the Maccabean period, and
that it refers to Simon Maccabeus the victorious
priest-king.   It is natural enough that the Psalmist
should suppose God to say this either of David
or of Simon, natural, too, that he should compare a
pious Jewish ruler to Melchisedek the ancient king
of Salem.   But Jesus and his followers imagined
that David wrote the Psalm, and was pointing here
prophetically to the Messiah, and on this sorry
illusion the author of the Epistle to the Hebrews
constructed his weak and fanciful argument of
similitudes, which the Mormon revelators have
improved upon by establishing their Aaronic and
Melchizedekan orders of priesthood.   See Voysey's
"Theistic Sermons," vol. xiv., Nos. 24 and 25, on
the "Misuse of the Old Testament by the Writers of
the New;" also Kitto's "Cyclopædia of Biblical
Literature," vol. iii. p. 624, &c., "Quotations."

CHAPTER V.

HIS REFORMATION CLAIMS.

Founders distinguished from chance beginners.   3. Reform not
   contemplated by those who believed the end of the world
   near.   4. The method of true reformers unlike that of
   revolutionists.   7. Observances and disciplinary regulations not needed by new sects as by old complex communities.   9. Formalism is not to be confounded with
   hypocrisy.   12. The Christian community corrupted by
   rapid and unguarded proselytism.   13. The Church's
   monstrous development not foreseen or designed by Jesus.
   14. It drifted blindly into the Sabbatic innovation and
   other changes.   15. He did nothing to promote much
   needed Jewish reforms, such as the abrogation of sacrifices.
   17. The Temple idolatry and Jewish iconophobia received
   no check from him.   18. Diabolism and the vaticination
   mania encouraged by him.   28. He had no communion
   with Dispersionist synagogues.   29. Modern Jewish reformation not indebted to his teaching.

LIBERAL Christian scholars, who have succeeded
      in emancipating themselves from much of the
idolatry in which they have been reared and in
drawing nearer to our own religious position, will
sometimes say : " We don't expect you to believe
that Jesus was divine nor yet that he was actually
a descendant of David and the Messiah spoken of
in the Scriptures, but you will at any rate admit
that he was the greatest religious reformer that ever
lived."   When, however, we ask what they
especially refer to, and desire to be made acquainted
with the principal religious reforms effected by the
prophet of Nazareth, their explanation simply
amounts to this, that he was the Founder of
Christianity, and therefore the originator of all the
good that has been effected by that system of

religion. We have already spoken of the veneration which mankind have generally felt for origins
and the illusions which modern Christians are in ·
this respect especially prone to (I. 20–23). It
must be observed that the term "founder" is often
very loosely and inaccurately applied so as to
become misleading. Strictly speaking, it means
not merely the chance beginner of a movement, or
the disturber who starts a rolling stone in the
world, but one who, like the constructor of a bridge
or a canal, designs a work and carries it out to
completeness, or at least aims at and insures its
completeness. Thus Alexander, Constantine, and
Peter may be said to have founded the great cities
which respectively bear their names, but it cannot
be said that the Australian settler who happened to
erect the first hut on the Yarra was the founder of
Melbourne. Romulus has been called the founder
of the Roman empire; all that he really did, however, was to found a petty Italian state : he cannot
be supposed to have had the remotest idea that his
rude stronghold would eventually become a magni-
ficent city, and the capital of the greatest civilizing
dominion in the world. And Jesus with his little
band of Judean communists preparing to establish
the "kingdom of saints" spoken of by writers of
spurious prophecies, had just as little foreboding
of the compact which a future generation of his
followers would make with Paganism in that
quarter and the wide diffusion in consequence of
their mixed system of religion.

2. If Jesus is to be held up as the author and
designer of Christianity in its entire growth of
nineteen centuries, it is clear that we shall have to
ascribe to him not only its good but its evil developments. Those who contend that he originated the
Sunday schools, the orphanages, the temperance
halls, the hospitals, the city missions, and other

benevolent institutions that confront us in every direction, will be equally bound to trace to his teaching the superstitions and barbarities which the Church has exhibited largely in past times. He must thus be made accountable for numberless pious frauds, frequent outbreaks of fanaticism, continual dissensions and religious wars, the deplorable witchcraft delusions, the burning and massacre of heretics, and the terrible persecutions which have not even yet wholly ceased to worry the Jewish community. But the eloquent clerical advocates, who thrust the claims of their religion upon us, will not consent to take fairly the good and the bad products together in their exhibition of the Christianity of Jesus, and endeavour to place before us with much skill only a very attractive selection. They dwell a great deal on some of the best pages of ecclesiastical history and contrive to skip others as though they had no existence. The contents of the Gospels are manipulated in much the same fashion; they make the most of a few good moral precepts contained in those writings and keep all the hard and unreasonable sayings of Jesus in the background, or otherwise contend that these did not really emanate from him, and must be regarded as later mythical accretions. Would they permit us to treat any other religious teacher in this manner for the purpose of embellishing his character and holding him aloft to attract the idolatrous homage of mankind?

3. Evidently the claims of Jesus must be judged by what he himself designed during his brief public ministry, and not by what those who took the name of Christian designed under very different circumstances long after the failure of his Messianic schemes. The Apocalyptic belief which he and his immediate followers held in reference to the impending doom of the world, however well calculated

to inspire them with an enthusiastic disregard of life, would entirely unfit them for the contemplation of any reforms to further human progress. For a man to be a reformer he must have a clear prospective vision of the present life and look confidently for a continuance of the existing order of the universe. An English agriculturist may be expected to improve his farm if he has before him the run of a long lease, but will be very unlikely to take pains for bettering its condition in the event of suddenly receiving notice to quit. When a vessel is wrecked in mid-ocean and in danger of being momentarily swallowed up by the waves, the passengers will perhaps utter agonizing shrieks, and be very prayerful and devout at the contemplation of their impending fate, but will not entertain any thought of effecting nautical reforms. A convict under sentence of death is never found making wise resolves to lead a better life in the future, the utmost that he may be expected to do is to feel sorrow and contrition for the evil life that is past. And Jesus seemed to aim by his teaching to make this spirit of the sinking ship and the condemned cell universal; people were to be brought into the solemn dying mood of the penitent thief and be got to renounce altogether the interests of this life for the attainment of salvation in paradise. In his view of the situation there was no time to contemplate improvements and set about training up a new generation in more salutary ways than those which then prevailed; all that could be done was to send forth an alarum cry of instant repentance, for the end of the world was at hand.

4. When a genuine reformer rises up in a community he follows the true method of reform, that is, endeavours to introduce the beneficial changes which suggest themselves to his mind in a

quiet, orderly manner, so as not to clash with authority or disturb in any way the constitution of society. ·An enlightened Englishman, who wishes to improve the laws of his country, exerts himself as a politician to become as speedily as possible a member of the legislative chamber, where he may stand and address the whole nation as from a vantage ground. In such a position he has only to gain the respect of his fellow-members, and make his plans known in clear and convincing language, and he will presently have with him a voting majority and see the measures which he advocates duly enacted and carried out. Now and then a reformer wishes to introduce an entirely new order of society, or propounds such advanced schemes that only a small fraction of · his country-men can be got to view them with approval, but he does not in consequence chafe at the opposition that confronts him and assume an irreconcilable and revolutionary attitude. He either submits patiently to the postponement of his projects, and helps on measures of a more moderate character, or he withdraws with a few enthusiastic followers to some distant colony, where they acquire an independent position and are able to realize their political ideal undisturbed. Every sensible religious reformer is accustomed to act on similar lines ; if he is unable with all his exertions to obtain a com-manding position, or finds it impracticable to move the whole Church through its governing council, yet can no longer submit to its doctrine and disci-pline, he quietly secedes with a small body of sympathisers, and they start an independent reform-ing community.

5. It was clearly open to Jesus to take one or other of these legitimate courses for promoting a great Jewish reformation. Hillel, who lived some years earlier in the same country, was a reformer :

how did he proceed? This celebrated rabbi is said to have been originally a poor woodcutter at Babylon, a position not unlike that which Jesus is supposed to have occupied at Nazareth. He journeyed to Jerusalem in quest of learning, almost starved himself in acquiring, under great difficulties, a profound knowledge of the Law, and made his way eventually to be President of the Sanhedrin, where he ably and successfully promoted reforms. This was then the position that ought to have been secured by the prophet of Nazareth for speaking to his countrymen with a voice of authority which they could not fail to respect. There was surely no better way of reforming the nation than by commencing at the Temple, and through its supreme council diffusing new religious light over every portion of the land. It was also especially desirable to acquire by such means the custody of the sacred writings, so as to let the people know as nearly as possible how the various authoritative books were actually compiled, and what was their relative importance. Indeed a leading reformer, at the head of the Sanhedrin, ought to have dealt as freely with the Scriptures as the Maccabean rulers had done 150 years before; he should have subjected the Canon to a thorough revision, both taking away and adding to effect its improvement according to the better light of his times. This was the fundamental reform to be effected in that age of primitive bibliolatry had there only been in the country a master mind. If, however, Jesus had considered it beyond his power to climb like Hillel to the presidency, or had resolved to conduct his reforming mission independently and not in any way acknowledge the authority of the Sanhedrin, it would have been incumbent on him as a true teacher to keep away altogether from the Temple and not even visit Jerusalem. He

should have taken up such a position as was held in
his day by many good Jews of the Dispersion,
and established a reforming synagogue in Galilee or
elsewhere. Thus he might have quietly gathered
about him a few enlightened and sympathetic
countrymen, and proceeded to admit Gentiles into
communion on the condition of their living
worthily and acknowledging the fundamental
principles of the Law. Such a course would not
have involved him in any strife with the Judean
rulers ; he would have held as strictly aloof from
them as from the Alexandrian and Babylonian
authorities, and his reformation might have
advanced peacefully from Asia to Europe on its
own intrinsic merits and gradually overspread the
world.

6. It is well known, however, that Jesus did
not call in question the authority of the Sanhedrin
nor that of the sacred writings in their custody; he
admitted that the seventy elders were the rightful
rulers of the Jewish church, yet, instead of working
as a reformer in accord with them that they might
be led to discharge their duties more worthily, he
studiously sought to discredit them in the eyes of
the country, and provoke their hostility.   He chose
from among his humble followers a rival Sanhedrin,
which was just as much an act of deliberate
revolt as we should consider any attempt of
disaffected politicians to set up here in England
a rival Parliament.   In taking this unconstitu-
tional course he was simply treading in the steps
of Jeroboam and others, bidding absolute defiance
to those who legitimately ruled from the seat of
David and creating a new division in Israel. When
the Zealots and Idumeans made a sanguinary
insurrection in Jerusalem during Vespasian's war,
they established there in like manner a fictitious
Sanhedrin for the purpose of competing with the

Temple rulers, and giving to their lawless proceedings a colour of authority. Although Jesus never
incited the populace to acts of open violence, nor
could do so consistently with his Essene doctrines,
he breathed all along a spirit of implacable sedition,
and made it clear that he was no friend of those on
whom devolved the duty of maintaining order in
the Jewish community. It could not be lawful nor
advantageous to have two Seventies in Judea at
the same time in direct opposition to one another;
the institution of a rival state council, however
humble in form, must necessarily tend in some
degree to weaken respect for government and
generate in a society already much divided
further confusion. There might have been a great
want of reformation in high places as everywhere
else, and a prophet endowed with power and
wisdom would have acted as another Moses, and
so purified the venerable hierarchy descended from
him as to gradually regenerate the nation. Jesus
took a directly opposite course : failing to influence
in the slightest degree his more intelligent and
thoughtful countrymen, he appealed as their
opponent to the weak credulous multitude; and one
who in this way rouses popular passions and turns
the ignorant tail of a community against its directing head, is not a reformer but a revolutionist.

7. Jesus has often been held up before the world
as a great religious reformer from the circumstance
of his being to some extent an anti-ritualist, as was
still more the case with St. Paul. But Jesus and
Paul were both in a very different position from that of
Hillel; they were simply sectarians drafting away from
the body of the nation, a small number of kindred
spirits. They were no better qualified to reform
the Mosaic economy or reduce the regulations which
had been introduced from time to time in the Jewish
Church than the members of a small Quaker or

H

Moravian colony are competent to frame a new code
to supersede the complicated laws of England.
The leader of a new enthusiastic sect, the members
of which are all of one mind, may easily rebuke the
formalism which he sees in an old complex community, as Jesus is said to have done on several
occasions, without being himself a genuine reformer
or even manifesting much spiritual discernment. A
national church, embracing all sorts and conditions
of men, is very much like an army of similar character; its members can only be held together and got
to maintain concerted action by strict disciplinary
arrangements. Any one who directs his attention
for the first time to military economy, will be struck
with the vast amount of drill that is required to
harmonize a mass of armed men and keep them in
a state of permanent efficiency. Only let the discipline get relaxed for awhile and the army will
become a confused multitude and be utterly unfitted
to take the field. But where a small body of volunteer fighters are banded together by a common
enthusiasm, as in the case of the Garibaldians in
Italy and the Boers in South Africa, discipline is of
comparatively little importance. Such rough and
ready combatants know each others' minds and are
so earnestly bent on attaining the object which they
have in view, that they can dispense with constant
drill, and the banners, music, pomp, and parade
introduced to foster a military spirit on a large scale
are for them unnecessary. In like manner the band
of enthusiastic brethren, the people of one sort com-
posing a new sect, will discard forms and ceremonies
as useless, and despise the ritualism which priests
maintain in older religious communities. It is well
known that both in an army and in a church disciplinary regulations may be too strongly enforced;
they may be so much insisted on that instead of
being regarded as simply a means to an end, they

shall be looked upon as the end itself, the very essence of duty, by weak superstitious minds. And this was undoubtedly a special fault of a large portion of the sect of Pharisees, but Jesus, who censured them from want of sympathy, did not enlighten them at all or take such wise steps as were calculated to promote their reform.

8. The ceremonies of public worship might be called the language of signs as distinguished from the language of words: they express the worshippers' meaning in a beautiful symbolic form, and if well chosen are very impressive. They may occasionally become obsolete just as words do, when the spirit or purpose which they were originally intended to express no longer exists or is expressed in other ways more correctly. Some Jewish observances were meant to impress the minds of rude people strongly with a love of purity and a loathing of all filth and defilement, and though outward cleanliness may not cleanse the heart, it is a manifest help in that direction. Other rites served the purpose of reminders, they put people in remembrance of the commands which they had received and thus helped to keep them faithful to their religious profession. A similiar kind of institution is the widely prevalent marriage custom of wearing a ring, which is kept up both by Christians and Jews. The wedding-ring is intended not merely to distinguish the married woman, but to be a token of constancy which shall remind her of her vows and strengthen her determination to keep them. It is true that there are women whose virtue is so robust that they do not require any suggestive emblem to aid in its conservation, while others are so frail or corrupt that no external device will sustain them in the hour of temptation, yet few would think of arguing in consequence that ring-wearing is a useless form. If it can be shown that it tends on

the whole to give people a stronger impression of the sanctity of marriage and is in a majority of cases of real efficacy in preventing a breach of its obligations, whether it is kept up or discontinued will not be a matter of indifference. Circumcision and the wearing of phylacteries have been often enough condemned, because it has been observed that many have not profited by these outward reminders and become inwardly pure. Too much importance has generally been attached to them : the Jewish church has long maintained them as helps to religion, but has not pretended that they were religion itself.   Rabbi Lipman testifies, " A certain Christian mocked us, saying, ' Women who cannot be circumcised cannot be reckoned among Jews ! '   Such persons are ignorant that religion does not consist in circumcision, but in the heart. He who has not true religion is not a partaker of the Jewish circumcision; but he who has true religion is a Jew, although not circumcised " (" Nizzachon," Num. 21, p. 19).

9. The going through certain prescribed religious forms without feeling the spirit which they are intended to arouse is not necessarily hypocrisy. Little children who are taught to pray, both in Jewish and Christian families, repeat their petitions mechanically or by rote for awhile as mere formalists, without knowing the sense of the words they utter, and are not on that account subjected to reproach. The great mass of people are scarcely better than children in religious development, and require a similar treatment; they are not expected to enter very heartily into the devotional instruction provided for them, and must be formal before they can be spiritual. It is a great thing if a rude population can be brought to respect public worship and so far master their animal propensities as to be outwardly religious;

those who have made this creditable advance may be expected to go further with good teaching and guidance, so as to reach at length the requirements of a righteous life. Jesus, therefore, might have reasonably stimulated any dull apathetic worshippers that he beheld and assured them that, unless they acquired through their religious exercises self-mastery and a real love of God and their fellow-men, their rigorous performance at appointed seasons would be labour expended in vain. But he had no patience with people whose outward religious demonstrations did not accord with their inmost thoughts; he seemed to regard all such as conscious deceivers endeavouring to obtain credit for what was not in their hearts, and his objurgations were rather calculated to wound and irritate formalists than to quicken their conscience and help them to the attainment of true spiritual religion.

10. We all like a person of honest and frank behaviour, one who is accustomed to say just what he means, and we detest the flatterer or pretender who misleads us through his outward professions being at variance with his inmost thoughts and designs. But when the words and acts of a formalist are not in accord with his real sentiments, it is not from any deliberate intention to deceive us, and it is seldom that he does deceive any but the simplest and shallowest observers of the ways of humankind. If, for instance, a neighbour is formally polite to us, knowing that it is is quite possible for a bad feeling to lurk under a courteous exterior, we accept his proffered civilities for what they are worth, and are not imposed upon and misled by them in the slightest degree. But George Fox, the founder of the Quaker community, and one of the most genuine followers of Jesus, made no distinction between a formal manifestation of

courtesy, and hypocrisy ; and, in his eccentric advocacy of a frank and honest deportment, thought it desirable to get rid of all the polite usages of good society. No man with a fair knowledge of the world can doubt for a moment the value of these regulation manners as a means of refining rude people, softening their asperities, and enabling them as neighbours to get on with less friction and strife. If they are not always accompanied by a humble, respectful, and obliging disposition, they make it clear that such a spirit is considered worthy of imitation, and to some extent encourage its attainment. To entirely discard them, therefore, and make people more churlish, rude, and uncouth, in order that their behaviour should be more genuine, so far from conducing to the improvement of society, would only be a step backward in the direction of barbarism. The same objection may be fairly urged against the total abolition of religious forms with the view to expose the short-comings of a large class of worshippers ; if such a sweeping change could be accomplished, it would only have the effect of seriously interrupting the religious education of mankind.

11. If men were all equally virtuous, intelligent, and devout, if the world were wholly peopled with saints, they would thoroughly understand each other, would say and do spontaneously the right thing at the right time, and laws, rules, and forms of procedure for their guidance would be wholly unnecessary. This was just such a harmonious world as Jesus and his communistic followers were constantly dreaming of and hoping to find in their forthcoming Millennium. To govern and help on a large complex community in different stages of religious progress was a task quite unintelligible to them : it was only people of their own sort that they knew well how to deal with ; they were not

educationists, but perfectionists. Had they been
placed in the position of Moses, instead of framing
suitable laws and regulations to bind all classes
together and contribute·to their gradual elevation
and enlightenment, they would have picked out a few
congenial spirits as being alone worthy of fellowship, and would have condemned all the rest to
everlasting perdition. Before the commencement
of their itinerant ministrations, neither Jesus nor
Paul had held any public office or acted in a
governing and directing capacity ; they had not
even had domestic servants under them, nor the
care of a young family, and so were utterly un-
conversant and unsympathetic with ·the means
which are found requisite for maintaining order in
a mixed community. It was easy enough for them
to wander from place to place and disburden their
thoughts for an hour or so to any idle crowd that
happened to collect in the streets, but they could
not at the end of the discourse have followed those
hearers with authority and got them to live
methodically and peacefully in their respective
homes. Had they been called upon as rulers or
magistrates to mediate between opposing factions,
to settle the contentions arising among families, or
restore a disturbed village to harmony, they would
have proved in such a judicial position altogether
useless to society.

12. If the early Christians had established somewhere an independent colony, they might well have
dispensed with most of the disciplinary regulations
of the Jewish law, but it was not wise or safe to do
so when they spread themselves abroad in every
direction to effect the conversion of the Gentile
world. Jewish rabbis, while admitting that their
system of ritual wants reforming from time to
time, have always valued it as a protective hedge
of thorns which has checked hasty and inconsiderate

proselytism, and so helped to keep their religion
from corruption. But Paul and those whom he
led were desirous of making accession to the
Church as easy as possible, that they might thus
secure a more rapid increase. They were not at all
scrupulous as to whom they admitted into their
body nor careful to subject those attracted towards
them to a long course of probationary discipline as
was done by the Essenes. The miraculous virtue
imparted by baptism and the laying on of hands
was supposed to be all that was needed to regenerate
the convert and transform his whole character and
habits of life. Consequently, what they effected by
wandering about the world excitedly preaching and
baptizing with water was for the most part a mere
surface conversion. By the end of the first century
a multitude of people of various races, sects, and
schools of thought professed themselves Christians
by believing in Jesus, but their religious sentiments
were of quite a different complexion from those of
the primitive disciples. During the second century
some of the most zealous and influential Christians
had been brought up as Stoics, Platonists, and
Pythagoreans, and they all imparted to the community more or less of their educational bias, so
that the Church which commenced in Galilee as a
simple homogeneous brotherhood became a Babel of
sects. The ablest minds, who wished to establish
some bond of unity and concord between these
divided worshippers, knew that it could only be
brought about by a representative council, and assemblies of this kind were therefore convened from
time to time to settle the principal matters in dispute
and decide on authoritative writings. Various compromises of Jew and Gentile doctrine were thus
effected; but at each succeeding council the
Gentile element had with further propagandism
increased in strength, and the majority of voices

carried Christianity a step further off from the primitive faith and practice of the Galileans. When established at length by Constantine as the religion of the Roman Empire, the Church had by the final triumph of its proselytism become a monstrous growth that would have been quite unrecognizable by the little society of kindred minds with whom it originated: it was no longer a religious sheepfold, but a huge menagerie, containing such a variety of species that the primitive gregarian arrangement was wholly inadequate to bring them to live together in tolerable harmony. Jesus desired his disciples to associate as a communistic brotherhood and "call no man master," but the time at length came when, having revolted against all other authorities, the once simple community became so complex that they required a High Priest of their own, together with a Cæsar, to balance and reconcile their party differences. In short, to settle all the rancorous disputes that were continually breaking out, and hold the European, Asiatic, and African churches together in some kind of doctrinal agreement, it was necessary to have a supreme judge or final court of appeal established somewhere, and a Papacy or monarchical form of church government became inevitable.

13. Had the conversion of the Gentile world and the consequent growth of the Church from a simple religious brotherhood to a great complex community been actually contemplated and designed by Jesus, he would have provided for such a mighty development in the institutions which he gave his disciples. Seeing what was in the distant future, he would have told them plainly that, so long as they were a small company of sympathetic friends, they could dispense with observances and would hardly require to be bound by any system of government. But when once they should become diversified with

continual increase and consist of many families—old
and young, learned and ignorant, rich and poor, all
sorts and conditions of people such as are gathered
in a great city—he would have assured them that
they would find it necessary to do as other citizens,
to have capable rulers for the settling of strife and
arrangements for holding their widely-dispersed
communities together in harmony. If the leading
Christians of the second and third centuries could
have found a passage to this effect in any of the
generally recognized authoritative discourses of
Jesus, they would have deemed the instruction
invaluable, and it would have afforded them a most
convincing proof of their master's wonderful
sagacity and foresight. But the Gospels, which
were then widely accepted in the Church, contained
no such text, and it was too late to improve them
by interpolations which should supply the defect.
Consequently the most able and influential ecclesiastics were compelled to do many things without
authority; they could only modify their institutions
from time to time as circumstances called for it by
disregarding the Gospels and acting entirely on
their own discretion. But thoughtful Christians,
unweighted with government responsibility, soon
perceived that these new arrangements were
totally at variance with the communistic teaching
of Jesus. The changes of polity introduced by
learned bishops were in their eyes not necessary
developments, but corruptions, and thus arose the
succession of revolutionary sects that disturbed the
peace of the Church by agitating for the restoration
of primitive Christianity. Jesus commenced his
religious mission as an opponent of ecclesiastical
rule, as a revolter against the Mosaic hierarchy,
and did not see that he was thus creating a
precedent for future revolts which should
tear his own community to pieces with intermin-

able strife when once it should reach a complex development.

14. Every great religious reformation is said to have its birth in a reformer's prophetic mind; some gifted individual more thoughtful and wise than his fellows sees the need of making salutary changes in the established system, and induces others to see it, and so they march steadily towards the realization of their views. But it is clear that the general renunciation of Jewish observances from the first to the fourth century and the substitution of other observances in the Christian Church were not in the mind of Jesus; the growing community that professed to follow him drifted into these changes as occasion arose, and did not adopt them in consequence of his authoritative direction. We might take as one palpable instance of this, the gradual neglect of the Jewish Sabbath, and the appointment in its stead of what Christians called the Lord's Day for the purpose of public worship and rest. Jesus never once hinted at such an alteration; he declared that it was quite lawful on the Sabbath to attend to any urgent business that would not admit of postponement; he showed, both by his teaching and acts, that he was not, like many Jews of that period, a Sabbatarian slave. This was the liberal doctrine and practice of the school of Hillel, and had he as well as Hillel continued a loyal member of the Jewish Church, his followers would not have been likely to make any needless departure from the Mosaic economy. But his revolt against the Sanhedrin, coupled with his anti-ritualistic leaning, led others to suppose that he was aiming at the entire abrogation of the Law. Paul reproved the Galatians for observing sabbaths and festivals, and told the Colossians to let no man judge them for the non-observance of the Sabbath. Laxity in this matter must have been very common

with the scattered Gentile Christians whom he visited, and the need of a regular sabbath was not generally felt till long after, when the Church was better organized and Christianity had become the established religion of the empire. Then, as some Christians consistently kept the seventh day and others the first, or rested equally on both, the bishops under Constantine decided, for the sake of distinction, to leave the ancient usage to the unconverted Jews, and render the observance of the Lord's Day universal. The breach which already existed between Christianity and Judaism was thus needlessly widened; and although one day might be considered as good as another for rest and worship, the institution of a rival sabbath was a revolutionary change, and could in no sense be considered a reform.

15. The early Christians drifted into some beneficial changes, such as the neglect of circumcision and the dietary laws, but they did nothing towards purging the Church of Israel from its Babylonian corruption, and promoting other much needed reforms. There had long been growing in the minds of the more enlightened and thoughtful Jews a wholesome distrust of the practice of offering sacrifices as a means of purchasing forgiveness of sins. It was felt that many people were thereby rather encouraged to continue in their evil ways than prompted to study right conduct, and set about earnestly to lead an amended.life. "To what purpose is the multitude of your sacrifices? . . . . Bring no more vain oblations. . . . Wash you, make you clean, put away the evil of your doings" (Isaiah, i. 11–16). "Will the Lord be pleased with thousands of rams or with ten thousand rivers of oil? Shall I give my firstborn for my transgression, the fruit of my body for the sin of my soul? He hath showed thee, O man, what

is good, and what doth the Lord require of thee, but to do justly, and to love mercy, and to walk humbly with thy God?" (Micah, vi. 7–8). It does not appear that Jesus caught this purer spirit which had manifested itself in the nation or said anything to the same purpose; he required his followers to offer sacrifices, with sincere repentance for what they had done amiss (Matt. v. 23, 24), which the priests also enjoined (Lev. v. 5), but did not show that repentance might become effectual without sacrifices. A real Jewish reformer, who rejected the authority of the Sanhedrin, should have kept away altogether from the sacrificial services of the Temple, and directed his utmost efforts towards increasing the congregations and advancing the purer worship of the synagogues.

16. It must be borne in mind that the Jews who returned from Babylon in successive migrations under the direction of Zerubbabel, Ezra, Nehemiah, and others, had no claim whatever to represent united Israel; they were only a poor fragment of the dispersed people—the sect of Restorationists. Nor could they, any more than modern Palestine colonists, be justly considered an enlightened or God-guided minority chosen for their superior character to act as exemplars and work out the redemption of the whole race. The immense influence which they exerted over their dispersed brethren was due not to their virtues or intelligence, but to the commanding position which they held as inhabitants of the Holy Land. There was much truth in an old rabbinical saying once current in Chaldea and other parts of the East, that "the chaff of the nation had returned to Palestine while the corn remained in Babylon." Not only on the Euphrates, but in Egypt and elsewhere, the more sensible of the Dispersionist community seem to have regarded those who went back to the old

home distrustfully as priest-led visionaries in pursuit of objects which were wholly unattainable. They could not restore the deposed royal family, they could not restore the lost ark and its sacred treasures, they could not restore their lost brethren without supernatural aid, and as such assistance was not forthcoming to make the work complete, a fragmentary restoration should not have been attempted at all.   There was not the slightest propect before them of regaining their ancient national independence in Palestine; they simply migrated from one Persian province to another and remained in a tributary condition.   To bring back in accordance with their dreams the dispersed twelve tribes to the respective territories occupied by their ancestors it would have been necessary to buy out the numerous Gentile families who had flown in and settled there, or otherwise expel them by force, and they were quite unable to do either. At the same time they assumed a jealous irreconcilable attitude towards those joint occupants of the country, which rendered future complications and wars inevitable.   The exclusive disposition which they manifested in carrying on the restoration of the Temple, was very unlike the large-hearted, charitable spirit in which it was originally erected by Solomon; they scornfully refused the offer of assistance from the neighbouring Samaritans, and would have been well pleased to destroy every other temple in the world to its last stone.   A more bigoted and intolerant community than these priest-led people never existed, and it was not progress that they aimed at, but retrogression towards ancestral conditions and usages.   The reputed holiness of Jerusalem did not in any respect improve the character of the inhabitants, and considering the pride, hatred, and jealousy which centred there, and the fratricidal blood which was often shed in the vicinity of the sacrificial services, it might well have been said by those Israelites who were content to pray and hear instruction in their quiet ˙synagogues, " the nearer the Temple the further from God."

17. The Restorationists professed to be very zealous in purifying the land from idolatry, that is, in reforming people from the superstition of honouring unduly the work ˌof men's hands so as to become spiritually blinded in conducting their worship and altogether forgetful of the Most High. But it was only against honour given to images or representations of living things that they stubbornly contended as being very prejudicial to religion. It never occurred to them that the work of an architect may become just as much an object of idolatrous homage as the production of a painter or a sculptor. Some of the world's renowned temples have been frequently venerated to excess, as well as the sacred emblems and relics contained within them, and this was especially the case with the restored sanctuary at Jerusalem. In an age when superstition was rampant under many forms, this building which attracted from afar immense crowds of people had become the idol of idols, yet those who bowed before it were so much afraid of giving honour to images, that they entirely prohibited the making of such things even for the innocent purposes of ornament. What was still worse, they could not be got to tolerate Greek and Roman sculpture, and from provocations thus arising, fanatical outbreaks attended with bloodshed were in some parts of Palestine of frequent occurrence. Even the ensigns, which were borne by the Roman legions, they resolved to expel from their country at any cost as a terrible pollution, although they could not resist the legions themselves, and this iconophobia probably did as much

as anything to precipitate the final ruinous conflict
with the forces of Vespasian.   There was great
need for a reformer to arise and tell the people that
they were polluted by their own iniquities; and not
by any customs and emblems which the conquerors
had introduced without their consent, and further
that the prejudice against images did not exist when
the first Temple was built, and had formed no part of
their primitive religion.   They certainly failed to
receive any instruction to this effect from the prophet
of Nazareth or from those who became his disciples.
The early Christians entertained just as strong an
aversion to painting and sculpture as any of the
Restorationist Jews; such productions of genius as
are now treasured in the galleries of Europe for
universal admiration, were in their eyes heathen
abominations hurtful to look upon, and having no
right to exist.   For the want of proper authoritative instruction on the use and abuse of works of
art the expanding Church not only committed great
injustice against pagans, but became eventually
divided and distracted itself, one party persisting
in a course of barbarous iconoclasm, while another
fell into a more or less debasing idolatry.

18. The Jews who returned from Babylon
corrupted the religion of Israel with many Persian
and Chaldean fables, especially with the doctrine of
the Evil Spirit and the entire mythological system
of Diabolism.   So far from Jesus perceiving this
serious lapse into error that had taken place, and
doing all he could to correct and reform his countrymen, he only helped to lead them further astray;
the religion which he taught was an outgrowth
of the prevalent Chaldean corruption.   An enlightened Israelite would have told his brethren
that God ruled uninterruptedly in heaven and
earth, and that whatever evils befel them were
wholesome corrections for what they had failed to

do or had else done amiss in order to promote their amendment. This overruling of divine justice in the constitution of nature and the affairs of men was unintelligible to Jesus; he imagined that diseases, accidents, and other ills, were caused by malignant demons that wandered about the world, or by the machinations of witchcraft. Satan, the Ahriman of the Persians, was supposed to be everywhere busy with his subject spirits, concocting mischief, and ignorant, vicious, and negligent people were thus furnished with a ready means of accounting for their troubles and adversities, and putting away blame in the matter from themselves. A notion also grew up among such people that they were entitled to receive for their various ills and misfortunes compensation in the future life : it was thought that in the great world-struggle then raging God would eventually overcome Satan and proceed to indemnify his saints for all the harm and loss inflicted on them by the great spiritual enemy. Hence, too, arose the insane idea of asceticism, that it is advantageous for people to court persecution, to expose themselves as much as possible to Satan's attacks, and suffer the utmost misery and wrong in the present life in order to be entitled to a proportionately large amends in the life to come. Nothing ever contributed more effectively than this pernicious superstition to warp the moral judgment of mankind and set up a false standard of righteousness. It tended, moreover, beyond anything else, to harden and exaggerate human differences, to separate the members of a community into what were supposed to be the perfectly good, and the entirely bad; people believed that those who opposed them were not simply erring brothers who might presently be enlightened and reconciled, but men under Satan's influence delighting in every conceivable

I

wickedness and doomed to suffer everlastingly in Hell.

19. One of the most heathenish and hurtful propensities that the Jews acquired during their sojourn in Babylon was the craving for supernatural foreknowledge ; the disposition to go beyond the limits of human calculation in anticipating future events. They were perhaps not entirely free from this weakness at any period of their history, for every ancient nation was more or less infected with it, and it seems to have been a superstition inherent in the whole race of mankind. But after their contact with the astrologers, diviners, and soothsayers who abounded in Chaldea, they certainly became more addicted to unreasonable attempts at reading their destiny than their forefathers had ever been prior to the Captivity. Their very circumstances as an exiled people, coupled with the recollections of their past history, would naturally dispose them strongly to look into the future for the opening of brighter prospects and the chance of recovering their lost national inheritance. But whether individuals or communities take to consulting oracles and anticipating the fortune that is supposed to await them, wholly irrespective of their present conduct and exertions, it is not likely to conduce to their real welfare. Why did the Restorationists, who returned to Palestine, persist so long in attempting to reconstruct their broken nation, and after all fail ? Or rather why were they not as successful as the wisest of their race had been at an earlier period in establishing an independent dominion ? One reason of course is, that they had to compete with far more powerful Gentile neighbours than the Philistines and other border communities who withstood the founders of the ancient monarchy. But a more especial reason is, that they consulted vacticinators, had always before them an impossible

programme to fulfil, and did not survey wisely the
situation presented to them, and take this or that
course for the advancement of their interests according to the turn of circumstances. David and
Solomon were sagacious rulers, who engaged in a
great enterprise when they saw that it was practicable and opportune, and not from its being predicted that such things should come to pass, or in
consequence of something similar being done by
their ancestors long before when in a totally
different position. Had they been influenced by
such superstitions as these, and induced to commit
themselves to undertakings so utterly dispro-
portioned to their powers that miraculous aid must
be considered indispensable to success, they, too,
instead of prospering, would have experienced a
long succession of sorrows and reverses.

20. The natural foreknowledge which sagacious
people displayed in a rude unscientific age was
invariably looked upon as supernatural and of unlimited extent by the more simple and credulous
portion of the community. When a person by
careful observation managed to foretell correctly a
change of weather, or the course which a malady
would take, or the result of an impending war, it
did not strike the ignorant that such prevision was
within the reach of all who would make a like
diligent use of their opportunities and powers: they
esteemed it, as they esteemed any other superior
knowledge, or skill, a gift or favour divinely conferred on here and there an individual, and by
ordinary mortals wholly unattainable. This superstition was readily taken advantage of by a class of
pretentious people who engaged in every conceivable form of empirical vaticination, and claimed to be
able to reveal fully all things of importance which
were marked out to occur in the fortunes of men
and the fates of empires. The failures of these

professional readers of destiny were soon forgotten, while their occasional successes were considerably magnified, and in one way and another they grew into such universal repute that monarchs and other persons of the highest rank were disposed to consult them in every important crisis of their affairs. A little more reflection might have convinced such people that the conferring of prophetic favours which seemed so desirable in their eyes would not really be conducive to human welfare. Those who want superior knowledge or special information of any kind, that they may see as prophets further than their fellows in this or that direction, must earn it by diligent study ; it is utter folly to expect to obtain it gratuitously. There is no royal road to effecting new discoveries and foretelling events any more than there is to the acquisition of ordinary school learning. The idle scholar who clandestinely obtains help in the working of his exercises and the solution of his problems, so far from being benefited by such favours, will only suffer loss in the end, since he will fail to effect the strengthening and development of his mental powers, which is the chief purpose of education. Every human learner, every student in the world's great university, would suffer in precisely the same way, if he were favoured with divine intimations about hidden things and forthcoming events which would save him from the usual course of persistent application and inquiry that is needed to procure enlightenment.

21. When we say that God rules the world, it does not imply that all human actions are divinely planned and prearranged as in a drama, so that every individual is bound to take a certain prescribed course. And even if the succession of events which are to make history were preordained it could serve no good moral purpose to have them

beforehand revealed. If the world's future could be clearly mapped out under the observation of mankind, they would not really become wiser in consequence, but would rather be prevented from acquiring wisdom, since they would no longer have any scope for the exercise of their reflecting powers in the calculation of probabilities. Their minds, too, would be so much taken up with the contemplation of a vast series of future events, that they would be unable to concentrate sufficient attention on the business immediately before them. An individual grappling resolutely with new circumstances as they arise from day to day might be not unaptly compared with a chess-player, who, whether he makes good moves or bad moves, is pretty sure to profit from the experience thus acquired and grow wiser as the game proceeds. But imagine a game of chess to be played in which the moves on each side should be all prearranged and written down consecutively for the players, there would in such case be no need for the continual exercise of their judgment, and the whole affair from beginning to end would be an idle mechanical exhibition. Those who believe in predestination and desire to have the future revealed would convert into just such a puerile stage performance the whole economy of human life; people would thus move as determined on in the manner of puppets; wise reflection would be no longer wanted in the ordering of their affairs, and they would be entirely freed from moral responsibility.

22. What has been the actual moral result of consulting oracles and believing in predictions of future events? what solid advantage have mankind ever gained by seeking to have their destiny miraculously revealed? A sensible person in deciding as to what course he shall take in any given circumstance, endeavours to keep his mind

as free and unprejudiced as possible, but a belief in vaticination inclines people one way more than another, or puts them under a strong bias which diminishes their scope of doing what will be for the best. The cultivator of the soil, who is guided in his operations from week to week by the weather predictions of an almanac, will not be found a model agriculturist. Superstitious peasants in this country, when in any doubt as to what they should do, occasionally resort to divination; they suspend a Bible from their door-key, and watch the direction in which it turns, or they open the sacred volume hap-hazard and place their finger unwittingly on a certain text, which if rightly interpreted is supposed to indicate their true course. Such expedients, like the casting of lots or the toss-up of a coin, enable the indolent and credulous to shirk the responsibility of making a proper use of their reflective powers, and commit them to a chance decision. Then, if they take some unwise step and suffer in consequence, instead of resolving to profit from their errors and act with more discretion in future, they console themselves with the thought that it was predestined that they should do what has been done, and there is no help for it. Many a person, from trusting to some flattering prediction of future prosperity, has failed to make the most of the opportunities presented to him for gradually ameliorating his lot, and has been reduced at length to a condition of beggary. Even those oracular assurances of success, which in all ages have been so much valued by politicians and military commanders as tending to inspire confidence and thus fulfil themselves, have not unfrequently made people neglectful in their preparations, or given rise to a spirit of headlong rashness which had ended in overwhelming defeat.

23. Those who have observed the pernicious

influence which the habit of seeking supernatural foreknowledge has had on mankind in general, may form a very good idea of its effect on the Jews of Palestine during that long struggle to recover their former glory when they were under a complete vaticination craze. The Restorationist prophets, only a portion of whose utterances are embalmed in Scripture, did good service so long as they simply rebuked the corrupt -tendencies of their age and admonished the people to turn from their iniquities. When, however, they no longer bore witness against the prevalent demoralization, and, yielding to the popular demand for political fortune-telling, predicted the doom of Tyre, Damascus, Egypt, and other countries, they spoke presumptuously, deceiving themselves and the sympathetic crowd. Moses, if correctly reported, very clearly taught his brethren to be guided at all times by religious principles and not to be ruled by predictions. To prevent the people from being influenced one way or another by hearing it said that such and such things were to happen, he enjoined them to wait awhile, and leave the value of predictions to be decided by events (Deut. xviii. 21). He further told them that even in the case of prophetic signs being given which should actually be fulfilled, they should not allow such fulfilments to govern their conduct or lead them away from their religion (xiii. 1-3). Another wise teacher of Israel said, "Whoso regardeth dreams is like him that catcheth at a shadow and followeth after the wind. The vision of dreams is the resemblance of one thing to another, even as the likeness of a face to a face. Of an unclean thing what can be cleansed? and from that which is false what truth can come? Divinations and soothsayings and dreams are vain, and the heart fancieth as a woman's heart in travail" (Ecclus. xxxiv. 2-5).

24. During the whole Restoration period there

120   THE REAL JESUS.

were probably always some few sensible Jews who
gave no heed to soothsaying and considered follies
of that kind inconsistent with the fundamental
truths of their religion, but they had not sufficient
influence to enlighten and reform their more credulous countrymen.   Plenty of vaticinators stood
ready to pander to the popular craving for a knowledge of the nation's future, nor was the superstition
checked in any degree by the continual failure of
predictions.   It was in vain that this rule had been
given for general guidance, " if the thing follow not
nor come to pass, that is the thing which the Lord
hath not spoken," for the priests as well as the
people had come to regard certain treasured
prophecies as the infallible word of God, whether
they were fulfilled or not.   From the record of what
was supposed to have been spoken to Nathan, " I
will establish the throne of his kingdom for ever "
(2 Sam. vii. 13), they seem to have been under the
impression that God was pledged in a manner to
perpetuate the dominion of David whatever might
be the conduct of his posterity or that of their
subject people.   And some devout Jews, in their
fervent outpourings, instead of blaming the pre-
sumptuousness of prophetic writers and showing
how they were confuted by the course of events, felt
inclined to half remonstrate with the Eternal for
having, as they thought, neglected to keep his word.
Thus the author of Psalm lxxxix. (probably Maccabean, and written evidently at a time when the
struggling people were depressed by defeat) says,
" My covenant will I not break, nor alter the thing
that is gone out of my mouth.   Once have I sworn
by my holiness that I will not lie unto David.   His
seed shall endure for ever, and his throne as the sun
before me.   It shall be established for ever as the
moon, and as a faithful witness in heaven.—But thou
hast cast off and abhorred, thou hast been wroth

with thine anointed. Thou hast made void the covenant of thy servant: thou hast profaned his crown by casting it to the ground. Thou hast broken down all his hedges, thou hast brought his strongholds to ruin. All that pass by spoil him : he is a reproach to his neighbours. Thou hast set up the right hand of his adversaries; thou hast made all his enemies to rejoice. Thou hast also turned the edge of his sword, and hast not made him to stand in battle. Thou hast made his glory to cease and cast his throne down to the ground " (35–44).

25. The difficulty experienced by pious Restorationists with respect to the non-fulfilment of predictions was in the course of time met in quite another way. It was still imagined that there could be no error or miscalculation on the part of the prophetic writer ; his inspired word could not fail under any circumstance, but those who read it might not be able to rightly comprehend its meaning. Where predictions seemed to be unfulfilled or contradicted by the course of events, they were supposed to have a mysterious spiritual significance which could only be expounded by the gifted and wise. There accordingly arose a school of mystical interpreters, the precursors of the Kabbalists, who engaged in a kind of Scriptural divination, and established fanciful rules for extracting the deep spiritual sense which was supposed to be hidden in every portion of the sacred records. Some of the prophets had spoken in hyperbolical language of terrible divine judgments which were to fall on the Gentile nations, and these predictions were believed at length to foreshadow an approaching general destruction of the world. It was further imagined that the restoration of the Twelve Tribes, which had been repeatedly foretold, would be fulfilled eventually, not in Palestine, but by the establishment of an everlasting Kingdom of Heaven.

As the author of Psalm xc. had said that a thousand years were only as one day to the Eternal, it was supposed that a prophetic day signified mystically a thousand years, and since the world, according to Jewish tradition, was created in six days, which were followed by a sabbath, so it was expected to endure just six thousand years, when there would succeed a sabbatical thousand, or what is commonly called the Millennium.

26. During the intense excitement of the Maccabean struggles another class of visionaries arose, who did not confine themselves to the interpretation of what had been written long before, but took the bolder course of writing mystical revelations of their own and passing them off as the productions of an earlier age. By far the most important of these in respect to the credit which they obtained and the influence which they exerted in the world, were the Book of Enoch and the Book of Daniel, which last even got to be admitted into the Hebrew canon. In both these Apocalyptic writings are predicted certain approaching supernatural events which many Jews of the Maccabean period were disposed to believe, namely, the impending destruction of the world, a general resurrection and judgment of the dead, and the establishment of the saints of Israel in an everlasting celestial kingdom. Concurrently with these views the ascetic delusion was making great progress among the people, as it seemed to accord well with their reverses of fortune and long succession of national calamities. It was thought especially meritorious to undergo hardship and wrong as the surest means of obtaining a future recompense: a life of much suffering in the present world was believed to furnish the best title to a blissful existence in the world to come. But if unjust treatment was necessary to prove the elect of

Israel and fit them for their everlasting reward, not only must each individual saint submit to this ordeal, but even the anointed ruler could not be exempted from it, any môre than the heir of David could escape the humiliation that fell on his subjects during the Captivity. Thus there was forced on the minds of those Jews, who were under the influence of the ascetic mania, the notion of a Suffering Messiah coming to gather and organize the saints of his kingdom prior to the impending destruction of the world, and they studied the sacred writings carefully with the view to find there a confirmation of their theory.

27. While the Restorationists were thus dominated by the vaticination mania, ever thinking of a glorious national future, and endeavouring to do all the unreasonable things which has been by wild dreamers predicted, the Dispersionist communities were for the most part free from their delusion and in a much more healthy moral condition. They fell under Palestinian influence eventually, and accepted the prophets of the Maccabean Canon as inspired writers for their authoritative guidance, but they were better guided by their own synagogue teachers, when they simply discharged their moral obligations from day to day free from all prophetic bias. Had then Jesus of Nazareth really been a great religious reformer, he would have set himself strongly against the Restoration movement as a radical error, would have denounced the whole line of vaticinators as misleaders of the people, and by travelling to Egypt, Babylon, Antioch, and other places, would have endeavoured to establish some bond of union between the uncorrupted Dispersionists. He would have taught the people to renounce the soothsaying folly entirely, to let the future alone and care for the present, which was clearly revealed, to go about their duty from day to

day as good Israelites, having peace among themselves and no quarrel with the neighbouring
Gentiles, since the country which God had now
given them to dwell in was not only Palestine but
the wide world. A council of the wisest teachers
in Israel would have been duly convened by him,
and they together would have purified the Law
from priestly corruption and effected a thorough
revision of the sacred writings, taking care that
every synagogue should be supplied in good time
with a copy of their work : there would thus have
been accomplished a fundamental religious reform
of inestimable value both for Jews and Gentiles.

28. It does not appear, however, that Jesus had
the slightest intercourse with the dispersed
synagogues, either by letter or otherwise, and it is
clear that he was entirely carried away by the
vaticination delusions of the Judean community.
The Restorationists were morally injured from the
belief that their destiny was revealed and that they
were bound to adhere to an inflexible programme,
and any one presuming to act as their predicted
leader must have been from the same cause
especially perverted. Jesus, the Suffering
Messiah, threw himself as a fatalist into collision
with his countrymen, just as they, the suffering
nation, continued from time to time to provoke a mad
conflict with the outside world. He felt that he
must go up to Jerusalem, not as a reformer, not as
a peacemaker, not as a reconciler of parties and
general benefactor of the nation, not simply to
observe the state of affairs there, and so do the
best he could under existing circumstances, but
deliberately to court hostility and suffer death,
else how could the Scriptures be fulfilled ? He said
to his disciples, " The Son of Man goeth as it is
written of him " (Matt. xxvi. 24). " It is written
of the Son of Man that he must suffer many things

and be set at nought" (Mark ix. 12). "When I sent you without purse or scrip, lacked ye anything? And they said, Nothing. Then said he unto them, But now, he that hath a purse, let him take it, and likewise his scrip; and he that hath no sword, let him sell his garment, and buy one. For I say unto you, that this that is written must yet be accomplished in me. And he was reckoned among the transgressors : for the things concerning me have an end. And they said, Lord, behold, here are two swords. And he said unto them, It is enough" (Luke xxii. 35–38). This punctilious endeavour to act in strict accordance to what was supposed to have been written prophetically rather than to do from time to time what conscience dictated as reasonable and just is one of the most pitiable exhibitions that religious delusion has ever presented to the world. Although Jesus was not fettered by the obligations of a rigid ceremonialism like some of the Pharisees, he was quite as much as they a slave of superstition, in being bound hand and foot by the mystical interpretation put on certain priestly documents. If he had been all along guided by principle and not by prediction, if, instead of going dramatically through the part which Scriptural divination had prescribed for the Suffering Messiah, he had simply done his best to serve God and promote the welfare of his fellow-men as a free Israelite, the superstitious world would have honoured him less, but his example would have harmonized with the eternal course of things and been of infinitely more worth to succeeding generations of mankind.

29. Jesus may be justly pointed to as a distinguished religious devotee, whose misunderstood and embellished death has greatly moved the hearts of the millions that are usually much

affected by mythical and dramatic representations
of murdered innocence, but there is not the
slightest ground for holding him before the world
as an eminent religious reformer. The greatest
reforms effected from time to time in the community
of which he is considered the founder have been the
renunciation or explaining away of his extravagant
precepts and the adoption of more rational and
practical views of life. Much religious progress
and enlargement of mind has been made not only
in the churches but in the synagogues. Enlightened
modern Jews are very far in advance of those who
were vainly striving eighteen hundred years ago to
reconstruct their nation in Palestine. We see now
no retrograde tendency manifested among them,
no disposition to build again the temple of their
forefathers, and restore the sacrificial services.
They do not allow themselves to be worked up to
a frightful pitch of militant fanaticism by the old
superstitious prejudice against images and pictures.
The notion of Satan and his legions of evil spirits
roaming about over the world to vex mankind with
diseases and other troubles has ceased to be a part
of their belief. They do not in any of their business
transactions resort to divination, nor consult
prophetic writings, nor manifest the least craving
for supernatural foreknowledge in reference to the
destiny of their race. There is some little amount
of difference between them in their conceptions of
the future life: some hold that it is useless to
speculate at all on what is absolutely beyond human
ken ; while others affirm that they find much ground
for consolation and hope in the contemplation of a
higher and purer existence. But the old barbarous
notion of dividing mankind sharply according to
their deserts into two sections—the sheep and the
goats—the former to be consigned to everlasting
bliss and the latter to endless torment, they are

quite agreed in rejecting as being well in accord with the ancient Egyptian mythology; but utterly inconsistent with the belief in a just God. Such is the course which Jewish reformation has taken, and will any unprejudiced person say that this reformation, which is still progressing, was initiated long ago or has been since helped on by the teaching of the prophet of Nazareth ?

CHAPTER VI.

HIS MORAL TEACHING.

Jesus more a poet than an ethical teacher.   2. In a family teaching and ruling are combined.   3. They were so combined by Moses the leader of Israel.   4. Jesus neither ruled nor helped others to rule.   5. While Moses took charge of the entire people, Jesus established a sect.   7. He had no idea of educating and training the young.   9. The poor results of his wayside discourses.   10. He did nothing to arrest the crying evil of brigandage.   12. While Moses sought to establish justice on earth, Jesus tried to introduce unjust equality.   13. He had not a well-balanced, but a lop-sided morality.   15. His golden rule condemns not only the wrong-doer, but the judge.   16. His doctrine of universal forgiveness considered.   19. Ill treatment of honest opponents.   21. Encouragement to suffer wrong with an eye to compensation.   22. Scourging the innocent and sparing the guilty.   23. Bitter invectives against the Pharisees.   27. The virtues practised by Jesus of a cheap petty character.   28. He did not befriend the industrious poor.   31. He taught people to beg and pray, but not to work.   33. His erratic teaching on marriage, divorce, and eunuchism.   36. His requiring the renunciation of property.   38. Dissembled asceticism.   39. True spirit of the Gospel.   41. Courting persecution and martyrdom.   42. Dr. Philip Schaff's remarks considered. 43. The Gospel inspired the martyr mania of Origen and Cyprian.

JESUS is commonly held up to universal regard at the present day as a great ethical teacher; from the nature of his discourses, however, he would be much more correctly designated a religious poet.   All the Jewish Restoration prophets were poets rather than moralists; they presented their visions to the world from time to time in lofty impressive language, but did not lay down very clearly and fully before the people the common duties of life. The wise Son of Sirach and the author of the Book of Proverbs gave a far greater amount of wholesome moral instruction to their countrymen than can be found in all the combined burdens of the prophets from Isaiah to Malachi. Jesus is not, as some have described him, a mystic having subjective visions; he does not in his discourses reveal celestial scenes and conjure up strange typical beasts like the writers of the Apocalyptic school; but he is clearly gifted with poetic talent of a better sort, continually deals in similitudes, and directs his hearers' attention to the surrounding beauties of nature. In some of his parables and short pithy sayings he reminds us much more of the ancient Jewish sages than of the prophets. And a large portion of these brief utterances, if taken separately, have much intrinsic excellence, whether they are to be considered entirely his own or common proverbs of the country.—"Cast not pearls before swine." "Set not a candle under a bushel." "New wine should not be put into old bottles." "They strain at a gnat, and swallow a camel." "Men do not gather grapes of thorns, or figs of thistles." "Where the carcass is, there the eagles will be gathered together." "Hypocrites are whited sepulchres." "They that are sound need not a physician." "A prophet gets no honour at home." "Before you begin to build count the cost." There is wisdom in these detached sentences, as we may find bits of wisdom in nearly every poet of ancient and modern times, but we must take into consideration the general design of a man's teaching to estimate its true worth. We may have pointed out to us in an ancient building a number of bright gems together with beautiful pieces of carved work and other ornaments; it will be necessary however, to have a more comprehensive view of the structure to form

K

a correct opinion of the ability and genius of the architect.

2. The first ruler that rises up among mankind is the father of a family who is also the first teacher; with him teaching and ruling go harmoniously together in moulding the young generation. If he gives his children wholesome advice and prays God to guide them aright, yet imposes no restraint on their vicious inclinations, and subjects them to no regular educational discipline, his duty will be only half accomplished, and they will not take to moral courses simply from hearing his admonition and prayers. A good father stands in the midst of his young dependent people both as a prophet and as a magistrate; he points out their failings and evil tendencies, warns them of the trials and temptations that await them when they go forth into the world, and enjoins them to persevere in faithfully discharging their duty before God and their fellow-men; at the same time he insists on their conforming to his household regulations, trains them carefully in moral habits, curbs their selfish and aggressive propensities, settles promptly the disputes which arise among them, and requires them to be at peace with their neighbours and respect the laws of their country. In some families the mother teaches and cannot rule, while the father rules and cannot teach, so that, though they would probably each fail alone to train up their children aright, they succeed well by working harmoniously together and supporting each other's authority. Such concord between the great educational forces which are directed towards the elevation and regulation of mankind ought to be maintained as far as possible in all communities— not only in every family, but in every nation. Owing, however, to conquests, revolutions, migrations, and the various other great social

changes which have been effected in the world, it frequently happens that the national teacher and the national ruler, the prophet and the magistrate, work independently of each other, and, instead of maintaining friendly relations, are altogether at cross purposes, so that their influence is weakened, and they fail to subdue disorder effectively and keep society in a healthy moral condition. Where a conflict or misunderstanding exists between a nation's teaching and ruling authorities it is generally owing to those who presume to instruct the people occupying a free competitive position which forces them into factious advocacy. They cannot afford to be impartial, and speak wholesome moral truths to all, as the father of a family, the master of a school, or the founder of a colony would do; they can only obtain an audience or following by alluring with blandishments people of one sort—a class, a party, or a sect—to whose crotchets and prejudices they must pander, when it is very desirable to do otherwise for their enlightenment.

3. The Israelites, who migrated from Egypt to Canaan under the leadership of Moses, resembled in some respects the Pilgrim Fathers who went from our own country to New England. They were driven to seek a new abode by oppression, and when encamped on independent ground Moses became at once their prophet and magistrate; in his hands instruction and government were just as effectively united as they would be by any father of a family. The Judges, who succeeded him, were both teachers and rulers of the people, so far as their authority extended in a period of great confusion and almost uninterrupted warfare. Under the early monarchy the same combination of educational forces continued, and the system may be said to have reached its fullest development during the

glorious reign of king Solomon. After the death
of that sagacious ruler the disruption and sad
decline of Israel commenced: the kingdom was
torn asunder by factious dissensions, and soon
scattered in subjugated fragments never more to be
brought together again. A class of teachers arose
to speak to the divided and confused people who
were called "prophets," but they were not
magisterial prophets as Moses and the Judges had
been; they did nothing towards settling men's
differences and causing them to live together in
harmony. They resembled greatly the dervishes,
marabouts, and other holy men who still abound
in the East, and the nearest analogues to them in
this part of the world would perhaps be the ranting
preacher, and the intemperate agitator or stump
orator. In short, they were visionaries, men of
wild theory, professing to teach without knowing
how to rule or having had the smallest experience
of government. No concord subsisted between
them; they competed one against the other for
popular support; every party, every faction, every
sect, had a prophet who was blind to its faults
while bitterly denouncing·the sins of the rest of
the community; and the rival prophets were
constantly flinging abuse and pouring forth
maledictions one against the other. They undoubtedly rebuked iniquity at times and did good
in a small way, but they were too fanatical,
prejudiced, and conflicting in their views to
command general respect and act beneficially as
teachers of the whole community.

4. Now it is evident that had Jesus any clear
conception of being called upon by God to reunite
divided Israel, he would not have taken up the
miserable rôle of these holy visionaries to add
to their confusion, but would have assumed the
magisterial office and set about to restore order and

build up the nation on just principles. For a prophet or any other man of superior intelligence to teach effectively and, bring a corrupt people to amend their lives, he should also, like Moses, be able to govern, or at least should be a respecter and upholder of government. But Jesus neither ruled himself nor assisted others to rule; when he went from place to place with a number of mendicant followers, delivering revolutionary discourses to those who gathered about him, he was really nothing better than an anarchist. The most serious defect that can be pointed to in his ethical system, if it deserves to be called such, is that it is virtually based on anarchy, so as to fail altogether to meet the requirements of civil society and the constitution of family life. It was impossible for him as a wandering preacher to do much for the moral elevation of his countrymen, when he did not understand the paramount duty of maintaining order in the world, and had not the least sympathy with those who were placed in authority and responsible for the administration of justice. If he did not choose to cultivate friendly relations with the Roman rulers of his country, he might still have done much to ameliorate its condition as a Jewish magistrate. He could have founded somewhere a small agricultural colony to serve as a pattern for the rest of Palestine, and thus commenced the regeneration of the whole community. There was nothing to prevent him from forming a settlement of this kind, and the people who gathered about him to earn a subsistence by honest labour would have been, with the exception of paying an annual tribute to Cæsar, in a position of independence. Under such an arrangement he could have far better instructed his countrymen in the common duties and obligations of life than in the position which he actually took of renouncing industrial pursuits and

wandering about with a company of celibate
religious beggars preparing for the end of the
world.

5. It must be borne in mind that the religion of
Israel was not sectarian in its origin and constitution, but national or rather pastorian : Moses did
not gather about him a band of kindred spirits, a
few sympathetic persons of one sort, but took
charge of the entire people without regard to their
opinions or sentiments, and did his best to reconcile
them and lead them on together in the path of
righteousness.   This was what every subsequent
Jewish teacher was expected to do, and it is what
we may see done more or less effectively now in
every modern synagogue. No genuine Israelite
would think of drafting off from the rest of the
community a portion of his brethren holding
peculiar views in order to establish a sect.   Perfect
uniformity between the synagogues is not to be
expected under the circumstances of a people so
varying in culture and widely dispersed throughout
the world as the modern Jews. In every congregation, and, indeed, in every family, there
will necessarily be differences of opinion and
diversities of taste with regard to theological
questions, and other abstruse subjects of human
study, as well as on matters of ritual; and the
important thing is, that the members should
manage, in spite of these divergences, to do their
duty mutually before God and get on harmoniously together. A narrow system of mystical
dogmatism which encourages petty disputa-
tions, and does not inculcate toleration of the
sentiments of honest people who are constrained to differ from us, is not worthy of the
name of religion.

6. Jesus took a course directly opposite from that
of Moses in establishing a sect.   If he had been

eminently successful in competing with other
sectarian teachers so as to gain by his persuasive
eloquence a hundred thousand followers, it would still
have been a very unworthy achievement for one
claiming to be the head of the whole community of
Israel. But in reality his attempts to influence the
people by preaching and exorcism produced but very
meagre results: during the whole period of his
ministry he obtained few disciples, and it is indisputable that he did very little for the instruction
and improvement of his countrymen. It has been
observed all the world over that like attracts like,
that the capacity of a religious teacher is invariably
denoted by the ignorance or intelligence of his
congregation. Those who gathered about the
prophet of Nazareth, so far from being the flower
of the nation, the most progressive and thoughtful
members of the Jewish community, were only
the dregs of the city population and a number of
credulous Galilean peasants. We are told by his
modern worshippers that he deliberately passed
by men of learning and ability, and sought out
by preference the poor, degraded, and uncared-for
—those belonging to the lowest stratum of society
—as being in the greatest need of his pastoral care.
It must be admitted that this notion is well acted
upon at the present day by many good clergymen
and others who are doing their best to reclaim the
outcast population of our large towns. But Jesus
gathered about him a crowd of poor vagrant people
wanting excitement and hungering for doles from
utter inability to attract those of higher intelligence
and superior worth. The sensible portion of his
countrymen, hearing him announce that the end of
the world was at hand and require them to abandon
in haste their property and industrial pursuits,
could not fail to regard him as a demented visionary.
Besides, if he was what he professed to be—the Good

Shepherd of Israel—it was clearly his duty not to confine his attention to any particular class, but to set about reforming the whole nation. The true way of reclaiming and elevating the degraded portion of a community is through the instrumentality of their more intelligent and less degraded brethren, and no worse method could possibly be devised than that of drawing the most ignorant class apart from the better educated and setting them at variance. A genuine reformer would have followed the example of Moses, would have selected for his assistants the most able and intelligent men that could be found, and by giving them proper instruction, and placing them judiciously where they could impart it to others, would have succeeded in harmonizing and enlightening the whole brotherhood of Israel.

7. Had Jesus only been the father of a family he might have gained from that responsible position some little knowledge of the constitution of society and of the need of a system of government. The desirability of establishing schools, and having special educational arrangements for training the young collectively in habits of virtue, would also have probably been impressed on his mind. Moreover, his own experience in ruling a household would have enabled him to give much sound practical advice to other parents as to the proper discharge of their kindred duties. But he was a celibate individual, an entire stranger to paternal obligations, ever seeking with his world-renouncing saint followers to break up family life, and such a teacher would not be likely to do anything, either by precept or example, to improve the fatherhood and motherhood of the country. On one occasion when Jewish parents brought their children into his presence, it does not appear that he gave them a word of good counsel on the subject of training

the young, but simply laid his hands on the little
ones and blessed them, just as an Italian priest
blesses the cattle that are brought to him on a
certain saint's day, and sprinkles them with holy
water.   Nothing was to be done by painstaking
labour for the strengthening and gradual improvement of their minds, but everything was to be
accomplished by miracle : prayers, charms, and
exorcisms were expected to dispel all distempers,
whether physical or moral, so as to render wise
training and the cultivation of new and better
habits of life wholly unnecessary.

8. The rude, slovenly, careless agriculture which
Jesus has depicted in the Parable of the Sower
very correctly typifies the character of his own
teaching.   There is no tillage described, no
ploughing and preparation of the soil, and careful
harrowing in of the seed; neither is there any water-
ing, hoeing, and weeding to strengthen the young
plant and insure its satisfactory growth.   The
husbandman goes forth and scatters the seed before
him indifferently as a blind man might do, no
matter where or how it falls, and imagines that his
work is fitly accomplished.   But see the result :
much that he flings carelessly abroad settles in wild
and stony places, where it cannot possibly germinate,
and some perishes for want of sustenance or is
carried off by birds, and only a comparatively small
portion strikes root in a good soil, so as to be
eventually productive.   Correspondingly poor issues
would be sure to come from his own irregular
wayside discourses—wandering from place to place
and imparting to groups of rude unprepared minds
instruction without education.   The hortatory
words which he thus delivered, whether wise and
reasonable or the reverse, might be expected to
produce but very little impression on the majority
of his hearers, and to pass in a little while from

their remembrance.   But if he had acted on
another system, if he had brought people together
in an industrial colony and carefully trained them
in the ordinary duties of life, the instruction which
he delivered would have been more effective, the
precepts which fell from his lips would have sunk
into their hearts and permanently influenced them
for good.

9. When any remark is made on the little that
Jesus accomplished as a teacher for the moral
improvement of his countrymen, we are commonly
told that this was due to their obstinate and
intractable disposition, their extreme hardness of
heart and unbelief.   But no people have ever been
more ready than the Jews to recognize men of
superior genius in their community, and they were
not less capable of discerning real merit when
Jesus appeared among them than at any other
period of their history.   Even supposing that they
had all the spiritual blindness and prejudice
ascribed to them, a teacher of transcendent ability
should have known how to treat them and gradually
effect their enlightment.   Those who visit the
Free School in Bell Lane, Spitalfields, the work of
which is annually tested by results, will see how
much may be accomplished by a real Jewish
teacher for the moral elevation of some of the most
ill-conditioned and intractable of his race.   Many
of the scholars there, children of poor immigrants,
have been reared in continental cities amidst the
worst possible surroundings, and are completely
dominated by foreign habits and prejudices.   A
mixed multitude more difficult to bring under
discipline and manage collectively in a large educational establishment it would be hardly possible to
conceive.   Yet this task is marvellously well
performed by the head master and his staff of
assistants ;   the children, however rough and

disorderly, are speedily organized, strongly impressed with a sense of their religious duty, and
encouraged to look forward with the good resolve
to earn a living by honest industry, and grow up
loyal and law-abiding citizens of England. Had
there been during the life-time of Jesus such a
school steadily operating on the poor neglected
Jewish population of Palestine, and made the
nursery of a wide ramification of industrial colonies,
there can be little doubt that it would have
completely regenerated and saved the nation.

10. All communities have their special moral
failings; the great vice of the English people is
intemperance, that of the French licentiousness, as it
was the reproach of the ancient Greeks and Romans
in a still worse degree. The Jews of Palestine
among whom Jesus lived were as a rule neither
drunken nor unchaste, but they were an excitable
and turbulent people, ever ready on the slightest
provocation to engage in fierce conflict either
against their own rulers or the Gentiles. It
happened with them as it as happened with many
other combative races; frequent insurrections and
a succession of wars unsettled their industry and
left behind them an evil inheritance of brigandage.
When hostilities ceased for a time and they
were enabled to disband their forces, some of the
most active fighters had got so accustomed to live
by forays and requisitions, that they preferred to
keep up the campaigning in a small way on their
own account rather than return to the quiet pursuits
of industrial life. During the whole period of the
Roman domination bands of freebooters were a
terrible pest to the country, not only in respect to
the depredations which they committed on the
villages and farms, but in the fact that they incited
futile attempts at revolt and brought on many
districts severe military repression. While affecting

a spirit of ultra patriotism, as is common with their class, and professing to fight for the liberation of their country, they were in reality its worst oppressors; it was chiefly through them that many cohorts had to be maintained and taxation was burdensome. As there was no powerful leader able to unite the people and give them independence, as irregular and spasmodic efforts against the forces of imperial Rome were altogether hopeless, the wisest Jews advocated patient submission to their foreign rulers and co-operation with them, so as to more effectually maintain order and tranquillity. Had the people, in agreement with these counsels, everywhere steadily devoted themselves to industrial pursuits, the Roman yoke would not have been heavy in Palestine; and by maintaining their national strength and virtue intact, they would have been certain eventually to gain a position of independence. It was brigandage that formed the great marplot to the realization of the hopes of liberty : the brigands, counterworking in every direction the efforts of the wise, would not allow the nation to bide its time and husband its resources, but kept it in a state of perpetual ferment, and in conjunction with equally mischievous fanatics they eventually lit up the flames of the great calamitous war.

11. During the whole period of his public ministry Jesus was never known to set his face strongly against brigandage : he not only took no special pains to diminish this crying iniquity, which more than anything else was discrediting and injuring the country, as a true moral reformer would have done, but he did not even vigorously denounce it at any time or make it apparent that he was very much concerned at its existence. Indeed he seems to have troubled himself just as little about the frequent depredations of robbers as about those which were committed by wild

beasts. He and his mendicant followers, being engaged in no industrial pursuit and having no property to lose, were not likely to worry themselves much at the occasional losses from pillage which others might suffer whom they persistently accused of covetousness. Had any Jewish farmers, after discovering that their cattle or sheep had been stolen, appealed to Jesus for redress, they would doubtless have met with just such a rebuff as he administered to the young man who complained that his brother had appropriated the whole of the family inheritance (Luke xii. 13). He did not positively take the part of the predatory class, but a great deal of his teaching, which undermined the foundations of property and discouraged judicial proceedings against the perpetrators of wrong, must have served their purpose indirectly even better than if he had been their avowed advocate. And so far as his influence extended in wandering about at the head of a band of communistic beggars, he quite as much as they helped to weaken the hands of industry, dissolve social and family ties, and keep the nation in that state of unhealthy excitement and longing for revolutionary change which precipitated unwise struggles and the final ruinous overthrow.

12. It is not possible to distinguish clearly the genuine legislation of Moses from the later priest legislation which was imputed to him, but it seems to have been his great aim to establish a reign of justice on earth; he was firmly resolved to protect his brethren from external wrong and not allow them to wrong one another. Such also was the disposition of every subsequent ruler of Israel who conscientiously followed in his footsteps and endeavoured to promote the welfare of the community. But Jesus, in claiming to be the head of the nation, was actuated by quite another spirit:

it was not *justice* that he was zealous for and
determined to extend to all classes of people, but
equality, that is, a levelling and subversive system
of communism.   He seems to have wanted all men
to live like the birds of heaven, in a state of natural
freedom, and take just what came to hand for their
daily sustenance.   It was not against the robber,
but against the rich man that his indignation was
chiefly directed : he who possessed two coats was
told to give one away, and he who was robbed of
anything was on no account to seek its recovery.
A person of provident habits who stored up the
fruits of his industry for the future wants of his
family and dependent people, he condemned as
avaricious and worldly, while the idle and thriftless,
who took no thought for the morrow, and permitted
their children to run about in a destitute condition,
were in his estimation genuine saints suffering here
on earth that they might have compensation in
heaven.   Jewish agriculture, from the unsettled
state of the country, was already sufficiently
depressed, but he, by requiring every diligent
farmer to sell his property and distribute the
proceeds in alms, would have ruined it outright.
It was his aim to overspread all Palestine with
mendicant preachers and self-mortifying ascetics
preparing for the end of the world, and if his
behests had been generally obeyed and his example
followed, there would soon have been no one left to
beg of ;   the cultivated lands would have relapsed
into the condition of a wilderness, and the
inhabitants, taking no thought for the morrow,
would have been reduced to the condition of
savages and wild beasts.

13. Moses was not only a legislator but a chief
magistrate, and no position is more favourable than
that of a magistrate for the cultivation of a consistent all-round morality as distinguished from a

lopsided morality. One who sits daily to determine
the causes that are brought before him will be sure
to learn much of human nature, will have constant
exercise for his reflective powers, and whatever
proclivity or impulse he may have in this or that
direction is likely to be kept· under wholesome
check. It will be his business to urge unremittingly
the paramount importance of those great virtues
of civil life—Justice, Honesty, and Truthfulness—
which no one ever strains unduly or practises in
excess. Other virtues, the impulsive virtues, if not
controlled by judgment, may be carried to such
immoderate lengths as to resemble at last vices, and
become in like manner positively injurious. Thus
it is well for people, especially for those in humble
circumstances, to be thrifty, but any one with too
strong a propensity in that direction will become
in awhile niggardly, and even acquire the grovelling
habits of a miser. Generosity is highly commendable, but an extremely warm-hearted liberal
man will sometimes become a victim of rogues, or
will impoverish himself and his family in endeavouring to assist those who are unworthy of
assistance, or will give away in inconsiderate
charity what ought in justice to have been given to
his creditors. Sensuality should be studiously
avoided, yet those who fly with excessive zeal from
the gratification of the senses may be carried to
an unwholesome extreme of asceticism. Courage,
if carried too far, will become reckless foolhardiness:
love may lead at length to idolatrous infatuation.
Cruelty is very shocking to all gentle and kindly
dispositions, yet an unreasonable abhorrence of
inflicting a little corrective pain has often had the
effect of increasing human misery a hundredfold.
Humane people have exerted themselves very
commendably of late to prevent the torturing of
dumb animals; there are some few, however, so

entirely carried away by feelings of tenderness
that they would abolish, if they could, the use
of spurs and riding-whips, and even prohibit the
destruction of vermin. It is evident, therefore,
that good impulses have just as much need of
control and regulation as bad impulses, in order to
avoid follies and extravagances in life and establish
a sound morality in every way conducive to human
welfare.

14. Jesus had certainly not a reflective mind
like Moses, but was very impulsive and enthusiastic;
he had no magisterial experience nor even the
inborn qualities which fit a man to undertake the
duty of judging the people. And, as might be
expected of such a prophet, the morality which he
set before his followers by precept and example
was not balanced and regulated, but ever running
to fanatical excess. In the avoidance of covetousness, the abstaining from concupiscence, the dispensing of charitable relief, and the forgiveness of
injuries, he is alike such a thorough going extremist
as to render his moral system wholly unfitted for
the requirements of a great complex community.
At the same time such virtues as industry,
providence, cleanliness, filial duty, urbanity, and
others of much importance in the economy of
human life, were either despised by him or
altogether overlooked, as though they had no
existence. The community that sprung from his
teaching—the primitive saints subsisting on alms,
undergoing rigorous penances, courting persecution
and martyrdom, calumniating all honest people
who held different views from their own; and
condemning them to the torments of hell-fire—
do not form by any means an edifying ethical
picture. They were in some respects a less lovable
people than even the Hindoo ascetics, and certainly
less harmless than the saints of the far East who

were brought to practise the mad morality of Buddha.

15. An ancient Jewish teacher said, " Do that to no man which thou hatest " (Tobit iv. 15). Hillel, the reforming rabbi and ruler who lived in the time of Herod the Great, said, " Do not unto thy neighbour that which thou wouldst not have him do unto thee " (Talmud. B Shabbath, 31a). So Jesus summarized human duty in these words, " Whatsoever ye would that men should do to you, do ye even so to them, for this is the law and the prophets (Matt. vii. 12). It must be observed, however, that the meaning of Hillel the ruler, and the meaning of Jesus, were not exactly alike. Hillel desired simply to inculcate true equity or the refraining from all aggressive acts; he meant, " Do not ill-treat your neighbour by violence, adultery, robbery, slander, or in any other way, as you would not like to be ill-treated yourself." And when we, and all modern Jews and Christians talk of people doing, or not doing, as they would be done by, we mean precisely the same thing, refer to equitable dealing or the want of it on the part of our fellow-men. But it is clear that this golden rule as it proceeded from the lips of Jesus was a repressive weapon that cut both ways; it not only struck at the transgressor, but was equally directed against the prosecutor and the magistrate. In his estimation it was wrong to condemn an offender, no matter how guilty, because those who condemn would not like to be condemned themselves. Christian rulers, of course, do not see his precept in this light, but such was nevertheless its unmistakable significance. What he taught in regard to doing nothing to others which we should dislike having done to ourselves, might be considered an attempt to mend the Decalogue by adding to it this new commandment, " Thou shalt not judge " (Matt. viii. 1; Luke vi. 37). And to carry out his

L

views effectively the courts should have been closed, the gaolers dismissed, the constables disbanded, and all administration of justice relegated to the final great day of assize, which prediction said was then near at hand.

16. There is no portion of the unbalanced moral teaching of Jesus that is more frequently held up to admiration than that which enjoins the universal forgiveness of injuries. But pardon exercised indiscriminately towards all who happen to wrong us without any regard to its probable results, means simply non-resistance, impunity for transgression, and therefore the delivering of society up to complete lawlessness. And if the passing over offences does not proceed from a truly generous spirit, if it is prompted by mere cowardice or expediency, or inability to inflict punishment, it cannot be considered a virtue at all, nor is deserving a shadow of respect. Thousands of people, who have sat regularly under Christian instruction, when they find it beyond their power to forgive everybody, end with hardening their hearts and forgiving nobody; or they put off all forgiveness of wrong till sickness and death overtake them, when the profession of it is absolutely worthless. It would be far better if such people were taught by their spiritual guides to order their conduct on lines of true equity, and discriminate carefully between just resentment and unjust revenge. There are too many selfish, ignorant, excitable brawlers in the world who harbour fierce vindictive feelings when they have scarcely anything to complain of, or even when their wrongs are purely imaginary. A neighbour, who simply does his duty by resisting their aggressions or bearing witness to their misdeeds, they regard not as a good citizen, but as an enemy whom they are entitled to visit with the severest retaliation. They entertain an unreasonable

spite against a rival in trade or competitor for the
same employment ; and, though he is only doing the
best he can to earn an honest living, will perhaps
stigmatize him as a "blackleg" and do all in their
power to requite him with evil. It is against all
savage unjustifiable vengeance of this kind that
Christian ministers ought to protest continually, yet
they frequently connive at it, and even palliate it
at the present day, if it happens to be perpetrated
by an organized mob whom they consider it im-
politic to censure.

17. It is where people have long been associated—
connected by kindred ties or industrial bonds—that
the forgiveness of injuries may be best cultivated
and practised with beneficial results, and if Jesus
had said nothing more on the subject than the
Parable of the Prodigal Son, his teaching might
have been considered unexceptionable. In every
case of people, who are unlike gifted and able to
supply each other's defects, agreeing to co-operate
for their mutual advantage and so become more or
less dependent on each other, it will be found that
they sometimes fall short of their duty, and are not
honest, truthful, respectful, patient, and diligent on
all days alike. In the marriage relationship the
most devoted of husbands will occasionally, from ill
health or some little derangement of temper, speak
and act with positive cruelty towards his wife ; and
she, too, however affectionate in general, will, from
similar upsets and infirmities, be no less inconsiderate and unkind towards him. These little
conjugal wrongs will be freely confessed by both
parties in their periods of calm reflection, and will
be very rightly and heartily forgiven. The
occasional hardships which masters inflict on
servants and the bad treatment which they receive
from them in turn, will in like manner, if the
parties are sensible, be mutually overlooked, and

worthier conduct will follow by way of atonement. Good humours may so continually make up for bad humours, as sunshine succeeds a storm, and the wrongs done be so thoroughly repented of, that an open rupture or dissolution of their compact will be deemed wholly undesirable.

18. But the forgiveness which is often exercised to good purpose on our friends and those who are closely associated with us will be completely thrown away upon strangers over whom we have no moral influence, and especially upon those who are habituated to crime. It is only the fear of being judicially punished and deprived of liberty that has a wholesome restraint on the seducer, the swindler, the burglar, and the pickpocket, and drives them occasionally to contemplate a reformed course of life. Their misdeeds are invariably found to become less frequent in proportion as they see the law regularly enforced, so that there is very little chance of their escaping from judicial retribution. And those weak-minded people, who plume themselves on their Christian virtues and make it a rule never to prosecute offenders under any circumstance, nor give any aid to the police, fail to do their duty to society. If their example were generally followed we should soon be left without protection, and the whole country would become a prey to criminal violence and lawlessness. The story of the woman taken in adultery (John viii. 3–11) is known to be an interpolation, and may be either a legendary addition or an authentic incident in the life of Jesus derived from some other source. In any case it truly represents the spirit of his teaching, which is entirely repudiated by the judicial mind of modern Christendom. He might on such an occasion very reasonably have condemned the barbarous and excessively severe punishment of stoning for adultery, but to forbid all

judicial correction for wrong-doing because neither judge, jury, nor gaolers will ever be found wholly immaculate, is only to deliver up the world to brute violence and unabashed licentiousness.

19. It is in dealing with political and religious opponents that people ought especially to cultivate a charitable and forgiving disposition. There is no reason why one honest man should feel angry and resentful towards another because they happen to take different views on some important question. The following observations in a recent sermon on the subject of "*Enemies*" are worthy of attention : "All friendliness between man and man is a mutual benefit ; like mercy it blesses him that gives and him that takes. Suffice it to say that this is one of our chief duties to God, and to our neighbour—to be as friendly as we can in all our dealings and relations. But in spite of this, some of us, I hope not many, cannot get through the world without having enemies, nay, without making enemies. Sometimes this is unavoidable and absolutely right. More often it is avoidable and grievously wrong. If we drive people into hostility by our own unamiable tempers, by our self-assertion and pride, by our crotchets and general contradictoriness, by our supercilious regard for trifles and conventionalities, by our manifest selfishness and preference for our own comfort over that of others; if we drive people into hostility by injudicious attempts to alter and improve them, by lack of sympathy with their ignorance and weakness, by doing to others and speaking to others exactly as we should wish them not to do, and not to speak to ourselves ; in short, if we drive people away by any kind of unfriendliness, we are manifestly doing very wrong both to them and to ourselves ; we are making enemies of those whom we might and ought to have made our friends, and

all possibility of contact is destroyed without painful friction and irritation. . . . . . We need God's help and guidance to make us just to our enemies, to enable us to see the better side of their characters, to see all the good that may lie even in their mistaken hostility towards us, to help us to make every possible excuse for them, and to impute no malice if we can at all avoid it. Still more do we need God's help in being absolutely truthful, straightforward, sincere, and brave, in saying plainly what we think and what we believe, and never tampering with our convictions. Our enemies are not to be subdued by mean evasions and compromises, by pretending to agree with them when we do not, or by passing over in silence methods of controversy which we know to be unfair. We need perpetually God's help to keep us in the path of righteous truthfulness, just as we need the divine guidance in finding it. If our enemies are hostile because of our fidelity and courage in what we believe to be the true service of God, all the more need have we for fortitude and perseverance, and that adamantine steadfastness that knows no fear and never breaks down. No less do we need the righteousness, patience, meekness, gentleness, and forbearance, which are the direct results of God's influence on our souls. If we are reviled, we must revile not again. If we suffer, we must not threaten. If we are tormented, we must not retaliate. We must bear all things, endure all insults with a silent patience, rendering only good for evil, blessings for curses, and melting even the hearts of our foes by the warmth of our compassion and sympathy" (Voysey's "Theistic Sermons," Vol. XIII. No. 20).

20. Many Christians at the present day will endorse these sentiments, and will affirm that they are wholly derived from the New Testament. But

a very different spirit really pervades that volume: for all that we read about patience, meekness, forgiveness, charity, and love of enemies, neither the founder of the church nor his immediate followers knew how to treat honest religious opponents with respect. Those who hold Jesus up before us as the moral exemplar of mankind, sometimes draw a distinction between the heroic and the martyr character to the decided advantage of the latter; they contend that while the bold, daring, vindictive, self-asserting temper has always been most in favour with the world, the meek, patient, forgiving, self-denying disposition which the Gospel enjoins is really much superior. There is really no proper superiority in either of these sides of character, which for the purpose of argument have been thus unwarrantably divorced from each other, and the wisest and best men in all ages have exhibited them both in due proportion. Every modern gentleman—that is, every intelligent and well-conducted person, whether Jew or Gentile—endeavours to cultivate the *suaviter in modo; fortiter in re* spirit; he learns both to yield and to resist on proper occasions in such a way as shall serve his own interest and conduce to the general well-being of society. He is ever ready to respect the feelings, tastes, and sentiments of those who conscientiously differ from him; he is too generous and magnanimous to entertain little spites and stoop to petty revenges, but when urged by a sense of duty to make a determined stand against wrong he becomes hard and inflexible as iron. The behaviour of the early Christians was exactly the opposite of this; they yielded without a word of remonstrance to any ruffianly assault or insolent demand which was made upon them by the criminal class, yet were extremely rude and uncourteous to honest citizens who happened to differ from them in certain points of religious belief. Then, again, instead of strengthening the hands of the magistrates, and helping them to maintain order and tranquillity, they became, by reason of the frequent tumults which their fanaticism provoked, a constant source of annoyance, and their sullen defiant manner before the courts, when seeking the glory of martyrdom, was only calculated to insult the administration of justice and bring it into utter contempt. Tertullian says, "while the love of friends is common to all men, the love of enemies is a virtue peculiar to Christians." But what amount of affection, tender consideration, and charitableness does he manifest towards his adversaries? "For his opponents, be they heathens, Jews, heretics, or Catholics, he has as little indulgence and regard as Luther. With the adroitness of a special pleader he entangles them in self-contradictions, pursues them into every nook and corner, overwhelms them with arguments, sophisms, apophthegms, and sarcasms, drives them before him with unmerciful lashings, and almost always makes them ridiculous and contemptible; his polemics everywhere leave marks of blood " (Milman's "History of Christianity," p. 516.)

21. The unconditional forgiveness of every injury or, in other words, the non-resistance of evil which the followers of Jesus were required to practise, tended, like their indiscriminate almsgiving, much more to demoralize than to reform and regenerate mankind. And it was not prompted by any really generous feeling, by any charitable consideration for other people's exigences and difficulties, but proceeded from a selfish calculation of purchasing in this way an abundant future recompense. An avaricious tradesman will sometimes overserve a customer, that is, will send him more than the quantity of goods which he has actually ordered

and expects to receive, not from any liberal impulse
to enlarge his stores, but solely with the view to
have a longer bill against him at the coming day
of reckoning. It was from a similar expectation
of advantage accruing to themselves at the great
judgment, supposed to be near at hand, that
Christians made it their study to overserve the
robber and the oppressor. They were to invite
those who smote them on the right cheek, to give
them a second blow on the left, to go two miles by
way of forced service when asked to go one, and to
induce the robber who should wrest their coat from
them to take away their cloak also, not with any
view to the offender's benefit, but in order that
they, the sufferers, should have heavier claims to
make at the approaching day of retribution
(Matt. vi. 12, 39–40). Jesus does not tell his
disciples to enlighten their adversaries, to remove
their misconceptions and prejudices, and so prevent
them as far as possible from acting unjustly and
having guilt to answer for, but bids them consider
their own prospective gains, and when wronged
and assaulted, "rejoice and be exceeding glad."
This can hardly be considered a more worthy
feeling than the joy occasionally expressed by a
litigious person when he learns that some
neighbour is inadvertently trespassing on his rights
so as to furnish an opportunity to sue him for
damages greatly in excess of the actual harm or
loss. There was as much selfish calculation in the
world-renouncing saint and persecution-seeker as
in the man who sinks a ship for the sake of the
insurance, or runs up in the line of a projected
railway a row of trumpery cottages so as to insure
their speedy demolition, and obtain from the
company as compensation far more than they are
actually worth.

22. There would have been a beautiful con-

sistency in Jesus preaching the doctrino of non-resistance if he had been in no way influenced by selfish considerations, still more so if he had manifested on every occasion a fine sense of justice, and his conduct towards all classes of his country-men had been uniformly gentle and kind. It might then have been said that he was a moral genius greatly in advance of his age, and that it only required for other people to follow his example and come nearer to the perfection of his character to produce a world of harmony and brotherly love, in which there would be no longer any need for courts of justice and stern repression. But in viewing him independently and apart from the incense-laden atmosphere of his worshippers, we cannot help being impressed with the belief that the superfine morality which he taught, like the supernatural power which he claimed, was mere pre-tentiousness. It cannot be made out that he was better prepared by faultless conduct to live wholly free from State control than other overwrought zealots of that period. Every saint, prophet, or holy man professed to set himself high above the magisterial standard of virtue, yet often sunk below it in reality. A Jewish or a Roman magistrate, if provoked at any time to inflict corporal punishment in the streets without authority, would at least have taken care to strike only genuine offenders. But Jesus, while remarkably tolerant towards the criminal population, was as capricious in the exercise of his wrath and entirely unjust as any barbarian despot could be, when he selected as the most deserving objects of punishment the harmless Temple merchants who were pursuing their lawful occupation of providing animals for the sacrificial services.

23. The little balancing and discriminating capacity possessed by the man, who in the common

belief of Christians is destined eventually to judge
the whole world, is sufficiently shown by the
sweeping denunciation which he hurled against
the Pharisees. Undoubtedly a large portion of
that sect were by no means a model people, some
of them were ultra-ritualistic, and they were in
general excessively conceited and sanctimonious,
but probably not more so than the holy men who
figured at that time among the Essenes and other
communities. There are known to have belonged
to the religious body, of which St. Paul and his
master, Gamaliel, were members, many upright
and conscientious Jews, and nothing could be
more unjust on the part of a rival teacher than the
holding them up to opprobrium as utterly base and
wicked without a single honourable exception.
Jesus did not convict the Pharisees of any flagrant
crime or immorality; did not expose any foul
misdeed which they had secretly committed to the
indignant reprobation of all Israel; but made a
series of loose defamatory charges against them
without seeming to care in the least for their being
substantiated—such, for instance, as their devouring
widows' houses, making long prayers for mere
pretence, paying tithe of mint, anise, and cummin,
and omitting the weightier matters of the Law
(Matt. xxiii. 14–23). Indeed, he seems to have
inveighed against these people with a great deal
of sectarian bitterness, just because they were rival
religionists who discredited his pretentions, and
could not be frightened by his predictions of the
coming doomsday into parting with their property
and joining his mendicant disciples.

24. The subtle distinctions which the Pharisees
are said to have made between the Temple and the
gold of the Temple, and between the altar and the
sacrifice, which Jesus carps at, were in harmony
with many other distinctions of the ceremonial law,

and could not reasonably be objected to unless the whole system were brought under revision. A true reformer would not have quarrelled about these little refinements, but would have pointed to the need of dispensing with sacrificial customs and weaning the people altogether from the Temple idolatry. If the Pharisee loved friendly salutations in the market and to be called Rabbi, he also loved to be greeted by his followers with the same title, and when told on one occasion to rebuke the noisy adulation of the populace, replied that if they were to be silent the very stones would cry out in his praise (Luke xix. 40). It was easy enough for him to censure the self-esteem and arrogance of others, but he should have first pulled out the beam from his own eye; for, like the ascetic Diogenes, whom Plato rebuked, it is evident that he trampled on the pride of his more learned and respected rival teachers with greater pride. He also charged them with giving the people good advice and not following it themselves; but did not he "say and do not"? Did not he, like Dunstan, Becket, and many another of his saintly imitators, preach humility and practise the very opposite? Did not he by precept teach his disciples to love all their enemies, while he set them an example of hurling against religious opponents a torrent of angry abuse. He even goes so far as to ascribe the zeal which the Pharisees manifested on various occasions to the worst possible motives. The public prayers which they offered up, and the phylacteries which they wore as a reminder of their religious duties, were to all appearance quite as genuine as the open-air services of this country, and the Scripture texts which are emblazoned on the walls of churches. As to the taunting charges that they compassed sea and land to make one proselyte, and having got him, made him twofold more the child of hell than themselves, and that they built the tombs of the prophets only to bear witness to the approval of their murder (Luke xi. 48), like accusations might be just as reasonably levelled against modern Christians, and they can only be regarded as an outpouring of wild and passionate invective.

25. Jesus accused the Pharisees of corrupting the Law of Moses with the traditions of men, which was manifestly quite beyond their power to do at that period: whatever modifications or corruptions of the Law then existed were the work of a former generation of rulers and priests. He was no more able than his religious rivals to say precisely what portion of the Law originated from Moses, and what was subsequently added by Ezra and other custodians. In observing what were said to be the unwritten precepts of Moses, handed down through the seventy elders by word of mouth, the Pharisees believed that they were only rendering strict obedience to their ancient legislator as though he were still in their midst. We have no reason to suppose that they attempted to neutralize or get rid of the Fifth Commandment by a traditional precept the meaning of which Jesus probably misunderstood (Mark vii. 11–12). It is certain that no people on earth have ever been more distinguished for filial duty than the Jews who have steadfastly adhered to their rabbinical traditions. On the other hand, Jesus and his followers were ever seeking to dissolve family ties, and weaken the obligations which parents owed to their children, and children to their parents : people were taught to consider it in the highest degree meritorious to abandon home and kindred, and take to a life of religious beggary for the kingdom of heaven's sake.

26. Jesus charged the Pharisees with being scrupulous in maintaining a decent exterior while they were corrupt and impure in heart. We have

no record to show what attention he and his
disciples gave to personal cleanliness, besides one
instance of feet washing (John xiii. 4) ; but many
generations of begging saints who professed to be
their faithful imitators were in a wretched condition
of filth and neglect.   During the middle ages
bathing was generally considered a pagan practice,
and under the influence of Christian teaching it
almost entirely disappeared from Europe.   External cleanliness among the Jews was meant to
conduce to internal purity, although it might have
failed to do so in numerous instances.   It is better,
however, that people should be only outwardly
clean and presentable than to wander about covered
with dirt and vermin, and breathe at the same time
a spiritual odour that is extremely offensive.   The
Scribes and Pharisees were generally a moral
people, and had Jesus, instead of reviling them, set
about to improve the conduct of those who did
acknowledge his claims, he would certainly have
been far better employed.   Most of his idle
followers probably hoped to enter paradise in
virtue of their belief, like the penitent malefactor,
and not through any reformation of character.
"Verily I say unto you that the publicans and
harlots go into the kingdom of God before you"
(Matt. xxi. 31).   It is true that he occasionally
preaches justification by works or words (vii. 19–
27 ; xii. 37), says that Heaven is to be obtained
by keeping the commandments (xix. 17), that
every minute thing which the Pharisees enjoined
is to be observed (xxiii. 3), nay, that their works
shall be exceeded, that the precepts of the Law shall
be obeyed in a more rigorous sense than at any
former period (v. 20–48), and that men shall be
judged even for every idle word that they speak
(xii. 36) ; yet his subsequent conduct and the
general drift of his discourses will lead an im-

partial observer to infer that this is only an out-ward display of doctrinal excellence which does not proceed from the heart. We never see him putting his superexcellent morality into serious practice, or taking any pains to elevate the credulous people who gathered about him and start them in a reformed course of life. That which he most esteems in man is a blind unhesi-tating belief in his pretentions, that which most provokes him is being put to the test in any way, or asked for more substantial evidence of his having a divine mission. Instead of commending people for being well on their guard against error and pretence, all honest doubt is ascribed to hardness of heart dooming men to perdition, while a ready and implicit belief in him entitles them to sit down in the Kingdom of Heaven (Matt. viii. 2).

27. The virtues which Jesus taught mankind by his own example were of a decidedly *cheap* character; they cost him little labour or effort. It is at all times very easy for a man to profess forgiveness of enemies when he is not in a position to take revenge ; such a profession can only be worth anything when he has them in his power and is strongly impelled to a vindictive course, as when David found Saul sleeping and yet refrained from taking his life (1 Sam. xxvi. 7–25). Modern Christians have magnified as much as possible all the little acts of old-womanly benevolence which he exhibited in the humble circle of his ministry, such as the dispensing of medical charms, the blessing of little children that were brought to him, and the washing of his disciples' feet. But it is very certain that there were greater and nobler acts of charity than these performed by many of his unconverted countrymen, and that he and his poor disciples received more assistance from other people than they gave in return. He

commended a poor widow on one occasion for having put two mites into the treasury, which he considered a greater act of liberality than the larger gifts of rich people, because it was all that she had, and he probably measured his own charitable performances by the same standard. Yet, had he the fine moral perception with which he has been accredited, he must surely have seen that when a pious beggar drops into a poor-box his last penny which he expects will soon be replaced and perhaps doubled by the charity of others, it indicates a less amount of virtue than the rich man's munificent donation, which has cost him much labour and care to obtain, and can only be made good to him by further prolonged exertion.

28. Many popular preachers at the present day are accustomed to hold Jesus up to admiration as the special friend of the poor, that is, as the benefactor of the humble working class, and their representations to this effect are doubtless very generally believed. But a greater delusion respecting him than this can scarcely be imagined, for, however much he may have been disposed to favour those who forsook their industrial calling and led a vagrant life, his preaching and the course which he took were prejudicial to all who honestly earned their bread. He did nothing with superior wisdom to develop the resources of the country and provide employment for the poor; all his efforts were directed to the unhinging of industry, the diminution of wealth, and the promotion of universal idleness and beggary. It was no part of his endeavour to see the peasant and the artisan better remunerated and more comfortably housed, for he despised domestic comforts as much as Diogenes, and believed that their enjoyment would disqualify people for obtaining the everlasting pleasures of paradise. A provident working man

who had managed to save enough for a few months'
subsistence, he would have classed with the covetous
rich, and required him to give away in alms all
that he had treasured as the indispensable condition
of discipleship. On one occasion he is said to
have distributed food liberally to the hungry
multitude, but the food was none of his providing,
since he was himself dependent on alms. Moreover,
the recipients of his bounty were not a band of
ill-fed labourers returning from work, not a
number of distressed farmers who had suffered
heavy losses from murrain or drought, but a
loafing crowd who had followed him about from
place to place and spent the day in idleness. Such
bestowment of largess would only tend to produce
a further relaxation of industrial effort; it would
induce credulous peasants to throw down their
tools and follow the wonder-working prophet for
the chance of a meal; they would see little wisdom
in plodding at their tasks from day to day, like the
ants and the bees, if people were to be fed by
wandering about trustfully for what should turn
up, as the idle improvident ravens (Prov. vi. 6;
Luke xii. 24).

29. In every great complex community, and
especially in large towns, there are many people
who, from not having a good early training, are
poor laggards of civilization, and both intellectually and morally not very different from savages.
Experienced philanthropists are constantly declaring that nothing can be done towards reclaiming
and elevating such sufferers from parental neglect
but by grounding them in habits of industry and
thrift, and thus rendering them self-supporting.
The charitable relief that is distributed from time
to time, however commendable in its aim, and
however indispensable in cases of emergency, is
only a poor palliative of their woes, and not un-

frequently has on the whole a hurtful influence. In every English reformatory the young people, whom it is desired to remove from evil surroundings and start fairly on a new course of life, are taught with especial emphasis to earn and to save, under the assurance that if the way to get an honest living is made plain and practicable to them, they will be delivered from constant temptations to prey on their neighbours by mendicancy, fraud, and theft. A wholesome industrial training of this kind was just as requisite for reclaiming the waifs and strays of society in the time of Jesus as it is now, yet he not only neglected to take such a course for raising his degraded countrymen, but fanatically opposed what others were doing in that direction. According to his view, improvidence was a virtue, poverty and rags were meritorious, and the greater the amount of privation and misery which people submitted to in this world, the greater would be their reward in heaven.

30. In the age when Jesus lived the free working population were enabled to prosper under some very tyrannical governments, because the hard blows that were struck at every hostile rising generally passed over their heads. Dangerous political rivals and seditious people were put to death with remorseless cruelty; bands of freebooters who dared to defy the law were hunted from place to place, and finally extirpated; but the cultivator of the soil, the artisan, and the trader, who had the good sense to mind their own business, were as far as possible protected and permitted to abide in peace. Jesus would not have improved the lot of the industrial population, but would have made it much worse, for instead of seeking to establish a better system of government, it was his aim to have no government at all. Consequently, so far from mitigating any hardships

that fell on the working class in the way of taxation, he would have increased their oppression a hundredfold. For anarchy in its worst form would have quickly overspread the country; a host of petty tyrants and rogues, hitherto held in check, would have been let loose to worry honest people with impunity. In short, although there would have been no central organized tyranny under his system, an infinitely greater amount of cruelty would have been inflicted by the strong on the weak in the opposite condition of lawlessness; thieves, beggars, and impostors of every kind would have speedily shown a bolder front, and poor plodding industry would have been robbed more and more, and maltreated on all sides till it was completely crushed out of existence.

31. What Jesus taught on the subject of prayer was not calculated to stimulate industrial effort nor prove in any other respect morally advantageous to mankind. Every enlightened Jew as well as Theist knows that God only helps those who help themselves, that the reforms which we require and the amelioration of our lot will never be brought about but in answer to our own hearty exertions. He does not therefore pray for external fortune, but for spiritual gifts—industry, sobriety, patience, courage, forethought—that will enable him to grapple successfully with any fortune. He does not ask God to change the wind or the weather for his accommodation, but knows that a moral change must be wrought within himself if he cannot contend effectively with the difficulties that happen to confront him. When an epidemic prevails, instead of solemnly fasting and offering up petitions for its removal, he bestirs himself and calls his neighbours together to devise what can be done to improve the sanitary arrangements of the city. The method of Jesus was exactly the

reverse of this, because he assumed the Eternal to be a great world-magician who, if he were only besought with importunity, stood ready to metamorphose the whole constitution of nature to humour the wishes of men. Instead of saying to his disciples, "Deserve, and you shall have," "Work, and you shall be rewarded," he taught them to take up a trustful, childish attitude, and persistently beg, that their wants should be supplied from day to day without their own labour and care (Matt. vii. 7; Luke xi. 9; John xvi. 7).

32. Prayers are at the best only the utterance of pious wishes, and to rely upon them alone for the effecting of any good upon earth is just as much of a superstition as the ancient custom of offering sacrifices; if they divert people from the performance of their duties or induce them in any way to slacken their exertions they are only a delusion and a snare. The faith in prayer which Jesus taught his disciples was nothing better than faith in prospective miracles. "For verily I say unto you, that whosoever shall say unto this mountain, Be thou removed, and be thou cast into the sea, and shall not doubt in his heart, but shall believe that these things which he saith shall come to pass, he shall have whatsoever he saith. Therefore I say unto you, What things soever ye desire, when ye pray, believe that ye receive them, and ye shall have them" (Mark xi. 23–24). How much better it would have been if he had taught his disciples to pray for industry, skill, patience, and perseverance to enable them to remove material obstacles from their path and earn their daily bread. Reliance on supernatural favours, which they were expecting to receive from time to time, undoubtedly had a demoralizing influence on the early Christians; they were not so helpful and active as they might have been for the improvement of their material

condition; they often became culpably reckless of danger, and, from failing to take the reasonable precautions which they should have done, deliberately sacrificed their lives. Modern Christians are in too many instances rendered supine and negligent in training the rising generation to habits of virtue from the same false trust. They pray that their children may become good and dutiful, without looking after them carefully and making any real educational effort to keep them in a right course, and are presently astonished at their delinquencies and more and more grieved at their depravity.

33. If Jesus had been the head of a family, and likewise the head of a large group of families forming an agricultural colony, he might have done much for the moral elevation of his followers by reforming and better regulating the institution of marriage. He might, for instance, have established a local council or court of amity, consisting of well-married people qualified to speak on sexual relations and give a decision both in respect to petitions for marriage and petitions for divorce. Sensible clergymen as well as medical men are pretty generally agreed that the present customary pairing of men and women with the view to procreation should be under much better social control. Our National Church very unnecessarily says, "A man may not marry his grandmother," and very unjustly forbids him to espouse the sister of his deceased wife, while in regard to many possible unions which are sure to prove injurious it makes no prohibition at all. In every Christian community this deplorable misarrangement is often seen to occur—a number of people enter into the marriage state who from youth, poverty, disease, insanity, or bad character, are wholly unfitted to take on themselves its

responsibilities, while others in every way competent to marry and rear children continue to lead a
celibate life.   So many circumstances have to be
taken into consideration in each case that it would
be hardly possible to frame a satisfactory law to
prevent the ineligible and the incompatible from
contracting alliances which must necessarily have
a bad result; but it would be quite safe to enact
that no marriage should be legalized till the
engaged parties proved their competency to undertake its burdens to the satisfaction of a local
council.   Young people have in many instances
been induced to break off hasty and inconsiderate
engagements which threatened to entail on them
life-long misery under the strong remonstrance
of their wiser friends, and if such admonitory
influence were regularly organized it would be
productive of much good to society.   Through the
benevolent guidance and control thus afforded
better marriages would be made, the hasty and
ill-considered unions which are now so fruitful in
trouble would be of comparatively rare occurrence,
and there would consequently be much fewer
appeals for divorce.

34. Jesus, while he introduced no regulation for
the purpose of preventing shortsighted marriages
which lead to misery and crime, absolutely prohibited divorce, deeming every wretched espousal
brought about by fraud, mercenary motives, or
impure lust as the inviolable work of God.   The
disciples on hearing him make a declaration to this
effect said, "If the case of the man be so with his
wife, it is not good to marry.   But Jesus said
unto them, All men cannot receive this saying,
save they to whom it is given; for there be some
eunuchs, which were so born of their mother's
womb; and there are some eunuchs that were made
eunuchs of men; and there be eunuchs which have

made themselves eunuchs for the kingdom of heaven's sake. ˹ He that is able to receive it, let him receive it" (Matt. xix. 10-12). This passage clearly shows that some of the Jewish as well as the heathen ascetics of that period thought it a great merit to become eunuchs in order to secure themselves more effectually from temptation to lead an impure life, and consequently obtain an exalted position in Paradise, like that of the chaste priests whom Æneas met in the Elysian Fields ("Æneid," lib. vi. 661). There can be little doubt that this further instruction which Jesus gives his followers is only a delicate and circuitous mode of enjoining the same practice. "Whosoever looketh on a woman to lust after her hath committed adultery with her already in his heart. And if thy right eye offend thee, pluck it out and cast it from thee; for it is profitable that one of thy members should perish, and not that thy whole body should be cast into hell. And if thy right hand offend thee," &c. (Matt. v. 28-31).

35. Thus good men—such as conducted themselves morally—were persuaded to lead a celibate life, that they might obtain a higher reward in heaven, when it was the bad who ought to have been restrained from marrying, with the view to the general improvement and elevation of the race. Religious people were also encouraged to make themselves eunuchs as a sure means of obtaining everlasting honour in the world of saints, when, if any class were required to sacrifice their virility it should have been the robbers and other hardened criminals, that they might no longer propagate their kind. It has been argued that the commands of Jesus to practise self-mutilation as a preventive of sin must not be taken literally, that they are simply strong rhetorical expressions enjoining the renunciation of valued friendships and other

worldly advantages lest they should conduce to our spiritual hurt. Modern commentators have done well to put this gloss upon them and disguise their offensiveness; a great doctrinal improvement has so been effected, but it cannot be accepted as correct by those who have no other object in view than the investigation of historical truth. It is well known that the early Christians understood these hard precepts in a literal sense, and some of the more zealous and austere literally obeyed them, which has even been done by here and there 'a fanatic in later times. The celebrated Origen, among others, made himself a eunuch for the kingdom of heaven's sake, and the insane practice had become so frequent in the time of the emperor Constantine that a special law had to be enacted at length for its prohibition.

36. Modern commentators have not less signally failed in their attempts to soften down and explain away those Gospel precepts which inculcate religious beggary and the abandonment of all worldly pursuits. It is said that Jesus here only intended to teach his disciples to avoid covetousness, and not to be too thoughtful about procuring the means of subsistence, when he positively tells them to take no thought at all of what they should eat, drink, and wear, to study their food and clothing no more than the increase of their stature, to leave husbandry, spinning, and other industrial pursuits to the worldly, and direct their own thoughts solely to the attainment of a happy existence in heaven (Matt. vi., Luke xii.). It is well known, too, that his injunctions to this effect were literally followed in the primitive church; great numbers of believers parted with their property, forsook their employments, and lived as wayfarers on what could be casually begged or found on the road. We are told that the command, " Sell all that thou hast and

distribute to the poor " (Luke, xviii. 22) was intended only for one rich young man who was exceedingly covetous ; .but what ground is there for
assuming that he was covetous above all the rest of
his countrymen ?   It is allowed that he was a good
moral man ; the very question which he asked
showed that he was not so worldly as to be forgetful
of his spiritual interests, and the request to sell
half or a less portion of his goods and distribute
to the poor would have been a sufficient corrective
for covetousness.   Some have said that he was
evidently self-righteous in declaring that he had
kept all the commandments from his youth up.   If
this had been the case, his self-righteous conceit
should have met with some reproof, yet we are told
that "Jesus, beholding him, loved him," which
denotes that his character was irreproachable, and
that it was only the refusal to part with his property
and adopt the mendicant life of the disciples that
excluded him from heaven.   In the Parable of Dives
and Lazarus it is taught just as clearly that in
the future retribution people's circumstances will
be reversed, the rich will be eternally abased, and
the poor exalted, without any regard to character
and conduct, wholly irrespective of the moral tenor
of their lives.

37. But it is sometimes asked, "If Jesus required
people to renounce their wealth entirely, and distribute what they had in alms, why did not he more
generally declare it ?   Why, for instance, did he not
require such a sacrifice from Zaccheus and other
rich Jews when he partook of their hospitality ?"
It must surely be admitted that any preaching
against wealth would have been greatly out of place
on these particular occasions, and the silence of
Jesus on the subject in the presence of his liberal
entertainers does not by any means imply that he
approved of his disciples holding property, or that

he would not have given any other rich man the same answer that he did the young ruler if he had come with a like inquiry. Some of the friends of Jesus may have entirely agreed with his communistic doctrines, and yet have deemed it expedient to retain their possessions for a time, that they might aid him occasionally and minister to the support of the poorer brethren. But that his strict followers (before Paul's modifying influence was felt) believed themselves obligated to sell whatever property they had and divide the proceeds, is clearly shown by their conduct after the day of Pentecost, when such as had goods and estates straightway disposed of them, and laid the price thereof at the apostles' feet (Acts iv. 34–35).

38. With just as little reason it has been argued that the presence of Jesus at the marriage feast of Cana shows that he was no advocate of asceticism. He did not enunciate any doctrine there to that effect, and his mere presence among festive people no more denoted a tacit approval of conviviality than his eating and drinking with publicans and sinners signified his acquiescence in their mode of life. The Pharisees were accustomed to practise their devotions and austerities openly, but Jesus believed that a higher reward was to be obtained hereafter by their concealment ; according to his view it was the perfection of saintship to fast and pray, and give alms secretly, and contrive to have the appearance of being undevout and sinful before the world. That he should eat and drink freely in public was quite in accordance with the dissembled asceticism which he taught his disciples, in order to incur the reproaches of men and obtain at length for their uncommended piety a more ample reward in heaven (Matt. vi. 16). Many of the early and medieval Christians acted in strict conformity with this policy. We are told

of St. Felix : " When he ate alone and thought no one saw him, he practised incredible austerities, but when he dined in company with others, he endeavoured ordinarily to shun any singularity that would be taken notice of. He disguised his penances under various pretences, and excused his going without sandals by saying that he walked more easily without them, but he suppressed the inconvenience that he suffered in that mortification. It was his study to conceal from others as much as possible all heavenly favours and to avoid whatever might give them a good opinion of him" (Butler's " Lives of the Saints ").

39. The Rev. Alban Butler, in his introduction to the interesting work from which the above is taken, has the following appropriate remarks : " 'The spirit of the Gospel,' says Massillon, ' is a holy eagerness of suffering, an incessant attention to mortify self-love, to do violence to the will, to restrain the desires, to deprive the senses of useless gratifications; this is the essence of Christianity, the soul of piety.' If you have not this spirit, you belong not, says the apostle, to Jesus Christ; it is of no consequence that you are not of the number of the impure or sacrilegious of whom the apostle speaks, and who will not be admitted to the kingdom of Christ. You are equally strangers to him ; your sentiments are not his ; you still live according to nature ; you belong not to the grace of our Saviour; you will, therefore, perish, for it is on him alone, says the apostle, that the Father has placed our salvation. A complaint is sometimes made that we render piety disgusting and impracticable by prohibiting many practices which the world authorises. But, my brethren, what is it we tell you ? Allow yourselves all the pleasures that Christ would have allowed himself, faith allows you no other : mix with your piety all the gratifi-

cations that Jesus Christ would have mixed in his,
the Gospel allows no greater indulgence. O, my
God, how the decisions of the world will one day
be strangely reversed! when worldly probity and
worldly regularity which by a false appearance of
virtue give a deceitful confidence to many souls,
will be placed by the side of the crucified Jesus
and will be judged by that model! To be always
renouncing yourselves, rejecting what pleases,
regulating the most innocent wishes of the heart
by the rigorous rules of the spirit is difficult, is a
state of violence. But if the pleasures of the
senses leave the soul sorrowful, empty, uneasy, the
rigours of the cross make her happy " (p. xxvi).

40. It is undeniable that the spirit of the Gospel
is correctly apprehended by the long line of
suffering saints and their sympathetic biographer,
and not by our modern rationalizing ministers,
who are only Christians in name, yet the latter,
in departing from the ascetic standards of the
primitive church, are genuine religious reformers,
plainly exhibiting in their walk and conduct a
higher morality. The philanthropic citizen who
in the course of an active industrial career
accomplishes much for the improvement of his
neighbourhood and the amelioration of the lot of
his poor countrymen, although professing nothing
more than " worldly probity and worldly regularity,"
is far more truly a servant of God than the world-
renouncing saint who turns his back on society and
concentrates all his thoughts on his own individual
salvation. The asceticism practised by the strict
followers of Jesus cannot be considered one whit
better, or holier, or worthier of being had in
everlasting regard than that of the Hindoo
sunniassi, the Buddhist phoongee, and the
Mohammedan fakeer. Such fanatics all experience a great deal of spiritual pride and inward

satisfaction at the sufferings which they voluntarily endure in order to acquire distinction and a high future recompense, while they are wholly indifferent to the interests of their fellow-men, and will not turn a straw to promote in any way the general good of their country. The miser, who deprives himself of the needful comforts of life till he is reduced to an absolutely starving condition, may equally boast of being happy in his miserable surroundings, and is sometimes more entitled to the respect of his fellow-men than either the mendicant friar or the anchorite. For such an individual, although without the slightest consideration for other people's welfare, manages at least to be self-supporting, and at length, when life fails, leaves his hoarded wealth for the benefit of his kindred and country, while the covetous heaven-soaring Simon Stylites lives idly on the charitable contributions of the credulous, and eventually bequeaths for their requital only his miserable bones.

41. But while the teaching of Jesus with regard to the renunciation of worldly pursuits and worldly pleasures is highly reprehensible, his very worst precepts are those which instil into the minds of his followers a fanatical longing for martyrdom. The anchorites, who deserted their families and selfishly fled away into the wilderness as the surest means of attaining eternal felicity, were under less moral obliquity than those who sought to get to heaven by provoking hostility and involving their fellow-men in guilt and perdition. The Christian Church has continually sung the praises of her martyrs, but very little disposition is now felt to imitate them, and apologies for their conduct are becoming more and more frequent as the motives which impelled them to rush out of the world by violence are getting to be more clearly understood.

Isaac Taylor, in his "Restoration of Belief," contends that those who suffered in the persecutions of the second century under the leadership of Origen and Cyprian, impressed upon the world for the first time what he calls "the religious obligation of truth." It is not a little singular that the credit of laying the foundation-stone of our modern regard for truthfulness should be given to Origen, above all others, that Origen whom Bishop Horsley has described, in his reply to Priestley, as "not incapable of asserting in argument what he believed not, and that a strict regard to truth in disputation was not one of the virtues of his character." And in another place, "Time was when the practice of using unjustifiable means to serve a good cause was openly avowed, and Origen himself was amongst its defenders" (pp. 23–160). There cannot be a doubt that all the Christian candidates for martyrdom were sincerely attached to their religion, and eager, from selfish considerations, to suffer for it, but they were by no means straightforward and truthful in their relations with the outside world. Like St. Felix and other ascetics, who disguised their austerities with the view to celestial gain, they did not scruple to damage themselves in public estimation by false appearances. When summoned before the magistrates, after refusing to comply with the Roman custom of manifesting loyalty to Cæsar, instead of endeavouring to explain their motives and remove the misconceptions of their accusers, they were only too happy to be falsely charged, and during their trials either maintained an obstinate silence, or gave such vague and sullen replies as were calculated to make them appear guilty of sedition and deserving of punishment. They were marked out as bad citizens by their general refusal to serve in the army, they were suspected, and in many instances not without reason, of being secret enemies of the Roman dominion and heartily desiring its overthrow. Had any of them taken pains to convince the magistrates that they were really loyal subjects of Cæsar, and only had religious scruples against the common mode of testifying loyalty, they would have been let alone or subjected to a fine at the worst. It is, therefore, very incorrect to say that those who could have honestly cleared themselves and refused to do so, suffered under a stern sense of "the religious obligation of truth"; so far from being constrained to die rather than prevaricate or dissemble their views, they notoriously practised dissimulation in order to obtain the martyr's crown.

42. Dr. Philip Schaff, in describing the great martyr conflict of primitive Christianity, says: "Among these confessors and martyrs were not wanting those in whom the pure, quiet flame of enthusiasm rose into the wild rage of fanaticism, and whose zeal was corrupted with impatient haste, heaven-tempting presumption, and sordid ambition; to whom that word could be applied, ' Though I give my body to be burned, and have not charity, it profiteth me nothing.' They delivered themselves up to the heathen officers, and in every way sought the martyr's crown, that they might merit heaven and be venerated on earth as saints. Thus Tertullian tells of a company of Christians in Ephesus who begged martyrdom from the heathen governor, but after a few had been executed, the rest were sent away by him with these words: ' Miserable creatures, if you really wish to die, you have precipices and halters enough.' Though this error was far less discreditable than the opposite extreme of the cowardly fear of man, yet it was contrary to the instruction and the example of

Christ and the apostles (Matt. x. 23 ; xxiv. 15-20 ;
Phil. i. 20-25 ; 2 Tim. iv. 6-8) ; and to the spirit of
true martyrdom, which consists in the perfect union
of humility and power, and possesses divine strength
in the very consciousness of human weakness.
And, accordingly, intelligent church - teachers
censured this stormy morbid zeal. The Church of
Smyrna speaks thus: ' We do not commend
those who expose themselves, for the Gospel
teaches not so.' Clement of Alexandria says :
' The Lord himself has commanded us to flee to
another city when we are persecuted, not as if the
persecution were an evil, not as if we feared death,
but that we may not lead or help any to evil doing.'
In Tertullian's view martyrdom perfects itself in
divine patience ; and with Cyprian it is a gift of
divine grace which one cannot hastily grasp, but
must patiently wait for " (" History of the Christian
Church," vol. i. p. 179).

43. The historian writes further on in reference
to what he considers the perversion of the spirit of
martyrdom : " Origen even went so far as to ascribe
to the sufferings of martyrs an atoning virtue for
others, an efficacy like that of the sufferings of Christ,
on the authority of such passages as 2 Cor. xii. 15 ;
2 Tim. iv. 6 ; Acts vi. 9. According to Tertullian the
martyrs entered immediately into the blessedness
of heaven, and were not required, like ordinary
Christians, to pass through the intermediate state"
(p. 182). It may justly be contended that these
and other notions respecting martyrdom and its
glorious privileges, which made ambitious Christians
eager to die by violence, were developed in the
Church during the second and third centuries. But
they were natural developments, quite in harmony
with the primitive Gospel teaching, and by no means
doctrinal perversions. Nothing can be further from
the truth than Dr. Schaff's apologetic plea that the

courting of persecution and martyrdom "was contrary to the instruction and the example of Christ and the apostles." The greater portion of those who sought a violent death at the hands of pagan opponents were notoriously stimulated in their fanatical zeal by the reading of the Gospels and other authoritative writings which were finally embodied in the New Testament. As to Clement of Alexandria, and one or two others, who sought to moderate the eagerness of their brethren to rush upon martyrdom, they anticipated to some extent the modern rationalistic method of treating the Gospels,—they were really Christian reformers considerably in advance of their age. If all the leading ecclesiastics had exhibited the same just and reasonable spirit, there would probably have been as few cases of seeking celestial glory at the cost of other people's guilt and damnation in the second century as in the nineteenth. But it cannot be denied that the generality of those who had most influence in the church were downright fanatics in their eagerness to suffer violence, and it is equally beyond dispute that from the teaching and example of Jesus, as embodied in the Gospels, their fanaticism had its real source. This is very clearly shown in Origen's celebrated Tract "Urging to Martyrdom," as well as in the "Epistles of Cyprian."

44. Epistle x. *To Martyrs and Confessors.*—" The combat is increased, increased also is the glory of the combatants. Neither have ye hung back from the conflict through fear of tortures, but the tortures themselves have more and more incited you to the conflict : courageous and steadfast ye have returned with eager devotedness to meet the extremest struggle. And of your own number some, I learn, are already crowned, some are closer and closer upon the crown of victory, but all whom the prison

N

has enclosed in one glorious bond are animated with an equal and common glow of courage to wage the strife as becometh soldiers of Christ. 'When they deliver you up,' he says, 'take no thought of what you shall speak, for it shall be given you in that hour what ye shall speak' (Matt. x. 19). The present conflict has afforded a proof of this. A voice full of the Holy Spirit burst forth from the martyr's mouth when the most blessed Mapalius, amid his torments, said to the proconsul, 'To-morrow thou shall see a fight.' And what he said with the testimony of courage and faith the Lord fulfilled. A heavenly fight was exhibited and the martyr was crowned."

45. Epistle lviii. After quoting texts from John and Paul, he continues : " All which things must now be considered by us, that no one may desire ought of the world now perishing, but may follow Christ. For the time is at hand which our Lord long since foretold. 'The time cometh, that whosoever killeth you will think that he doeth God service' (John xvi. 2). But the apostles taught us these things, which they also learned from the Lord's precepts and the commands of God our Lord himself, namely, strengthening us and saying, 'There is no man that hath left house, or parents, or brethren, or wife, or children, for the kingdom of God's sake, who shall not receive manifold more in the present time, and in the world to come, life everlasting' (Luke xiii. 29–30). And again he says, 'Blessed are ye when men shall hate you, and when they shall separate you from their company, and shall reproach you, and cast out your name as evil for the Son of man's sake. Rejoice ye in that day, and leap for joy ; for, behold, your reward is great in heaven' (vi. 22–23). The Lord would have us rejoice in persecutions, and leap for joy, because when persecutions come, then the crowns of faith

are given, then the soldiers of God are proved, then the heavens are opened to martyrs. For we have not so given in our names for warfare as to think only of peace, and decline and refuse warfare. He will confess those before his Father who confess him, and deny those who deny him (Matt. x. 32–33). If we could escape death we might rightly fear death, but since it must needs be that one subject to death should die, we should embrace the occasion offered by divine promise and favour, and accomplish the ending of life with the reward of immortality, nor fear to be slain who know that when slain we are crowned."

46. Epistle xxxi. *Moyses, Maximus, Nicastratus and Rufus to Cyprian.* "We repeat it again, therefore, we have received, brother Cyprian, great joy, great consolation, great ease, especially that you have described in such fitting praises the glorious—I will not say death, but immortality of martyrs. For such a close ought to be accompanied by such words that the things related may be described as they were really done. In your letters, then, we have beheld those glorious triumphs of the martyrs, and with our own eyes have followed them, as it were, on their way to heaven. We, in a manner, too, have heard with our own ears the Lord giving the testimony promised them before the Father. This it is then which day by day raises our courage and inflames us to the attainment of so great an honour. . . . For to this battle the Lord, as it were, with the trumpet of his Gospel, rouses us, saying, 'He that loveth father or mother more than me is not worthy of me; and he that loveth son or daughter more than me is not worthy of me; and he that taketh not his cross, and followeth after me, is not worthy of me' (Matt. x. 37–38). And again, 'Blessed are they that are persecuted for righteousness' sake, for

N 2

theirs is the kingdom of heaven' (v. 10). And again, 'Ye shall stand before governors and kings for my sake.' 'And the brother shall deliver up the brother to death, and the father the child.' 'And ye shall be hated of all men for my name's sake, but he that endureth to the end shall be saved' (x. 18-22). And 'To him that overcometh I will grant to sit with me on my throne, even as I overcame, and am sat down on the throne of my Father' (Rev. iii. 21). When we read and compare these things, and the like in the Gospels and in our Lord's words, we feel, as it were, torches put under us to kindle our faith; not only do we no longer dread the enemies of the truth, but we even challenge them, and in the very fact that we have not yielded, we have already conquered. And though we have not yet shed our blood, but are prepared to shed it, no one may think this postponement clemency, for it injures us; it interposes a hindrance to our glory; it puts off Heaven; it delays the glorious sight of God. For in a contest of this sort, in a battle of this sort, where it is the fight of faith, not to put off martyrs by delay is true clemency," ("Epistles of Cyprian." Pusey's Edition).

47. We may pick out certain texts from the Koran which, taken by themselves, tend to show that Mohammed was a courteous, tolerant, peaceable man; and it might be argued therefrom that he never contemplated propagating his religion by force, and that his less enlightened followers evidently perverted his doctrine when they took up the sword. It will be found, however, when we come to read chapter after chapter that fell from his pen, that the Prophet was not always in the same amiable mood, that he was at times very warlike, strongly inciting his followers to fight against unbelievers as

the sure means of attaining the joys of paradise.
In like manner, there are a few Gospel texts which,
when viewed separately, indicate that Jesus desired
his disciples to be meek, gentle, and benevolent
towards all men, whether friends or enemies. But
there are other portions of his discourses which
breathe a spirit of animosity and combativeness,
which make it clear that hostility is to be welcomed,
persecution considered a cause for rejoicing, and a
violent death at the hands of opponents esteemed
the greatest good fortune, from its offering a pass-
port to the endless felicity of heaven. And it is
these contentious militant precepts pointing to
prospective glory which so strongly influenced
Cyprian and the other martyr leaders in their
systematic efforts to raise a commotion and provoke
judicial punishment during the great religious conflict of the second century. There were undoubtedly
some Christians of superior character who suffered
involuntarily when disturbances occurred and the
vengeance of the Pagan rabble was excited ; but it
is clear that the majority of the martyrs eagerly
sought death, and were just as much guilty of self-
destruction as the fanatical Hindoos who pros-
trated themselves in the fatal trackway of the car
of Juggernaut. Indeed, a certain portion of these
zealots, in the intervals of calm, when it was
difficult to find persecutors, bravely accomplished
their own martyrdom without casting on other
people any stigma of guilt. Several of the Donatist
sect (spoken of by Gibbon) when they were impatient to gain by violent suffering the joys of
paradise, fixed a certain day for publicly laying
down their lives, and then threw themselves from a
neighbouring precipice, so as to die in the presence
of a sympathetic multitude. However abhorrent
the conduct of such people, it was less reprehen-

sible than that of the combative martyrs, who contrived to suffer at the hands of opponents, having
no hesitation to provoke a breach of the commandment "Thou shalt not kill," and gain eternal
honour, as they thought, by fastening on others
eternal infamy.

CHAPTER VII.

FICTITIOUS MARTYRDOMS.

The Crucifixion called " the greatest crime in history." 3.
But an act of concert is not a crime. 4. The voluntary
death of Socrates. 5. The Christians in general courted
martyrdom. 8. Jesus desired to be crucified. 9. The
Jews charged with killing prophets, but they only stoned
such as were political opponents. 10. Jesus could not
have been obnoxious to them either from his predictions
or his doctrines. 12. M. Renan's unjustifiable charge
against Annas the high priest. 14. The murder of the
younger Annas. 16. Real crimes distinguished from
imaginary. 17. The Christians charged all their opponents
with Diabolism. 18. The child crucifixions and other
strange offences fastened on the Jews. 20. The Massacre
of the Innocents imputed to Herod the Great. 22. The
equally extravagant charge against the Sanhedrin. 23.
Ex parte statements of faction strife always untrustworthy. 24. The Christian calumnies easily propagated.
25. Gradual exposure of baseless medieval martyr stories.
26. Dr. M'Caul shows that they were from first to last
entirely fictitious. 27. The evidence of Christian character
thus throws discredit on the earlier kindred accusations of
the Evangelists.

ARCHDEACON FARRAR, in the preface to
his well written and very popular work, " The
Life of Christ," earnestly bespeaks the attention
of all unbelievers in Christianity, all who reject
the supernatural claims of the religion which he
so ably and eloquently defends. He continues his
appeal as follows: " It is possible that this book
may fall into the hands of some Jewish readers,
and to these particularly I would wish this remark
to be addressed. I have reason to believe that
the Jewish race have long since learnt to look with

love and reverence on Him whom their fathers
rejected; nay more, that many of them, convinced
by the irrefragable logic of history, have openly
acknowledged that he was indeed their promised
Messiah, although they still reject the belief in his
divinity.   I see in the writings of many Jews a
clear conviction that Jesus, to whom they have
quite ceased to apply the terms of hatred found in
the Talmud, was at any rate the greatest religious
Teacher, the highest and noblest Prophet that
their race has produced.   They therefore would be
the last to defend that greatest crime in history—
the Crucifixion of the Son of God.   And while no
Christian ever dreams of visiting on them the
horror due to the sin of their ancestors, so no Jew
will charge the Christians of to-day with looking
with any feeling but that of simple abhorrence on
the long, cruel, and infamous persecutions to
which the ignorance and brutality of past ages
have subjected their great and noble race."

2. Probably most English Jews, who know anything of the Archdeacon, respect him as a zealous,
hard-working minister and kind Christian neighbour, and reciprocate the good wishes which he
has expressed for the establishment of a better
understanding between the Jewish and Christian
communities.   But very few are likely to endorse
his strong partisan statements or submit to be led
captive by his earnest apologetic pleading as
though they had been schooled from their earliest
infancy in Christian prejudices.   Without entertaining the slightest feeling of hatred towards the
prophet of Nazareth, who is worshipped by so
many millions as " the Son of God," they are quite
unable to admit his supernatural claims, or even to
recognise his moral pre-eminence, and as to the
wide propagation of the faith in him, or what is
called the " irrefragable logic of history," it is just

FICTITIOUS MARTYRDOMS. 185

as unconvincing in his case as in that of Mohammed. Nor can they for one moment allow that his immense Gentile following entitles him to be considered "the greatest religious Teacher, the highest and noblest Prophet that their race has produced;" any sober, thoughtful Jew who reads the Gospel discourses carefully and with clear eyes must regard him as a mistaken visionary. The fanatical doctrines which he promulgated, and especially what he said in reference to courting persecution and martyrdom, help to explain his own death, and it will become manifest in time to all unprejudiced people that the Crucifixion, which has been turned to such wonderful account in the Church, so far from being "the greatest crime in history," was in reality no crime at all.

3. For a crime to be perpetrated, for a rape, a robbery, a burglary, a murder, or an assault to be committed, it must be clearly shown that there was neither mutual aggression nor mutual consent; it must be proved that the suffering party did not deliberately provoke nor encourage what was done, but was really and truly aggrieved. When a soldier is struck hard in battle and wounded, his assailant has simply committed an act of war and cannot be regarded as a criminal. If the same wounded soldier, being in great agony, induces a comrade to strike him afresh and mercifully terminate his sufferings, the blow inflicted in such case is an act of concert and not a crime. We are told that when king Saul was suffering from wounds in his last battle with the Philistines, he vainly entreated his armour-bearer to kill him in kind consideration, and at length fell on a sword and slew himself (1 Sam. xxxi. 4). According to another version, he induced an Amalekite to despatch him with a spear, and this man went at once and honestly reported what was done to David,

his son-in-law and successor. Assuming the last account to be correct, the poor Amalekite, although he may have acted indiscreetly, was clearly free from criminal guilt, yet David, judging his conduct under strong excitement, had him capitally punished precisely as though he had been a murderer.

4. In another country, and at a later period, Socrates was just as desirous of quitting this world by violence as Saul, only for somewhat different reasons; he was not longing to be released from physical agony, but had become weary of the life which he led at Athens, and was hankering for the higher spiritual existence of the Elysian Fields. When people are in such a mood and hope for the compensatory gain which is supposed to await those who suffer unjustly, they do not call on friends to kindly release them from earthly trouble, but prefer to be put to death by their enemies. Socrates accordingly set about with much study and deliberation to provoke his political opponents to sentence him to imprisonment and execution. Instead of endeavouring to remove their prejudices and conciliate them, as he easily might have done, he uttered the most aggravating language against them, which he knew well would make him seem in their eyes a dangerous character and call forth their indignation and resentment. He was not aggrieved, but greatly obliged, by their condemnation; it was just what he wanted, and he drank the hemlock brought to him with the utmost good will; his death was partly an act of war, partly an act of concert; there was culpability in the matter on both sides, but no criminality; his admirers have had no good ground for holding him up before the world ever since as a victim of injustice.

5. No discredit attaches to Socrates for believing in a higher spiritual existence, but in rashly provoking a judicial death for the purpose of advancing

himself prematurely to the better world of his
hopes, instead of patiently discharging as long as he
was able the duties of the present life, his conduct
must be considered altogether reprehensible. In
the eyes of the early Christians, however, the
culpable last acts of the Athenian philosopher
constituted his crowning merit, and they felt
assured that in thus voluntarily sacrificing himself he was entitled to share the glory of their own
suffering saints. They were prepared to go much
further in the way of provoking hostility and taking
the kingdom of heaven by force (Matt. xi. 12).
A sensible man who simply did his duty in an
unostentatious manner, and by kindness and civility
got on smoothly in the world, was certain to receive
no honour in their community. They thought it
indispensable to be surrounded by enemies, to be
continually buffeted by Satan, and suffer in various
ways much trouble and wrong that they might
become worthy of the everlasting compensation of
heaven. Indeed a suffering Christian had a rather
difficult part to play ; he desired to avoid sin, yet
was anxious to incur suspicion of guilt, and draw
upon himself unjust punishment ; he especially
sought in some way or other to render himself
obnoxious to the authorities. If he could only
succeed in creating an uproar by some intemperate
harangue, and get himself imprisoned as a disturber of the public peace, he rejoiced exceedingly
in having won so great an honour. Then if he
could further behave rudely and defiantly as a
prisoner, and put on such a semblance of unsub-
dued wickedness as to provoke the magistrates
eventually to sentence him to death, his vision of
glory was consummated, and he felt assured of
being rewarded quickly with a heavenly crown.

6. In the great struggle for religious ascendancy
which was maintained so long in the Roman

empire, the Christians, when they formed a weak
minority, were occasionally murdered, just as Pagans
were subsequently murdered and ill-treated when
fortune turned against them and their numbers
declined. But it cannot be made out that those
saints who are specially held up to honour as
martyrs were criminally assaulted and slain,
because it is clear that they wished to die by
violence, and were consenting parties to the
shedding of their blood. When a man goes to
have a tooth drawn or a limb amputated, however
painful the operation may be, he is very well
satisfied with what is being done, and assured of
its conducing to his permanent benefit. The
Christian saint was equally well pleased with the
scourging which he occasionally received. When
any one could be induced to smite him on the cheek
he smarted momentarily under the infliction, but
was so sure of profiting from it eventually that he
begged the smiter to favour him with a second
blow. Whether the stroke so repeated wounded
him, or stunned him, or killed him outright, he felt
certain to benefit in proportion to the hurt, and it is
absurd that an act of concert which afforded him
so much inward satisfaction should be represented
as a crime. When the martyr Cyprian went to his
voluntary death he was filled with thankfulness
and joy at the great honour which was being conferred upon him, and requested that twenty pieces
of gold should be given to the executioner who
struck off his head. Many other Christian saints
felt equally obliged by the services of those who
liberated them forcibly from their fleshly tabernacle
to attain for such brief suffering, as they thought,
the compensation of everlasting glory in paradise.
"I would rather die for Christ than rule the whole
world," said Ignatius of Antioch, "I pray that the
beasts may be found ready for me. Nay, I will fawn

upon them that they may devour me quickly. Yea, and if they will not voluntarily do it, I will bring them to it by force."

7. Even those of the primitive Christians, in whom the love of life was so strongly implanted that they had no desire to become martyrs themselves, were ever ready to encourage the attainment of martyrdom by others. For the ancient martyr, like the modern emigrant, was considered to better at the same time both his own position and that of his brethren whom he left behind. It was well known that the Christians who suffered in this way attracted a large amount of popular sympathy towards their community, and brought in additional converts. The blood of the martyrs was rightly said to be the seed of the Church. To the unreasoning multitude no more convincing proof of the truth of a religious system could be offered than the spectacle of a man voluntarily laying down his life for it. Polycarp's one final act of sacrifice was of more worth for the advancement of proselytism than all his preceding discourses. Reflecting Christians, therefore, when they saw clearly how every martyrdom strengthened their cause and discredited that of their opponents, rightly considered that they were engaged in a successful warfare, and urged on their boldest spirits, as a general would encourage his soldiers, to provoke further collisions which were sure to result in fresh victories. Indeed the martyrdoms of primitive Christianity were of more evidential value even than its miracles; so much glory came to the Church from these tragic scenes that imaginative writers not only embellished them, but were induced to create some of a purely mythical character.

8. In modern times political agitators are often known to exhibit great astuteness in earning the honour of martyrdom to such a moderate degree as

is afforded by their being subjected to the penalty
of imprisonment. They long to get arrested and
shut up in a dungeon in order thus to gain distinction and excite in their behalf a strong manifestation of popular sympathy. It is necessary,
however, to disguise their self-seeking ambition
as well as they can, and present an appearance of
being real victims of injustice, otherwise they
would entirely fail to win sympathy, and would
only become objects of contempt. Their design in
seeking to put their opponents in the wrong and
gain honour from suffering will perhaps be clearly
seen through by a few shrewd observers, and yet
not in the least suspected by the credulous multitude on whom they rely for support. The early
Christians were actuated by similar motives in
courting persecution and death: they expected to be
well recompensed for their transient pains; they
dreaded the scaffold just as little as the scourge;
in their eyes the tomb was only a prison from
which they would soon have a glorious deliverance.
Admitting, then, that Jesus, in going up to
Jerusalem at the Passover feast, deliberately aimed
at provoking hostility there and earnestly desired
to die a martyr, the story of his trial and crucifixion, stripped of the colouring which it might
be expected to receive from partisan scribes, is
perfectly natural and intelligible. But on the
theory that he went about as an ordinary righteous
man intent only on doing all the good in his power,
and thus quite undesignedly drew upon himself
the enmity of the Jewish rulers who at length
conspired to put him to death, we find ourselves
confronted by so many insuperable difficulties that
any parallel case of that kind presented to the
world would be deemed wholly unworthy of belief.

9. When a crime is said to have been committed,
it is usual to take into consideration the character

of the accused as a very important evidence pointing to the probability of their innocence or guilt. Such judicial treatment is accorded both to individuals and to communities; any fresh report of their doings is considered more or less credible according as it agrees with or differs from what they have already done. Those who look upon the crucifixion as "the greatest crime of history," and want to make it appear in this light reasonable and probable, will tell us that the Jews were a reprobate people, who repeatedly stoned and killed the prophets that were sent to them long before the advent of Jesus. But in point of fact it was only political prophets whom they thus occasionally ill-treated, as that class of men were liable to be ill-treated in all countries by those whose interests happened to be prejudiced by their predictions. Every ancient nation had its political vaticinators, and what they said in favour of one party and against another frequently produced such an impression on the popular mind as led to their words being fulfilled. When, for instance, a prophet of good reputation declared that a city would be soon captured, or that a king would be overthrown, it was pretty sure to cause discouragement and perhaps defection among some of those who were desirous to avert such an eventuality. The more stout-hearted would then entreat some other prophet to contradict what he had spoken and arrest the panic, or would otherwise clamour for his imprisonment and death as a dangerous enemy to their cause. The princes of Judah spoke to their king concerning Jeremiah, "We beseech thee, let this man be put to death, for thus he weakeneth the hands of the men of war that remain in the city, and the hands of all the people, in speaking such words unto them" (Jer. xxxviii. 4). At a later period, when the civil war was raging between the rival princes, Hyrcanus and

Aristobulus, which led to Pompey's intervention, the prophet Onias was brought into the camp of Hyrcanus, and asked to pray for the defeat of the opposite faction. The good man, on refusing to comply with this request, was treated by the soldiers of Hyrcanus as a political enemy, and speedily stoned to death ("Ant." xiv. ii. 1).

10. Such cases of punishing adverse or unfriendly prophets were common enough among both Jews and Gentiles in times of war when men's passions were strongly roused, and, however cruel the stone-throwers may have been, their conduct under the circumstances was not at all strange or unnatural. They were only a little more barbarous than our own political mobs, who pelt their opponents freely, and break both windows and heads during the excitement of a fiercely-contested election. They did not conspire to put any prophet to death from pure love of wickedness, and when there was not the slightest prospect of his removal advancing their interests or improving their position. It is well known, too, that during the public ministry of Jesus, Palestine was free from any great internal strife, and he had not, like Jeremiah, to encounter the hostility of a fighting faction, which had been weakened by the tenor of his words. What he predicted was not the defeat of one armed party by another, but a series of general calamities—wars, sieges, famines, earthquakes, the wreck of the sun and moon, and the near approaching end of the world. He was not likely to make himself obnoxious by setting forth afresh the apocalyptic visions of the pseudo-Daniel and others; doomsday predictions had been hazarded long before his time, and have been often enough repeated since in each succeeding century, and although they have occasionally excited alarm in superstitious minds, neither from the credulous nor from the in-

credulous have they ever called forth hatred and resentment.

11. The religious teaching of Jesus was no more calculated to give sérious offence to other Jews than his predictions. His doctrine was very much like that of the Essenes, who enjoined non-resistance, the prohibition of oaths, the communion of goods, and the renunciation of wealth and worldly pleasures. Such notions have been very extensively promulgated throughout the world, and, if not very attractive to the energetic and prosperous classes, have always been well received by the saintly, the ascetic, and the poor improvident multitude. It was the brigand leaders, men appealing to physical force, such as those who troubled the country much after the death of Herod the Great, that law-abiding people were likely to regard with fear and abhorrence. Jesus, with his poor mendicant disciples, might have been despised more than they, but while he did nothing worse than practise exorcism and faith-healing, and exhort people to prepare for the coming kingdom of heaven, it is morally impossible that his conduct should have kindled a feeling of deadly hatred among any section of his countrymen. In all parts of the world a harmless religious devotee, wandering without a home and renouncing the ordinary comforts of life, has ever commanded the respect of some people and the commiseration of others; and if we are to believe that the Jewish rulers were moved with malignant wrath against such a character, they were an exceptional class of beings very differently constituted from the rest of mankind. The only proceeding of Jesus in the least likely to create a bad feeling against him was his violent behaviour and vituperative language in Jerusalem during the feast of the Passover. But it is clear that on that occasion he had a purpose

to serve; he believed that the time had arrived for
him to attain the full glory of martyrdom, and he
was deliberately aiming to get himself arrested and
condemned to death.

12. Ernest Renan professes to explain the origin
of Christianity by natural causes, and yet is quite
prepared to accept the most monstrous of all the
miracles recorded by the Evangelists—the preternatural wickedness of the Jewish Sanhedrin.
In his pretty historical romance called "The Life of
Jesus," he has endeavoured to make the popular
belief in their malignity somewhat less unreasonable by charging it especially on a single individual,
supposing that among the assembled rulers there
was one very bad man who had great influence,
and that chiefly through him the others were
brought to acquiesce in the shedding of innocent
blood.   The person whom he selects to play this
ungracious part of persecutor, monster, and arch-
devil is Annas, the father-in-law of Caiaphas, the
high-priest, and this is what he says of that ruler's
character: "Like all the aristocracy of the
Temple he was a Sadducee, 'a sect,' says Josephus,
'particularly severe in its judgments.'   All his
sons also were violent persecutors.   One of them
named, like his father, Annas, caused James, the
brother of the Lord, to be stoned under circumstances not unlike those which surrounded the
death of Jesus.   The spirit of the family was
haughty, bold, and cruel; it had that particular kind
of proud and sullen wickedness which characterizes
Jewish politicians.   Therefore upon this Annas
and his family must rest the responsibility of all
the acts which followed.   It was Annas (or the party
he represented) who killed Jesus.   Annas was the
principal actor in the terrible drama, and far more
than Caiaphas, far more than Pilate, ought to bear
the weight of the maledictions of mankind" (p. 254).

13. The only evidence, apart from the New Testament, that M. Renan has been able to discover respecting Annas is contained in the writings of Josephus, and what that historian says of the Jewish ruler, so far from affording any ground for a belief in his extreme wickedness, is altogether favourable : "This elder Annas was a prosperous man, for he had five sons who successfully filled the high-priest's office, and he had himself formerly held that dignity a long time " ("Ant." xx. ix. 1). " The people having risen against the conspirators at the instance of Annas, the senior of the high-priests, a man of consummate wisdom who might have saved the city only for those who plotted against him " (" War," iv. iii. 7). But as M. Renan's object is to blacken the reputation of Annas, he finds it convenient to overlook these testimonies, and endeavours to make it appear that he must have been a cruel persecutor because he belonged to the Sadducee party, who, according to Josephus, were "severe in their judgments." The fact is, the Sadducees were, in a political sense, the Tories, and the Pharisees, to whom Josephus belonged, were the Liberals of Judæa, and the latter, as a magistracy, were more inclined than their rivals to cultivate popularity by mild and lenient sentences. He does not represent that the Sadducees were corrupt, or partial, or inclined to punish the innocent, but only that they were severe in chastising the guilty. Besides, it does not follow that Annas was severe—much less unjust—because he belonged to a party that had a reputation for judicial severity; and neither can it be proved that he was tyrannical by any evidence showing that tyranny prevailed in his family. But is there such evidence ? " All his sons also were violent persecutors." Where is it so stated ? How does M. Renan make this out but by his own busy fable-

building imagination ?   " One of them named like his father, Annas, caused James, the brother of the Lord, to be stoned."   This is only a modern conjecture based on an ancient forgery.   The words now found in Josephus, " James the brother of Jesus who is called Christ" ("Ant." xx. ix. 1) are allowed by all unbiassed scholars to be an interpolation of the fourth century, and are of no more value as evidence than that other interpolation quoted by Origen, which represents that the destruction of Jerusalem was admitted by the Jews to be a retribution that fell upon them for the murder of this James.

14. In the genuine narrative of Josephus we are not told who the persons were that suffered capital punishment at the instance of the younger Annas, nor what they were charged with, but it is highly probable that they were some of the robbers who then greatly troubled the country.   The only fault of Annas seems to have been his acting unconstitutionally in an emergency by taking upon himself a power which could only be legally exercised by the absent procurator.   Not a shadow of evidence does the narrative furnish to warrant the supposition that his attempt to enforce the Jewish laws without sufficient authority was aggravated by cruelty and injustice.   If somewhat rash and haughty when comparatively young, we are informed that he afterwards became distinguished as a moderate and liberal ruler.   It is clear from the testimony of Josephus (who was not of their sect) that both the elder and the younger Annas were estimable high-priests—men of probity, generosity, and public spirit, and endowed in their riper years with much discretion ; men who were sufferers from injustice and not its perpetrators; and the latter at length died a genuine martyr while endeavouring to save the city from the violence of the zealots

and the Idumæans. " I might justly say," writes
Josephus, in reference to this event, " that the
death of Annas was the beginning of the city's
destruction, and that from this very day might be
dated the ruin of her affairs, when the people saw
their high-priest and preserver slain in their midst.
He was also in other respects a venerable and just
man, and, notwithstanding his exalted position, was
an admirer of democratic government, and a great
lover of liberty and equality, condescending to the
level of the humblest of the people. He ever
regarded the public welfare before his own advantage, and preferred peace above all things, for he
was thoroughly convinced that the Romans were
not to be conquered. He foresaw that of necessity
a war would follow, and that unless the Jews
arranged matters with them very dexterously they
would certainly be destroyed " (" War," IV. v. 2).

15. After having murdered the high-priest
Annas and his associate, Jesus, son of Gamalas,
the revolutionary faction at Jerusalem put many
other people to death who opposed their wishes,
and proceeded to commit every imaginable excess.
To give a semblance of legality to their lawless
proceedings, they chose seventy men from among
the populace and set up a mock Sanhedrin, before
which tribunal every one who became obnoxious to
them was tried. Among other eminent citizens
one Zacharias was thus presented for trial, chiefly
because he was a man of property who had great
influence in Jerusalem, and they were eager to get
possession of his wealth. They accused him of
having a design to betray the insurgent city to the
Romans, but the seventy judges finding no evidence
in support of this charge, and fearing to condemn
him wrongfully, brought in a verdict of acquittal.
The armed rabble were exasperated at this decision,
and struck the rulers whom they had elected with

the backs of their swords, while two of the most
violent fell upon Zacharias in the middle of the
Temple, and slew him with reproaches and insults
("War," iv. v. 4). If these shameful mockeries of
justice and savage atrocities had been perpetrated
by Annas the elder, Caiaphas, Gamaliel, and other
members of the real Sanhedrin during Pilate's
procuratorship, it would have afforded some
support for the terrible charges of the Evangelists;
it would have shown that the Jewish rulers were
cruel and unscrupulous men, capable of going to
any length in the abuse of their judicial power.
But the fact of their being committed by fanatical
revolutionists and levellers, the sworn enemies of
the governing class, furnishes a strong ground for
believing that the latter were moderate and reasonable men, anxious to preserve order and not disposed to punish offenders rigorously or without
necessity. The horror, too, that was manifested by
the orderly inhabitants of Jerusalem on this occasion shows that they were quite unaccustomed to
such outrages, and that nothing of the kind would
have been tolerated in the preceding quiet period
while they had a stable government. Even the
mock sanhedrin, which had been selected from the
city populace, had too good a sense of rectitude to
condemn a man in the absence of incriminating
evidence, and thus burden their conscience with
innocent blood.

16. Archdeacon Farrar expects modern Jews to
see the crucifixion of Jesus with his own eyes, to
regard it as "the greatest crime in history." But
they are not very likely to do this: most of them
will be disposed to consider the murder of the high-
priest Annas by the city rabble an act of greater
wickedness. For it is clear that this murder, like
the many that followed it, was a real crime, and
cannot by any construction of motives be made to

appear an act of concert. Annas would have saved his life if he could; he was not deliberately courting martyrdom and fulfilling Scripture; he did not studiously provoke his opponents to condemn him to death, but suffered involuntarily at their hands while faithfully discharging his duty in endeavouring to maintain order and peace. There will also probably appear to modern Jewish minds a greater amount of criminality in "the long, cruel, and infamous persecutions" which the Archdeacon admits their race to have suffered in past times from people of his own faith. For they are known to have died unwillingly in those persecutions; they were not fanatics eager to rush out of the world by violence for the attainment of a blissful recompense, but sober conscientious citizens desirous to do all they could to conciliate their opponents and avert an unjust death. Moreover, in respect to these and all other genuine crimes that have darkened the pages of history, we are in no way at a loss to understand the motives of the perpetrators. Annas was struck down by the rabble of Jerusalem because they wanted freedom to plunder the city, and he stood in their path as an obstacle to the carrying out of their anarchical designs. So the many families of Jews who were unjustly tortured and put to death during the middle ages generally had some amount of property, and the multitude trumped up terrible charges against them, that would insure their condemnation, in order to get possession of their wealth.

17. The crucifixion of Jesus, viewed as a crime, does not stand alone; it is simply one of an immense series of preternatural crimes which Christians imputed to Jews and other religious opponents from the first century down to the period of the Reformation, and which have been

occasionally heard of in later times. They believed in Diabolism, believed that those who opposed them or did not hold their doctrine were in league with the Evil Spirit, and as his agents were bound to work mischief, and carry on an unrelenting war against righteousness. When people thus acquire the superstitious notion that their neighbours, who differ from them a little, are under the domination of Satan, they are sure to regard their conduct with suspicion and distrust, and imagine them to be guilty of malignant misdeeds. The first opposition encountered by the Christian sect was from the Jewish authorities at Jerusalem, who consequently appeared in their distempered fancy full of devilishness, monsters of wickedness and cruelty conspiring day and night to destroy Jesus. They soon after, in their career of proselytism beyond Palestine, met with an occasional check from Pagan rulers and magistrates, and every one of these was more or less calumniated by them, and represented as a fierce, evil-minded persecutor of the saints. Prior to the conversion of Constantine the greater portion of those who composed the militant church were accustomed to regard all earthly potentates as feudatories of Satan at deadly war against the kingdom of Christ. When once they came under the protection of Christian emperors they looked distrustfully on their Pagan fellow-subjects as children of the devil, who were constantly having recourse to sorcery and plotting their ruin. In the fourth century the Christian emperor Valentinian had many Pagans, some of them persons of high position, condemned and executed because they were suspected of injuring Christians with magical arts. "A general charge of magic hung over the whole city. Maximin poured these dark rumours into the greedy ear of Valentinian, and obtained the authority which he

coveted for making a strict inquisition into the
offences, for exacting evidence by torture from
men of every rank and station, and for condemning
them to a barbarous and ignominious death"
(Milman's "History of Christianity," vol. iii. p. 37).

18. As the Pagan population throughout the
Roman empire were generally converted or driven
into the churches after having their temples
destroyed, the hostility of Christians was con-
centrated more and more on their earlier opponents,
the unbelieving, unrepentant Jews. The devilish
hatred of Christ which they were thought to
entertain was supposed to break out regularly at
the season of Easter, when they crucified any
Christian children that they were able to lay their
hands upon, and insulted the consecrated Host.
And as this belief was generally held both by
learned and ignorant, it is not surprising that
unscrupulous people who wanted to injure the Jews
should occasionally get up fictitious evidence in its
support. A church was now and then found
broken open on Good Friday, and the sacred wafer
treasured therein was seen to be removed from the
pix and pierced with knives. The body of a dead
child was also sometimes discovered at the same
season nailed up against a wall, a tree, or a wooden
cross, with a ghastly wound in its side to suggest a
re-enactment of the crucifixion of Jesus. Suspicion at once fell on the Jews, who were alone
considered capable of perpetrating such hellish
deeds, and they were forthwith arrested, imprisoned,
tortured, and sent to execution, while their houses
were pillaged by the mob. Perhaps here and
there a sensible magistrate deemed the outrages a
great mystery, since the accused people were not
mad, and it was clear that they could derive no
earthly advantage from such acts even if they
escaped detection or were suffered to go un-

punished.   But it would have been said that the
Jews were not ordinary human beings, that they
were emissaries of Satan, and were incited by him
to war against Christ, as their fathers did, from pure
love of wickedness.   They were supposed to inherit
the devilishness of the original crucifiers and to
long for an opportunity to repeat at any cost the
same nefarious deeds.

19. Not only were the crimes imputed to the
Jews irrational and contrary to human nature, but
the Christian imagination invariably connected with
them a variety of other miracles.   Thus in the year
1250 the Jews of Saragossa are said to have
nailed a child named Dominic to a wall in the form
of a cross and then to have pierced its side with a
spear.   We are told that they buried the body to
conceal the crime, but in the night time the place
of sepulture shone with such a brilliant light, that
some   Christians   found   the   martyred   child's
remains, and they were deposited in a church where
many wonderful cures were performed.   About
five   years   later,   according   to   the   monkish
chronicler Matthew Paris, the Jews of Lincoln
stole a boy eight years old—the celebrated St.
Hugh.   They   then invited the principal Jews
from all parts of England that they might attend
the crucifixion of the child, and appointed one to
sit in judgment on him, as Pontius Pilate.   They
afterwards scourged him till he was black and
blue, spat in his face, crowned him with thorns,
mocked   him   in   reproachful   and   blasphemous
language, calling him Jesus the false prophet.   At
length,   after   giving   him   gall   to   drink   and
loading   him   with   every   kind   of   abuse, they
crucified him and pierced his side with a spear.
Afterwards they took out the bowels of the child
to be used for magical purposes, and privately
buried the corpse.   The earth, however, vomited

forth the innocent body; as often as they tried to bury it securely, it revealed itself the next day above ground. Fearing that their crime would be discovered by this miracle, they threw it into a well, where it was at length found by the mother. On its being drawn forth it became a wonderful spectacle to the people. There happened to be among them John Lexingtone, a man of much learning and discretion, who said, " We have sometimes heard that the Jews have dared to attempt such things to discredit the crucified Jesus our Lord." Then one of the Jews near whose house the child was last seen, on being apprehended and put to the torture, confessed the whole plot. He was soon fastened to a horse's tail and dragged to the gallows. Eighteen of the richest and most influential Jews of Lincoln were executed in the same way, and ninety others were sent in chains to London. The body of the child was given to the canons of Lincoln cathedral in compliance with their petition, and it was there honourably buried and enshrined as a precious martyr. .

20. It is scarcely worth while to attempt to separate fact from fiction in the above abridged narrative of the learned monk. Hundreds of such martyr stories were at one time current throughout Christendom; they generally originated in fictitious evidence, which was got up to incriminate the Jews and involve them in punishment, and they were subsequently embellished and made more wonderful by a mythopœic imagination. Let us now go back from the record of Matthew Paris to that of an older and more venerated monkish chronicler— Matthew the Apostle—and see what he says on the subject of preternatural crimes committed by the enemies of Christ. Archdeacon Farrar deems the alleged propensity of the Jews to kill Christian children during the middle ages wholly incredible;

but he has not the least doubt respecting the reality of the Massacre of the Innocents at Bethlehem by Herod the Great. It is not easy, however, to see how King Herod, any more than the Jews, could expect to derive the slightest temporary advantage from his Christ-hatred and monstrous criminality. If he occasionally inflicted severe punishments, even on his own relatives, he at least had a clear motive for so doing : he was universally admitted to be a sagacious ruler, and no tributary king in his right senses would have ever thought of slaying a multitude of infant children in this wanton manner with the view to safeguard his throne. Had this monarch, whom the Roman Senate elected and upheld, subject to his good behaviour, actually been fool enough to believe that his position was endangered by the birth of some wondrous peasant child, and, for the chance of removing his supposed rival, mad enough to command a sweeping massacre of young Bethlehemites, those about him would have readily perceived that his mind was disordered, and would not have ventured to carry out his extravagant behest. It is quite certain that such a slaughter could not have been effected without the consent and aid of a large number of capable men, and how could the king obtain their co-operation and at the same time escape the consequences of his mad misgovernment? We might search through all history and the whole range of fiction beside, for anything to match the utter imbecility, to say nothing of the monstrosity, of this ill-invented political crime. The author of the legend and those who first received it as an authentic record must have been in point of intellectual development and knowledge of the world's affairs, nothing better than dreaming children.

21. Even if the reported Massacre of the

Bethlehemites could be regarded as a rational crime, as a bold and able stroke of Eastern statesmanship, it would still, without abundant corroboration, be wholly unentitled to belief. For Herod was a famous ruler of that period, only second in importance to his great patron Augustus Cæsar ; and, had he committed the unparalleled outrage on an innocent population ascribed to him, it would soon have been in everybody's mouth and would have resounded through the whole Roman empire. Yet there is not the slightest allusion to it in any of the numerous writers of the Augustan age whose works have come down to our own times. Moreover, Josephus, a writer strongly antagonistic to Herod, in the great historical work dealing with the whole period of his reign, makes no mention of any such child massacre. He tells us, too, that after the death of that monarch fifty deputies of the faction opposed to him went to Rome for the express purpose of decrying his rule and blasting his reputation, in order to create a prejudice against his son Archelaus, who was then petitioning to have the succession. These deputies, in their fruitless appeal to Cæsar, raked up everything that they were able to remember to Herod's disadvantage, and did their utmost to represent him as a merciless tyrant and oppressor, yet of the massacre—which if true must have been very recent and more to their purpose than anything else—they said not a word, which makes it clear that the legend of Matthew was then not in existence.

22. The alleged mad attempt of Herod to slay Jesus when a child is a pure fiction ; the alleged wicked conspiracy of the Jewish rulers to crucify him when a grown man is a misrepresented fact, just as we have fictions and distorted facts bound up together in the stories of child martyrdom which arose in the middle ages. Even if there had been

no crucifixion and Jesus had died from some natural ailment, his death would probably have been ascribed to the evil devices of the Sanhedrin. The charge of murderous malignity fastened on this religious assembly is in some respects more outrageous and incredible than that made against the king. For Herod was a military ruler, who had both the power and the disposition to put people to death for state purposes, and was known to have ordered many to execution. Whereas the Jewish elders had no corresponding power nor like sanguinary record, and, even if one or two had not borne the high character which befitted such an assembly and had desired from pure malice to kill a righteous man, they would have been severely restrained by the rest. Everybody who has the least knowledge of human affairs and is capable of looking round on the world with unprejudiced eyes, must be convinced that under such moral conditions as those depicted by the Evangelists a religious government able to command respect would be impossible; a council of elders at the head of a nation so utterly abominable and at the same time so idiotic could not exist. During the witchcraft persecutions of the seventeenth century men of good reputation were frequently tried and condemned to death for perpetrating extravagant Satanic crimes on the testimony of silly fanciful children. The early Christian saints, who persistently calumniated people in authority and suffered their imagination to run wild were, in point of intelligence and truthfulness, pretty much on a level with these child witnesses whose revelations startled the world. And if those whom they accused were not immediately injured in consequence an endless amount of injustice was thereby eventually inflicted on their posterity, or rather visited on their dispersed race.

23. Even where people are not crazed by the superstition of Diabolism, *ex parte* statements of cruelty and wrong committed by an opposing faction are notoriously untrustworthy. When a community is sharply divided by political or religious strife, it is not in human nature for one of the contending parties to lay aside all prejudice and give a fair and accurate report of that strife. It will be sure to get up a more or less coloured and distorted account of what took place, embellishing a little here and blackening there, leaving out entirely or diminishing some things which ought to have been mentioned, and introducing others for which there is scarcely any other basis but imagination. Hence the necessity of confronting every such one-sided story by the statements of opposition witnesses, in order that independent inquirers may make a fair judicial decision or arrive as nearly as possible at the truth. In the accounts which have come down to us of the English Civil War, the French Revolution, the origin of the Quakers, the Wesleyans, and several other sects, we have this requisite completeness of testimony, each side of the conflict or movement is well represented in literature, and one historian rightly corrects the partiality of another. But the contention which long ago existed between the humble Nazarene sect and other religious Jews who could not be won over by their proselytizing efforts is only reported to us in the one-sided sectarian story of the Evangelists. Their narrative may seem credible enough throughout by those who have been carefully trained from childhood to regard it as a divine revelation, yet any similar story coming to them afresh on its own intrinsic merits would be instantly rejected as untrustworthy, and partisan testimony of such a character would entirely fail to command respect in a modern court of justice.

24. The monstrous charges which the first
Christian writers made against the Sanhedrin were
not published openly at Jerusalem during the lifetime of the accused, so as to challenge criticism
and refutation.   Oral statements to the same effect
were probably uttered there by disciples of Jesus,
under the shelter of obscurity, and they would not
be treated seriously or considered worthy of
notice by educated and sensible people.   Then, as
the missionaries of the sect wandered into other
countries to propagate their doctrines and announce the coming end of the world, they could
tell their pitiable tales of persecution and martyrdom
to sympathetic audiences without the least fear of
contradiction.   In this way their sectarian slanders
soon struck root in a congenial soil, and before the
lapse of a century were carried by ignorant,
sensation-loving, gossiping converts into all parts
of the Roman empire.   Whatever independent
documents might have existed in Jerusalem to
check or confute them were probably destroyed
during Vespasian's war, so that after the death of
that generation the Christian story would remain in
almost undisputed possession of the field.   The
dispersed Jews did occasionally meet with Christian
preachers, and indignantly deny the calumnious
statements they were propagating, but they had
not the requisite information to controvert them
satisfactorily, and even if they could have done this
it would not have availed much to arrest a story
which had got the start of them in every direction
and was winged with fanaticism.   Some Jewish
writers, having no authentic knowledge of the
origin of the Nazarene sect, very unwisely replied
to Christian falsehoods with fables of their own
invention, just as Christians themselves at a later
period attempted to disprove by fiction the claims
of Mohammedanism.   And the time at length

arrived when the proselytizing Roman Church, backed by the secular power, became so aggressive and intolerant that its one-sided sectarian testimony had to be listened to in humble silence: those who ventured to question the truth of the charges which its early chroniclers made against the Sanhedrin answered for their temerity with their lives.

25. The monstrous charges of shedding innocent blood which used to be brought against the Jews regularly at Easter time, at first broke down, not from their intrinsic unreasonableness, but from its being clearly demonstrated that they were based on fictitious evidence. Unprincipled men were occasionally detected in the very act of craftily fabricating appearances of guilt with the view to incriminate them, and on this becoming known it induced the magistrates to give all such cases a more careful investigation. The celebrated Manasseh Ben Israel, writing in the seventeenth century, says, " I cannot but weep bitterly and with much anguish of soul lament that strange and horrid accusation of some Christians against the dispersed and afflicted Jews that dwell among them, when they say that the Jews are wont to celebrate the Feast of Unleavened Bread by fermenting it with the blood of some Christian whom they have for the purpose killed, when the calumniators have found one dead, and cast the body as if it had been murdered by the Jews into their houses and yards, as lamentable experience has proved in various places. Then with unbridled rage they have accused the innocent Jews of doing what has only been done in appearance, which detestable wickedness has sometimes been perpetrated that they might thereby take advantage and exercise their cruelty upon them, and sometimes justify former massacres " (" Vindiciæ Judæorum "). ✗

26. The repeated failure of these accusations when subjected to a thorough investigation did not for awhile in the least weaken the popular belief in former charges which had met with success. It was thought that the Jews, although now and then accused falsely, had certainly been often enough guilty of killing Christian children, as was shown by the unimpeachable testimony of many holy shrines. There was no questioning that St. Hugh of Lincoln, St. William of Norwich, St. Werner of Bacharach, St. Robert de Pontoise, and others were genuine martyrs who had suffered from the malignancy of the hereditary enemies of Christ. People began to suspect at length, however, that even these charges were probably of the same baseless character as those which had been recently exposed, and that they only obtained credit at the time from not being subjected to a like searching criticism. And this has now got to be the general opinion of educated Christians; the numerous child martyrdoms of ecclesiastical history are regarded as being from first to last calumnious fabrications which have only brought disgrace on the church. Dr. M'Caul, who laboured long and earnestly to convert the Jews, wrote some years ago of the repeated attempts made to convict them of Diabolism as follows: "In the first place, the charge has been only made in the times and regions of ignorance, and in countries where justice is not impartially administered. How is it that during the last two centuries the sound of it has gradually died away in Europe? Why is it that no case of the kind now occurs in France, Holland, Prussia, or England? . . . . This accusation is brought forward among others now universally acknowledged to be gross and ridiculous falsehoods, and almost every case of child murder recorded is itself inter-woven with a narrative of lying wonders, so that of

each such history one part is confessedly fabulous, and if the one part be rejected why should the other be believed ? . . . . The enormous lying and profound ignorance of Judaism and the Jews, as well as degrading superstition involved in some of these charges, throw discredit on all. The mere recital of these follies shows that they are the offspring of an unenlightened imagination, if not the invention of a malignant heart. The total absence of all credible testimony compels us to refuse our belief. The only evidence to be had is that extracted from the victims of torture. But that mode of examination would have made the same persons confess that they were metempsychoses of Judas Iscariot or Pontius Pilate—that they had caused the ruinous convulsions of an earthquake or the devastations of the cholera " (" Reasons," &c., pp. 2–24).

27. Dr. M'Caul, after giving a list of blood accusations accompanied by lying wonders extending from the sixth century to the sixteenth, admits that during this whole period Christians were for the most part credulous, untruthful, and much disposed to calumniate their Jewish neighbours, and that they only ceased to bring false charges against them when the growth of intelligence and the improved administration of justice rendered it difficult to get their absurd stories believed in the courts. But the martyrdoms and miracles of the thousand years which preceded the Reformation are manifestly akin to those of the first century recorded by the Evangelists ; and as their supposed truthfulness was then thought to prove the unbroken succession of Christian truth, their known falsity now proves the unmistakable continuity of Christian falsehood. It must be clear to every unprejudiced mind that the evidence of character has turned more and more against the accusers

and in favour of the accused. The alleged propensity of the Jews to shed innocent blood has been repeatedly and abundantly disproved, while to precisely the same extent the Christian propensity to calumniate those who are not of their faith has been confirmed and established. We have therefore a very strong presumptive ground for believing the original charge of devilry—the unsupported story of the Jewish rulers conspiring from pure malice and envy to put Jesus to death—to be no better founded than the numerous horrifying murder tales which gave from time to time additional martyrs to the church during the middle ages. It is not to be supposed that Christians of the first century were in point of intelligence and veracity superior to those of the sixth. Fairness towards opponents, careful investigation and accuracy of statement, are no more to be looked for from the credulous and excited community forming the primitive church than from any modern group of Catholic peasant children to whom the Virgin Mary has recently appeared. Christianity in its earliest stages had in a marked degree those moral weaknesses which are characteristic of the age of infancy; it believed in its own wild dreams and revelled in exaggeration and fiction. Then after awhile it learned the wisdom of putting a rein on its imagination, and to some extent bridling its tongue, from the repeated checks and corrections which it received from the outside world. Like every individual human being, as it grew in strength and importance and found its extravagant assertions more subjected to criticism, it became gradually educated in truthfulness. The reasoning capacity of such men as Origen and Tertullian was poor enough, as their works testify, yet it was much better than that of the earlier and less instructed

saints; and, besides, they wrote under a sense of
greater publicity; they knew that they were confronted and watched by educated unbelievers, and
they had not such a chance as some of their obscure
predecessors to impose on the credulous world by
misrepresentation and miracle-mongering.

CHAPTER VIII.

THE CRUCIFIXION DRAMA.

Subjective and objective visions of revelators.   2. The Pagan
mysteries.   3. Christian masked dramas.   4. Personated
and forged authorities.   5. The Transfiguration vision
in Galilee.   6. Jesus there instructed to prepare for martyrdom.   7. Stratagems of his instructors.   8. It was
clearly not the chief priests and rulers who plotted his
death.   10. Dr. Geikie's surmise that he was tried before
a fictitious sanhedrin.   12. The fickle behaviour of the
populace towards him shows that they were a hireling
mob.   13. The part acted by Judas Iscariot is dramatic.
14. Jesus troubled at his approaching death.   15. No
defence offered at his trial.   16. Remarks of Dr. Benisch
on his supposed trial before the Sanhedrin.   18. Dr.
Philippson's mistaken theory of his punishment by the
Romans as a political offender.   20. The Crucifixion as
dramatic and artificial as a modern Passion-Play.   21.
Imaginary wrongs and real ones.

THE apparitions or spectres, which we read of
or hear of as being now and then seen but
much less frequently than in past times, are known
to be of two kinds—subjective and objective.
In the former case a person evolves spirits from
his own mind as in a dream, that is, believes in the
pictures produced by his imagination; in the latter
case he sees in external nature real objects which
he supposes to be ghosts.   There is precisely the
same difference of character in the revelatory
visions which have effected at one time and another
very important results in the religious world.   The
ancient prophets who obtained recognition as
revelators were for the most part mystics who had,
as they firmly believed, direct communication with
Heaven.   Ezekiel says at the commencement of

his revelations, "the heavens were opened, and I saw visions of God." The prophet's visions on this occasion were evidently subjective; he fell into a reverie and saw with a powerful imagination what was not apparent to any one else. The author of the Apocalypse, Mohammed, the Druse prophet, Swedenborg, and hundreds of other revelators of ancient and modern times, thus beheld independently with their mind's eye the spiritual pictures which they afterwards described to the world. And the visions of many distinguished poets, such as Virgil, Dante, and Milton, have been of a similar character; their much exercised imagination has completely overmastered their reflective powers, so that they have as thoroughly believed the reality of the celestial scenes presented to them as though they were observations made in the course of travel.

2. The great bulk of mankind are neither poets nor mystics; their imagination is feeble or so much under control that if they are to see in their waking hours what they shall deem visions, these must be clear objective visions or phenomena outside themselves. Mohammed complains in the Koran of certain heathen Arabs saying to him, "We will not believe thee unless thou make thy paradise appear and show us the torments of hell." These people wanted objective revelations to satisfy them, but the Prophet thought they should take his word; he would do nothing in the way of wonder-working to meet their requests, which he considered altogether unreasonable. Many other religious teachers have, however, differed from him in this respect; some of his followers, who established in Persia the heretical sect of Ismaelites, obtained immense influence over a certain number of credulous people by taking them while they slept into beautiful gardens so that they might behold on awaking objective visions of

paradise. And long before his time the priests in some of the Pagan temples got up mysteries or religious dramas in which were skilfully exhibited the punishment of the wicked in Tartarus and the reward of the righteous in the Elysian Fields. White-robed spectral forms appeared who delivered to the trembling audience very impressive moral discourses, as though they had been messengers from heaven. Thousands of people believed in the supernatural character of these dramatic visions, when they would not have given a moment's credit to what any individual revelator might profess to have heard and seen by himself. The mysteries were undoubtedly the most powerful instrumentality ever devised for the religious instruction of a rude people, but they were greatly abused by some profligate persons, and they fell at length into complete discredit on that account, and from their being employed more and more by unscrupulous priests for the advancement of their own selfish ends rather than for the moral guidance and elevation of the community.

3. In every age when the sacerdotal class have wanted to get influence over credulous people and persuade them more powerfully than mere preaching could do either to reform their lives, to devote themselves to some special undertaking, or perform an act of self-sacrifice for the advancement of a religious cause, they have repeatedly sought to attain their end by getting up objective visions. For there have always been many who would not do this, that, and the other thing against their inclination at the request of any fellow-mortal, yet would instantly obey a voice that was thought to come from the spirit world. And it has not been necessary to have a sacred edifice or any special place for the production of such visions, as in the case of the Pagan mysteries; they have occasionally been

exhibited to good purpose in private houses and in all sorts of obscure localities. In Roman Catholic countries a few simple peasants have occasionally been favoured with a surprise visit of the Virgin Mary, who has given them a message requiring the neighbouring people to erect a sanctuary there, or attend to their religious duties better in future, and the instructions thus delivered as divine have been believed and acted upon with a great deal more promptness than if they had emanated from the Pope. A searching investigation has in some few instances exposed these masked dramas and identified the personators of the Virgin, as was the case at La Salette in 1846, but for all that the popular belief in their supernatural character has been generally maintained. The Rev. Alban Butler, in his "Lives of the Saints," has given an interesting account of the discovery of the relics of St. Stephen through a revelation from the ghost of Gamaliel, that is, from some venerable man clothed in a white garment professing to be Gamaliel. Such revelations were common enough at that period; the early Christians in general were well disposed to use deception for what they considered a good purpose; if they wanted to palm anything off on the credulous multitude they did not hesitate to bring in some eminent authority to vouch for it by personation or forgery. Dramatic apparitions of departed saints and spurious epistles from them testifying in behalf of this and that doctrine or institution were, in their eyes, perfectly justifiable, because, when everything else failed, these stratagems produced conviction.

4. The resort to pious frauds for the purpose of influencing the credulous did not commence especially in the fourth and fifth centuries, as the historian Mosheim would make it appear; they were equally, nay more, practised in the first century, and

at earlier periods. It is well known that the
dominant ideas of primitive Christianity were
derived mainly from two forged revelations of
Maccabean times—the Book of Daniel and the Book
of Enoch. Jesus and those associated with him in
his mission never entertained the least suspicion of
those writings being forgeries, they received them
as unquestionably genuine. Indeed he seems to
have valued them above all other Scriptures, from
their revealing the doctrine of the "kingdom of
heaven," and it is from them that he derives that
favourite designation, the "Son of Man," which he
applies to himself. Would not enthusiasts so
destitute of the critical faculty have been just as
readily imposed upon by any designing people who
might craftily personate the dead ? Had two men
clothed in white garments appeared to Jesus in the
night time representing themselves respectively as
Daniel and Enoch, and bringing him divine
messages, he would have been sure to place the
same implicit credit in the oral revelations thus
delivered as he did in those of the spurious books.
And there are very strong reasons for believing
that he really was influenced by secret messages of
this character : indeed it is hardly conceivable how
he could have been brought in any other way to
act the extraordinary religious part which he did.
Some writers persist in calling him a mystic, but
there is nothing of that character about him ; he
was no more an independent revelator than his
disciples were ; he was clearly instigated and moved
by others who would of course enjoin secrecy upon
him ; his whole line of conduct affords evidence of
his being a credulous zealot schooled by objective
visions. The Jews of that period, who believed
in the coming "kingdom of heaven," seem to have
thought that with certain dramatic preparations
and fulfilments of Scripture many others would be

brought to believe, and that the predicted events would thus be accelerated. It was needful in their estimation that the suffering nation should have a suffering Messiah who must die as a martyr and rise again in appearance, foretokening the general resurrection. And it was not by mere persuasion and argument that a pious Galilean peasant would be led to believe that he was the Messiah specially pointed to in Scripture and was required to undertake a mission which would involve the laying down of his life.

5. One of the most important events which the Evangelists record is what is called the Transfiguration of Jesus—that is, the interview which he is said to have had with "Moses and Elias" on a mountain of Galilee, where three of his most trusted disciples were permitted to accompany him (Matt. xvii. 1-9). Expositors of the school of Strauss have been accustomed to explain this remarkable interview as a purely mythical picture, but, judged by internal evidence and in connection with those closing events of the prophet's career which are allowed to be historical, it is much more likely to be the report of an objective vision especially designed to prepare him for martyrdom. As in the case of several well-known Roman Catholic apparitions, the whole scene is strictly mundane and plainly within the reach of human contrivance, and there are several suspicious circumstances connected with it, such as the seclusion and elevation of the spot, the fewness of the spectators, their previous sleep, and the charge of secrecy imposed upon them, which remind us of the old mystery performances and forcibly suggest dramatic design. It seems to have been the object of those who appeared on the mountain in a spiritual guise not only to influence and instruct Jesus, but to furnish the chief disciples with very

strong and impressive evidence that their master had communion with the greatest of the prophets, and was really the divinely commissioned Messiah. We are told that when Peter, James, and John had ascended the mountain to some distance they were fatigued with the exertion and lay down to rest. While they were sleeping, the "Moses and Elias" of the drama, whom Jesus would have been prepared to meet by arrangement, came forth from their concealment and clothed him in a garment beautifully white. The disciples were then awakened to witness with astonishment their master thus gloriously robed and the risen prophets who accompanied him, while a voice from the height above, which they supposed to be no other than God's voice, said, "This is my beloved son, hear ye him." The three disciples, like those initiated at the Greek mysteries, were naturally enough frightened at what they had seen and heard, and Jesus came at length and spoke with them familiarly, and aroused them from their prostration. When they looked up they found their master standing with them alone, so that they neither witnessed the advent nor the departure of the apparitions, and came down from the mountain as fully confirmed in their faith, and as much enchanted with their foretaste of paradise as the devotees who in an interval of freedom from intoxicating stupor passed through the delightful gardens of Alimoot.

6. At this mountain drama or vision of the Transfiguration, it is worthy of notice that the personators of Moses and Elias spoke to Jesus of his decease, which he should accomplish at Jerusalem (Luke ix. 31) ; and about this period he seems to have first revealed the serious undertaking which he had in prospect to his disciples. We are told, "From that time forth began Jesus to

show unto his disciples, how that he must go unto
Jerusalem, and suffer many things of the elders,
and chief priests, and scribes, and be killed, and be
raised again the third day " (Matt. xvi. 21). " Tell
the vision to no man, till the Son of Man be risen
from the dead " (xvii. 9). " And Jesus, going up to
Jerusalem, took the twelve disciples apart by the
way, and said unto them, Behold, we go up to
Jerusalem; and the Son of Man shall be betrayed
unto the chief priests, and unto the scribes, and
they shall condemn him to death " (xx. 17, 18).
The disciples, or most of them, were not prepared
for this grave information, and seem to have had
great difficulty in believing that their master
would really suffer an ignominious death. But
Jesus told them that they must not only soon see
him suffer, but be ready also to lay down their
own lives in order to obtain life everlasting.
" Whosoever will save his life shall lose it, and
whosoever will lose his life for my sake the same
shall find it " (xvi. 25). Thus the trained
devotees of the Nazarene sect, the simple con-
fiding men, who hoped ere long to sit on twelve
thrones judging the twelve tribes of Israel, were
taught at length that the high places in paradise
were only to be obtained by submitting to persecution and martyrdom. It is not at all probable
that Jesus would of himself have entertained the
idea of rising again after being buried three days;
but the real heads of the sect, Joseph of Arimathea
and others who had secret intercourse with him,
had an obvious reason for predicting this as though
it had been revealed from heaven, that he might
the more readily devote himself to martyrdom, and
his disciples be the more disposed at the appointed
time to believe in the projected miracle of the
Resurrection.

7. The Nazarene confederacy, in arming their

suffering Messiah with evidences, relied in no small degree on what they considered the fulfilment of Scripture texts, and they seem to have taken especial care that he should conform to the sacred writings in the important acts that were just about to close his career. He was instructed to make his public entry into Jerusalem on a young ass, that he might thereby seem to fulfil a passage (Zechariah ix. 9) which is supposed to refer to the humble condition of Zerubbabel when he came from Chaldea to rebuild the city walls. In connection with this fulfilment of Scripture it is interesting to notice the dramatic artifices resorted to for convincing the simple disciples of their master's prophetic foresight. As they approached Jerusalem, Jesus, probably from some information conveyed to him by "Moses and Elias," sent two of his disciples in advance, telling them that at a certain place they would find a colt tied, which, by delivering a given message to the keepers, they would be suffered to bring away (Mark xi. 3). They went forward to a place where two ways met, and found everything precisely as their master had foretold. When they gave the correct answer to the keepers' interrogations, "The Lord hath need of him," they were permitted to remove the animal, and they would be sure to regard this as an unequivocal proof of their master's divine fore-knowledge and power. Again, on the day of unleavened bread, Peter and John (probably the same two disciples that brought Jesus the colt) were sent into the city to engage a room for the Passover feast. They were told that on entering the city a person would meet them bearing a pitcher of water, whom they were directed to follow home and say to the occupant of the house, "The master saith unto thee, Where is the guest chamber where I shall eat the Passover with my disciples?" (Luke xxii. 11). They went accordingly, and found every circumstance as Jesus had foreshown and made ready as he had directed. The room which they prepared belonged probably to Joseph of Arimathea or one of his colleagues; but the simple unsuspecting disciples would imagine that the engagement was brought about by a supernatural power which their master had over the minds of strangers to induce them to minister to his wants.

8. Soon after eating the Passover feast with his disciples Jesus is said to have been arrested and brought to trial, and there can be little doubt that the same secret chiefs of the Nazarene sect, who got up the mountain vision and spoke of the martyrdom which he was soon to suffer, were really instrumental to its accomplishment. They had, under the guise of messengers from heaven, directed their Messianic devotee to go up to Jerusalem, and there die, to rise again according to the Scriptures, and now that he had arrived within the city they laboured craftily and assiduously for the completion of their design. The intemperate harangue which Jesus made against the Temple authorities, commencing, "Woe unto you scribes and Pharisees, hypocrites!" (Matt. xxiii.) was undoubtedly intended to provoke the Jewish rulers to get him arrested and condemned to death, just as many tumultuous Christians of the second century forced from the hands of Pagan priests and magistrates the martyr's crown. His noisy and triumphal entrance into the city, his rude interference with the arrangements of the Temple court and the privileges of the merchants, and lastly his collecting a crowd of people and coarsely denouncing their educated teachers, must naturally have given considerable offence. But there were many sects

at that time and much freedom of speech, and it
is not likely that the chief priests and rulers
would have cared greatly for anything that the
prophet of Nazareth might say so long as he
did not commit any serious breach of the peace.
At the Passover season prophets, devotees, and
fanatics flocked into the city from every quarter
(as, indeed, they do at this day), and they were
allowed great indulgence, if they only abstained
from open rioting and inciting to insurrection.
The Jewish ecclesiastical authorities, acting in
concert with the procurator, were not likely to be
more alarmed or exasperated at the violent
behaviour of Jesus than they were at the temporary
indiscretions of other excited zealots. They might
naturally suppose, from what usually happened
with such characters, that in the course of a few
days his enthusiasm would evaporate, and he would
quietly return to his native province.

9. If the chief priests and scribes had really
been moved with "envy" against Jesus, and had
sought how they might take him by craft and put
him to death " (Mark xiv. 1), as they are falsely
reported to have done, they would beyond all
doubt have tried to assassinate him, and not
have plotted to obtain the punishment of an
innocent man by the tedious and hazardous process
of a public trial, which would have been likely to
expose their malevolence to the reprobation of
all honest people. They could have hired secret
murderers just as readily as they are said to have
procured false witnesses, and the agency of the
former would have been infinitely the safer and
surer means of terminating the prophet's career.
For Jesus was not a resident citizen, but a houseless
wanderer, far away from his native province ; and
as he was often alone, or only accompanied by a
few simple unarmed disciples, must have offered

on such occasions the most accessible mark for an assassin. Now the fact that no stealthy dagger assault on his life .was ever attempted, that he went where he pleased in the neighbourhood of the city unmolested either by day or by night, is a convincing proof that the chief priests and rulers were not, as they have been represented, always plotting and seeking how they might by subtlety seize and destroy him. It is manifest, too, that if they took any hostile part against him at last, they were not conspirators, but more truly the victims of a conspiracy, for they never would have incurred the trouble, risk, and obloquy of delivering one of their countrymen into the hands of the Romans to be publicly crucified, when they might have watched their opportunity and taken him off secretly in his retirement. The real conspirators in this affair were those who got up the masked drama on the mountain of Galilee, and persuaded Jesus to go up to Jerusalem and seek death at the hands of men who had then, probably, never heard of him, could certainly have no enmity against him, and, however strange his conduct might seem when he at length thrust himself under their notice, so long as he behaved as a law-abiding citizen, would not have hurt a hair of his head.

10. Dr Geikie has the following remarks on the constitution of the Jewish Sanhedrin—the court before which Jesus is alleged to have been tried : " The accused was in all cases to be held innocent till proved guilty. It was an axiom that the Sanhedrin was to save, not to destroy life. No one could be tried and condemned in his absence, and when a person accused was brought before the court, it was the duty of the president at the outset to admonish the witnesses to remember the value of human life, and to take care that they forgot nothing that would tell in the prisoner's

Q

favour. Nor was he left undefended; a Baal-Rib,
or counsel, was appointed to see that all possible
was done for his acquittal. Whatever evidence
tended to aid him was to be freely admitted, and
no member of the court who had once spoken in
favour of acquittal could afterwards vote for
condemnation. The votes of the youngest of the
judges were taken first, that they might not be
influenced by their seniors. In capital charges
it required at least two to condemn, and while the
verdict of acquittal could be given at once, that
of guilty could only be pronounced the next day.
Hence capital trials could not begin on the day
preceding a Sabbath or public feast. No criminal
trial could be carried through in the night; the
judges who condemned any one to death had to
fast all the day before, and no one could be executed on the same day on which the sentence
was pronounced. Rules so precise and so humane
condemn the whole trial of Jesus before Caiaphas
as an outrage. It was, in fact, an anticipation of
the prostitution of justice which Josephus records
as common in the later days of Jerusalem. 'Fictitious tribunals and judicatures,' he tells us, 'were
set up, and men called together to act as judges,
though they had no real authority, when it was
desired to secure the death of an opponent.' As
in these later instances so now in the case of Jesus,
they kept up the form and mockery of a tribunal
to the close " ("Life of Christ," p. 680).

11. The mock tribunals which Josephus speaks
of as being instituted during an insurrection in
Jerusalem have been referred to in the preceding
chapter (vii. 15), and it must be borne in mind that
they were not set up by the chief priests and rulers,
but by their revolutionary enemies, who even went
so far as to kill without trial Annas, the brother-
in-law of Caiaphas. So, if Dr. Geikie is right in his

very reasonable surmise that Jesus was tried before a fictitious sanhedrin, it is quite certain that the president would not have been the high-priest, although it might have been some one who simulated the high-priest. Some of the Nazarene confederacy, who wanted to bring about the martyr-dom of Jesus for the advancement of their cause, might possibly have gone to the Jewish rulers and besought them to arrest Jesus as a preacher of sedition and disturber of the public peace, just as French magistrates during the great Revolution were occasionally persuaded to arrest or attempt to arrest a mob leader, in the hope that such a proceeding would turn against them the vengeance of the people. On the assumption that the genuine Sanhedrin did take some kind of judicial action against one who was seeking a condemnation to death, they must have been inveigled into doing so by their designing enemies, but the narrative of the Evangelists points rather to the probability of a counterfeit court being got up in some part of the city to make an exhibition of injustice that would cast on the true rulers opprobrium. As Dr. Geikie points out, this tribunal did not conform to the rules which the Jewish Sanhedrin was bound to observe, and there are indications of a dramatic show and marks of semblance and unreality in the whole of their proceedings. In a genuine trial we see two parties earnestly opposing each other like the contending hosts on a battlefield: one side labours hard to obtain a conviction, and the other spares no effort of reasoning and persuasion to get an acquittal; but in what is presented to us as the trial of Jesus a regular concordance is maintained—it is all accusation, unreasonable accusation, and no defence.

12. The contradictory behaviour of the populace towards Jesus on the day of his public entry into Jerusalem, and immediately afterwards, can only

be explained on the supposition of their being a
hireling mob under the direction of a managing
confederacy.   The people who strewed palms for
Jesus and shouted hosannas received no provocation from him after his entrance into the city ;
the sudden and violent change of sentiment manifested towards him must, therefore, have been a
dramatic display, and could not have proceeded
from any natural impulse.   If such marvellous
instability of temper were not dramatic, we should
be forced to consider it mythical, and some commentators have actually endeavoured to explain it
in this light, although not with the same amount of
reasonableness.   Dr. Philippson, in his journal,
Allgemeine Zeitung des Judenthums, says : " The
same people that a day before received Jesus with
a festive procession and gave him the greatest
homage, of whom the priests, and the Sanhedrin,
and the Pharisees were afraid, so that they would
not lay hands on Jesus, that gave him the power
to act the part of a master in the Temple of God,
and drive from its courts the whole crowd of traders
and vendors, together with all their followers ; the
same people stand on the next day before the judgment seat of the governor and clamour most
terribly for the blood of Jesus, refuse all requests,
repudiate all compassion, prefer the release of a
notable robber, and even desire that the responsibility of the crucifixion may rest on their heads
and on the heads of their children.   And here it
must be remembered that the same people had
prepared that triumph for the popular speaker and
Messiah, and must therefore have known what they
were doing.   However changeable the temperament of a populace may be in general, we have
here a contradiction which proves the statement of
a fact to be untrue."—The populace who are said
to have demonstrated in this strange fashion are

likely to have been a very small number of people, perhaps less than a hundred.

13. The singular part acted by Judas Iscariot in this crucifixion drama is a further proof of its being entirely under the direction of the Nazarene confederacy. If Judas had been a real traitor employed by the chief priests and rulers to compass his master's destruction, he would have been persuaded to poison him or strangle him while he slept, or at least to betray him into the hands of some other secret assassin. The mere act of publicly kissing Jesus and pointing him out in the midst of his disciples when he was well known and did not attempt to conceal himself, would have been a useless service to his religious opponents had they wished to arrest him, and could only have served the purpose of those who were directing all his movements, urging him to martyrdom, and getting up dramatic spectacles to fulfil Scripture and impose on the credulous multitude. The confederacy would naturally desire to test the apostles previous to their master's death, and see if they were also prepared for the yoke of martyrdom, or likely to be induced by any worldly considerations to abandon their cause. Secret agents pretending to be adversaries of Jesus had probably frequent conversations with them for the purpose of proving their real sentiments. If they found any of the number inclined to apostatize they might deem it advisable to anticipate his defection and eject him from his office as a perpetual example of punished faithlessness, which could in no way have been more thoroughly effected than in the casting off and punishment of Judas. That this man was not a very sincere ascetic and devoted follower of Jesus, that his character and disposition were such as to unfit him for discipleship is very probable ; but that he should suddenly become so

wicked and reckless as to plot against his master's life is highly improbable. The story that he went of his own accord to the chief priests and agreed to reveal Jesus to them for thirty pieces of silver is absurd, for even if he had made the proposal it is certain that they would not have accepted on any terms such idle services. But on the supposition that one of the Nazarene party, pretending to be a servant of the chief priest, came and offered the condemned disciple to accompany him on the Passover eve to the place where Jesus was waiting and there salute him with a kiss, the formal act of betrayal is perfectly intelligible. The simple and unfortunate man would readily comply with such an offer, not imagining that any harm would come from it till the dramatic salutation was accomplished, when he would suddenly find himself pointed at by his apostolic brethren, cast off and spurned as a traitor.

14. The behaviour of Jesus when awaiting his arrest in the garden of Gethsemane (which probably belonged to Joseph of Arimathea) was very unlike that of a genuine martyr, hunted by implacable enemies, from whom there was no possibility of making escape. Men in such circumstances have generally conducted themselves like a brave shipwrecked mariner, who, having exhausted every effort to save himself from drowning, becomes perfectly calm and resigned to his fate. But Jesus had a consciousness that his fate depended upon his own will, and was convulsed by the internal struggle of desiring to become a martyr and wishing to avoid death. His agony was something like that which used to be occasionally experienced by a weak, irresolute Hindoo widow, who, having promised the Brahmins that she would sacrifice herself on the body of her dead husband, when the hour of trial came was distracted by conflicting

passions, and led to feel that she had imposed on herself too great a task. The instructors of Jesus might naturally be apprehensive that his martyr courage would fail him at the last moment, unless he should be assured by some means that spiritual messengers were near. The "angel" who, as Luke informs us, came to strengthen him in the garden, was probably a real person related to the white-robed visitors who conferred with him on a mountain in Galilee. When the party who arrested him at night moved from the garden towards the house of Caiaphas, and the disciples dispersed or timidly loitered at some distance in the rear, Mark tells us that "there followed him a certain young man having a linen cloth cast about his naked body, and the young men laid hold of him, and he left the linen cloth and fled from them naked" (xiv. 51–52). Some orthodox commentators have conjectured that this young man spoken of was Mark himself. But it is very improbable that Mark, if he had been present, would have been clothed in this manner, or would have been separated from the other disciples. It is more reasonable to suppose that the mysterious young man in a linen cloth who followed the procession from Gethsemane was the same as Luke's "angel," or a companion messenger. The eagerness which he manifested to get away from his pursuers at all costs affords ground for suspicion that he was really engaged in a serious religious ghost plot, and was fearful of being caught and identified.

15. When brought to the judgment-hall before Pilate, Jesus had recovered his firmness, and, like a true seeker of martyrdom, made no attempt to defend himself against his accusers and save his life. Pilate said, "Hearest thou not how many things they witness against thee? And he answered him to never a word; insomuch that the

governor marvelled greatly" (Matt. xxvii. 13 14). Neither did any of his friends nor followers come forward to speak in his behalf, which abundantly shows who were the parties really interested and active in bringing about his crucifixion. The procurator was anxious to give him a fair trial, extremely reluctant to condemn him, suggesting all he could think of to afford him a legitimate path of escape, so that if any of his friends had come forward to testify of his innocence and of the good which he had wrought among them, as they should have done, they might have easily obtained for him an honourable acquittal. But that nothing of this kind was attempted, that no expression of sympathy was manifested, that not a single voice was raised in his defence could only have been because Jesus, at the instance of his secret white-robed instructors, had strictly forbidden his followers to plead in his behalf, or give themselves any concern for his safety. Joseph of Arimathea is said to have been one of the Jewish rulers, but he is more likely to have been a member of some fictitious sanhedrin. It was reported that he dissented from the verdict of the other rulers who delivered Jesus over to Pilate (Luke xxiii. 51), and Joseph would have been likely enough to represent that he had opposed their wicked designs ; there can be little doubt, however, that this man who refused to appear before the governor and plead for the life of Jesus, but "went in boldly" and begged for his dead body (Mark xv. 43), was one of the most active, if not the chief, of the mystic confederacy who contrived and brought about his crucifixion.

16. It is commonly believed among Christians that Jesus was tried and condemned by the Jewish Sanhedrin previously to being taken before Pilate, and this opinion is maintained by Mr. Taylor Innes in his two articles on "The Trial of Jesus

Christ," which appeared some years ago in the *Contemporary Review.* If there really was a Jewish trial, it must have been, as Dr. Geikie has suggested, nothing better than a mock trial before a fictitious sanhedrin. Dr. Benisch, as well as this Christian scholar, points to the irregularities attending it, and is convinced that they would never have been permitted by the genuine Temple authorities. He says, "To conclude that there was a Jewish trial, we have to assume that the Sanhedrin which condemned Jesus undertook an utterly useless, and even senseless task, since a Jewish court at the time had no longer the power to carry out its sentence; that this court was presided over by Caiaphas, the high-priest, consequently of the seed of Aaron, when we know from history that the presidency of the court was hereditary in the family of Hillel, certainly not descended from priests, and are acquainted with the name of every one of these functionaries until the court was closed by the Romans. . . . . And what was the crime of which he was accused, and for which he was sentenced to death? Was he condemned because he called himself the Son of God? Every Judean addressed God as his Father in heaven. All Israel are called in the Bible God's children; God distinctly called David 'My son.' How, therefore, could a Judean be condemned for an utterance which might have been, and no doubt was, in the mouths of thousands of his countrymen? Surely no one will maintain that when Jesus called himself the Son of God, and his disciples assented to that designation, they understood it in a sense subsequently given to it by the Council of Nice or in the Apostles' creed? Of such a sonship the disciples could have had no idea. Now if there was no crime, how could a sentence have been passed?" ("Judaism and Christianity," pp. 31-33).

17. I quite agree with Dr. Benisch up to this point, that there was no actual trial of Jesus before the Jewish Sanhedrin, which held its sittings in the Temple, and not at the house of Caiaphas. It is very certain that the absurd charges which are said to have been brought against him, such as his calling himself the Son of God, and saying that he would destroy the Temple and rebuild it in three days, would not have been made by the real Jewish authorities. Men experienced as they were in the administration of justice would have either found a reasonable accusation to advance against him or would have said nothing. Is it to be supposed that they could have found no true witnesses to accuse him amongst the merchants on whom he had recently committed an assault, or that they would have entirely forgotten to mention that clear breach of the peace, while they paid false witnesses to say what was irrelevant, and altogether ridiculous ? The false testimony which the chief priests and rulers are said to have bought for the purpose of this prosecution would have been of just about as much value to them as the kiss of Judas. It what the Evangelists describe to us is not purely mythical, it can only be reasonably explained as a mock trial, a mere dramatic performance got up by a confederacy to impose on credulous people. Dr. Benisch does not seem to entertain any suspicion of Jesus being taken before a fictitious tribunal, and endorses the theory propounded by Philippson, in 1865, that he was really prosecuted and punished not by Jews, but by the Romans as a political offender. While holding both these distinguished scholars in very high estimation and giving careful consideration to their opinion, I am unable to accept it as correct for the following reasons.

18. Jesus, although claiming to be the Jewish Messiah, differed entirely from the warrior chiefs,

such as Judas of Galilee and Barcochebas, who made themselves obnoxious to the Roman authorities. He was · not only non-military, but he preached non-resistance and looked for the redemption of Israel wholly by supernatural means, so that he could not be considered dangerous in a political sense nor expected to raise a standard of revolt. The Romans, who had so many robbers and insurrectionists to contend with, would be likely to regard with the greatest tolerance a harmless zealot of this kind, and to believe that his parading about with a few unarmed peasant followers as king of the Jews would be a very likely means of bringing the aspirations of the national party into contempt. Then it is well known that Jesus had no quarrel with the Romans on the score of their unbelief, he did not seek to effect their conversion ; he regarded them as aliens, but not as enemies, and · passed them by · without feeling any more concern for them than he would have done for the horses of Cæsar. Dr. Philippson believes that it was a leading object of the New Testament writers " to clear the Romans from the guilt of the death of Jesus and charge it altogether on the Jews." I am quite unable to see any such disposition in those chroniclers ; they undoubtedly did their utmost to blacken the Jewish authorities, but they were equally ready to calumniate the Roman governors of the country. The Herods—not even excepting the amiable Herod Agrippa—are represented as persecuting monsters, ever seeking occasion to shed the blood of the saints. Pilate, we are told, " took Jesus and scourged him," even while admitting him to be an innocent man. The Christian creed says expressly that Jesus " suffered under Pontius Pilate," and from the first century to the nineteenth this Roman governor has been held up to the execration of all Christendom. The Nazarene

saints were revolutionists opposed to all government beyond their own circle, and delighting to
calumniate every ruler and magistrate whose
shadow came across their path, and it must be
admitted that they bestowed their abuse with the
strictest impartiality.

19. Dr. Philippson contends that the Evangelists—whom he supposes to have written in the
second century—had this capital reason for
exculpating the Romans and inculpating the Jews.
" Christianity found no favour at all among the
Jewish people; hence the proper scene of conversion had to be removed into heathen nations.
But then it was of vital importance to controvert
the belief that Jesus had been executed by the
Roman authorities," &c. This political reason
which the Evangelists are supposed to have had
for colouring their narrative seems to me wholly
imaginary. In the first place it is incorrect to say
that Christianity found no favour at all among the
Jewish people, when it originated among them, was
in complete harmony with the Essene teaching,
and notoriously found favour with the poor and
ignorant. Jesus and his apostles and their true
successors, the Ebionites, were thoroughly Jewish,
so was Paul, though widely differing from them,
and indeed every one of the writers of the New
Testament. Then it is a completely mistaken
view of the character and aims of primitive
Christianity to suppose that in whatever quarter it
hoped to obtain proselytes it must needs endeavour
to conciliate and flatter the authorities, for the
very reverse of this policy was actually pursued.
The revolutionary sect was not conciliatory,
but combative, and always contrived to stir up a
persecuting enemy in its field of proselytism.
During the lifetime of Jesus, and so long as it
only sought to lay hold of Jewish converts, it had

no quarrel except with the established teachers of
Judaism, and then in the second century, when
Jerusalem had fallen and the Sanhedrin had ceased
to exist, it found a new enemy to challenge in the
rulers of Paganism.   The overthrow of the Seven-
hilled city—the great Babylon, as they called it—
was ardently desired and predicted by the Christian
writers of that period, and the Satanic powers
constantly held up to execration were the Pagan
Beast, the Antichrist, and the Man of Sin
(2 Thess. ii. 3; 1 John ii. 18; Rev. xiii. 2; xvii. 8).
"O haughty Rome!" says one of the Christian
Sibyls, "the just chastisement of Heaven shall
come down upon thee from on high; thou shalt
stoop thy neck and be levelled with the earth, and
fire shall consume thee to thy very foundations,
and thy wealth shall perish; wolves and foxes shall
dwell among thy ruins, and thou shalt be desolate
as if thou hadst never been."   It is therefore to
the last degree improbable that just when the
struggle with the organized priesthood at Jerusalem
had ceased, and a new and terrible conflict had
commenced with the Pagan magistracy and priesthood, the Christians who then wrote would be
disposed to take a burden of infamy from off
Pontius Pilate and cast it on the shoulders of
Caiaphas.

20. The way in which the Crucifixion was
carried out, no less than the whole course of
preparation for it, clearly shows that it is what
neither the Roman nor the Jewish authorities
would have designed for the punishment of one
who had become obnoxious to them.   If real
political adversaries or religious opponents had the
plotting of his death, it would have taken place
as quietly and privately as possible, and without
any of the laboured dramatic display which
actually accompanied it.   They would never have

entertained the notion of crucifying him between two thieves, of giving him vinegar to drink as he hung on the cross, of piercing his side with a spear, of parting his garments and casting lots for his vesture, so as to establish a mystic agreement with certain texts of Scripture. And they would have been wholly unable to disarm the opposition of his disciples and friends, or prevent a demonstration being made in his favour by the shouting crowd who had recently welcomed him into the city. But all this, which would have been the greatest infatuation and childishness on the part of the chief priests and rulers, or would otherwise have exceeded their power, was on the part of the Nazarene confederacy a well-devised scheme and one which they were well able to carry out. It was to them simply the getting up of a masked drama to impose on the world; they stood behind the scenes and commanded the whole of the movements; they had only to engage a number of people to act certain parts, to do this, that, and the other thing, for a small payment as they directed, and the religious mystery was performed with entire success. Those who crucified Jesus, mocked, and insulted him, no more acted from natural impulse than do their modern imitators in the Bavarian Passion-Play; they did as they were told, just to fulfil Scripture and produce a strong impression on the minds of spectators; the whole story is dramatic, coloured to some little extent with mythical embellishment. Nothing else so powerfully moves mankind as a harrowing representation of murdered innocence, and there is little need of its being well founded and truthful; the bodies of Christian children that were occasionally nailed up during the middle ages served just as effectively to work on the feelings of credulous people as the dramatic crucifixion which took place long before on Mount Calvary.

21. Imaginary wrongs are often made a great deal more of than real ones. Just as sentimental people are sometimes affected to tears by an ordinary theatrical performance having no foundation in fact, so still more strongly are devout Christians moved by contemplating the tragic scene of the Crucifixion as exhibited in the Gospels, and converted by St. Paul's mystic teaching into a divine sacrifice. A succession of religious painters and poets have for many centuries expended all their powers in embellishing and idealizing the wondrous death of the Messiah on Mount Calvary. And any realistic interpretation which detracts in the slightest degree from the dignity and solemnity of the transaction, as they have been accustomed to regard it, will, as a matter of course, be intensely repugnant to Christian feelings—not only unbelievable, but almost unendurable. There is no other martyr festival but that of the Mohurrum that can distantly compare with the Good Friday commemoration, which imparts a dolorous mood to so many millions of worshippers throughout Christendom. Both these festivals, and especially the latter, have been fruitful in calling forth unreasonable vengeance and the shedding of much innocent blood. If the devout people who keep the Crucifixion day with a great show of mourning and sorrow could only be got to shed a few tears for the thousands of poor Jews who have been murdered at this time of the year in consequence of an imaginary crime of their ancestors, Christian grief would be expended to much better purpose. And those who wear crosses and believe that sacrificial magic will cleanse them from all sinfulness, would serve God far more worthily by looking steadfastly to the straight path of duty which lies before them, and resolutely reforming their lives.

CHAPTER IX.

THE RESURRECTION DRAMA.

The measures taken ostensibly to prevent a false resurrection must have been a mere blind devised not by the chief priests but by the Nazarenes. 5. The soldiers more likely to report a fictitious miracle than deny a real one. 6. The Sanhedrin would have been not only wicked, but mad to reward the utterance of useless falsehoods. 7. Those who buried the body evidently bore it away. 8. On what grounds the personator of Jesus obtained credit. 10. His mannerisms and crucifixion wounds. 15. His appearing by appointment. 14. The disciples' doubts, and difficulties of recognition. 15. The rising of Lazarus contrasted with that of Jesus. 16. Evidence of the great Christian miracle less complete than that of Mormonism. 19. The Ascension. 20. Conversion of Paul by an objective vision. 21. The success which Christianity derived from its obscure origin.

WHEN Joseph and Nicodemus, two of the confederacy called "rulers," who had secret communion with Jesus, had taken his body and put it into a new vault or cavern prepared for the purpose (John xix. 38–39), we are told that "the chief priests and Pharisees came together unto Pilate, saying, Sir, we remember that that deceiver said, while he was yet alive, After three days I will rise again. Command therefore that the sepulchre be made sure until the third day, lest his disciples come by night, and steal him away, and say unto the people, He is risen from the dead: so the last error shall be worse than the first. Pilate said unto them, Ye have a watch: go your way, make it as sure as ye can. So they went, and made the sepulchre sure, sealing the stone, and setting a watch" (Matt. xxvii. 62–66). It is highly improbable that the chief priests and rulers ever resorted to such a foolish and clumsy contrivance as this for the purpose of strangling the supernatural evidences of Christianity at its birth. If they, or any rational and intelligent men, had known of Jesus having promised his disciples that he would rise again after three days, and had seriously resolved to prevent them from effecting a pretended resurrection, they would have petitioned Pilate not to suffer the body to be buried at all during that time, or would have had it divided as the relics of saints have been treated, and placed here and there in safe custody. But the common belief that they were expecting a surreptitious removal of the body to be attempted, that they were anxious to do all in their power to prevent its abstraction, and that they yet permitted the partisans of Jesus to conceal it in their private vault, which might possibly have more than one entrance, is manifestly absurd; still more so is the supposition that they were so infatuated as to entrust the watching of this Nazarene tomb to a party of Pagan soldiers, who could only be expected to discharge such a duty from mercenary motives.

2. If the Jewish rulers and their friends had been actively engaged in contriving and bringing about the death of Jesus, and had now at length got him in their hands as a fallen enemy, it is evident that they would no more have delivered him up into the hands of his disciples after the crucifixion than before that event, while they had him under arrest. For as he was not considered permanently dead, as it was believed by many that in three days he would rise again and effect his escape from the tomb, or, as others supposed, that his body would be stolen, and that a pretended Jesus would go forth and deceive the people, he must have been under these circumstances regarded and

R

treated as a prisoner, and it would have been utter madness to deliver such a prisoner into the custody of his own partisans.   Fancy Charles I. falling into the hands of Cromwell's forces during the Civil War, and being delivered by them into the custody of Prince Rupert; and the English Parliament sending a company of foreign mercenaries to the residence of that distinguished royalist, charging them to lock the doors carefully and prevent the king's escape, and we should have something like a parallel case to that of the Jewish Sanhedrin delivering the body of Jesus into the safe keeping of Joseph of Arimathea, and sending a hireling Roman guard to seal the entrance of that Nazarene leader's private tomb, so as to prevent the removal of the crucified Messiah.

3. On the other hand, if the religious confederacy to which Joseph belonged had the placing of the Roman watch at the sepulchre, we can readily perceive their motives for it, and it was a prudent and well-arranged measure.   In the raising of Lazarus and other important miracles which they had enabled Jesus to perform, they chose their own convenient time and suitable spectators; but now, if the report had begun to spread that Jesus after three days was to rise again—if the time and place of the miracle were fixed, and there was, in consequence, a probability of some of their religious opponents being present at the sepulchre, how, in the face of such hostile supervision, could the intended resurrection be accomplished ?   It might naturally seem advisable to them under these circumstances to place a guard at the sepulchre to keep away all impertinent and hostile intruders.   And who could be more fitted for such a task than their late hired assistants, the Roman soldiers, who had so well acted their part of fulfilling prophecy at the crucifixion ?   Moreover,

by getting a military guard placed at the tomb for the ostensible purpose of preventing the expected fraudulent resurrection, it might tend to lull suspicion, to quiet and satisfy those who were really apprehensive of a secret abstraction of the body, and who might otherwise have deemed it necessary to be present and watch for themselves. That the confederacy were apprehensive of an unwelcome intrusion on this occasion is manifest by the premature haste with which they effected the pretended resurrection. The body ought to have remained in the tomb till Monday evening, but it was borne away early on Sunday morning, "when it was yet dark," so that instead of rising "after three days," Jesus was actually made to rise before the second day was completed.

4. It is commonly assumed by Christian writers that the band of soldiers stationed at the sepulchre were acting in behalf of the Roman government, so that they dare not abandon or betray their charge, must necessarily have been hostile to the partisans of Jesus, and would have presented an invincible obstacle to their bearing away his body. They have, however, a totally mistaken view of the soldiers' position. If those men had been unfaithful in their duty to Cæsar they would most assuredly have been punished by the procurator; but Pilate cared no more than Gallio for the religious quarrels of the Jews, and if either the chief priests and rulers, or a sectarian confederacy at enmity with them chose to engage at their own expense a number of his men to frustrate the designs of their opponents, he would have been wholly indifferent to their fidelity and vigilance in such a cause, and the soldiers' only care would have been to get as much pay as they could from either party of contending Jews who might happen to solicit their services. It is evident, then, that the

Roman watch placed at the sepulchre, instead of preventing, must rather have facilitated the fraudulent abstraction of the body. For if, as we believe, they were in the hire of the religious party to whom the sepulchre belonged, they would have been ready enough to quit their post whenever their employers might require them to do so. On the other hand, had they been engaged by the chief priests and rulers, they might easily have been bribed by the proprietors of the tomb to go away "when it was yet dark." And even supposing the soldiers had been in any danger of punishment for not performing their duty on this occasion, they would have incurred less risk by telling a lie for the confederacy, reporting a miraculous resurrection which no power could prevent, than by falsely declaring for the Jewish council that they had slept at their post and suffered the body to be stolen. For although the chief priests and their friends would not have believed the reported miracle, they might have thought it probable enough that the soldiers had been frightened from their post by the sudden approach of white-robed men, whom they mistook for angels. Whereas the absurd story of their sleeping on duty, and thus permitting the tomb to be broken open and emptied by the disciples, would at once have convicted them of unpardonable negligence or perfidy.

5. It is further infinitely more probable that the soldiers and other people then living in Jerusalem would report a fictitious miracle than deny a real one. They might easily fancy and say that they had seen angels or spirits approach and open the sepulchre, as miracles of this sort have been imagined and reported times without number. But what if angels had descended in reality; what if the heavens had opened and the earth had quaked

and given up her dead, as poets have described the last judgment—would those who had witnessed the awful spectacle easily forget it, or be in any humour to go forth and declare to the neighbours that nothing of the kind had taken place? No; such utter callousness and indifference to miraculous manifestations of this astounding character would not be in human nature. The soldiers, who are said to have been so appalled at the tremendous scene which they witnessed that they " became as dead men, " when somewhat recovered from the shock and able to walk and speak, must have been in a very serious frame of mind. Having this actual commencement of the end of the world and the coming kingdom of heaven made visible to them, they ought to have been the fittest and foremost Christians to part with their temporal possessions and travel up and down in all countries preaching and bearing witness of the resurrection. So far, however, from their setting out on such a mission, we are informed that they had the hardihood to go straightway into the city and deny what they had seen, and, for a few pieces of paltry coin, renounce their prospect of wearing everlasting crowns. It is by no means rare for men to lie both consciously and unconsciously in agreement with their passions and their apparent interest, but it is very unusual and unnatural for them to start a falsehood in the opposite direction. In our own times it now and then happens that a ghost story is created either by some credulous person who is dominated by superstitious fears, or by a more crafty individual who wishes for some purpose to get it believed that a certain place is haunted. But there is no well-known instance in this or any other country of people having seen what they took for a real ghost and been nearly frightened to death by it, and yet denying their terrible experience before the world.

6. Not only would it have been morally impossible for the Roman soldiers to see Jesus raised from the dead by an angel descending from heaven, and then go and report that his body was stolen by the disciples, but we may be sure that the Jewish Sanhedrin would not have suggested and paid them to utter such a monstrous falsehood. Some of the members of that assembly might justify the practice of deception occasionally in the service of religion, as was common with all sacerdotalists at that period, others might not exhibit the strictest probity in their private life, but when they were all solemnly acting together in their official capacity, they would be sure to respect the ninth commandment, and would never so far renounce their moral dignity as to bribe a number of heathen wretches to lie for them in the face of Heaven. "It is a difficulty," says Strauss, "acknowledged even by orthodox expositors, that the Sanhedrin, in a regular assembly and after a formal consultation, should have resolved to corrupt the soldiers and put a lie into their mouths. That in this manner a college of seventy men should have officially decided on suggesting and rewarding the utterance of a falsehood is too widely at variance with the decorum, the sense of propriety inseparable from such an assembly." Moreover, the council must have known that the lie which they are said to have purchased would not, after all, avail them for concealing the truth and obstructing the cause of their opponents. For if they deemed the report of the resurrection false, they would know it to be far better to examine the men publicly and expose their lie than to pay them to contradict it by a second lie which no rational person would be found to believe. On the other hand, had they been

convinced of the truth of the miracle, they would have been further convinced that they could not by any contemptible falsehood which they might start against it prevent it from becoming manifested to the world. They would have known that if Jesus had really broken forth from the bonds of death and the sepulchre, and was become as a king escaped from prison, he would soon, by his personal presence among the people, give any report which might be circulated of the stealing of his body a triumphant refutation. The lie, then, which the Evangelists tell us was set going by the Sanhedrin and the soldiers to arrest the Christian faith must be considered a preternatural lie, and the Resurrection itself was scarcely more miraculous.

7. There is little room to doubt that the same confederate party who had stealthy communion with Jesus, and who deposited his body in a receptacle which they had prepared for the purpose in their garden, also secretly bore it away. But they would not think of carrying off and concealing the dead prophet of Nazareth without providing a living representative to go forth in his place and fulfil the prediction of his rising. In order to complete their resurrection drama it would be necessary for one of the confederacy to personate the revived Jesus before some of the leading disciples, as they had on a former occasion personated Moses and Elias in Galilee. Accordingly we find in the Gospel narrative an account of a mysterious visitor presenting himself to a few privileged beholders in that character. It is generally supposed that this person, who obtruded himself on the notice of the disciples occasionally, soon after the evacuation of the sepulchre, was believed by them to be Jesus, on the ground of his perfect identity in form and feature with their late master. This assumption is, however, quite

incorrect, as the narrative plainly shows that they did not believe him to be Jesus in consequence of any striking natural resemblance, but for other and chiefly the following reasons.

8. The resurrection and reappearance of dead persons was not antecedently so incredible to the immediate followers of Jesus as it would be to modern Christians. If any one were now told that his deceased friend had risen from the grave he would at once deem it impossible, because such a thing is contrary to all present experience, or at least is never reported and looked for in modern times. In the age of the apostles, however, there were frequent rumours of the rising of interred bodies as the commencement of an expected general rising, and fleshly apparitions were as readily believed by superstitious people as disembodied spectres are among the ignorant population of our own country. The disciples of Jesus had seen the pretended Moses and Elias, Lazarus of Bethany, the daughter of Jairus, and several others, who either professed to have been raised themselves from the dead, or to have witnessed other resurrections. It was believed by some, as the Evangelists report, that the martyred John the Baptist had risen out of his grave and reappeared in the person of Jesus. At the very time of the supposed reappearance of Jesus we are told that " the graves were opened ; and many bodies of the saints which slept arose, and came out of the graves after his resurrection, and went into the holy city, and appeared unto many " (Matt. xxvii. 52–53). This story may be nothing more than a mythical embellishment, but it would not have been written in that age nor believed, if such a thing as the rising of the dead had been considered a very rare occurrence demanding very clear and positive evidence for

its credibility. The disciples were also fully expecting their master's reappearance; for Jesus, acting under the direction of the confederacy, had told them repeatedly that three days after his death he would rise again and revisit them (Matt. xvi. 21; Mark viii. 30; Luke ix. 22, &c.). Bearing these promises in mind, they were looking forward to the appointed day and fancying him back again with such confidence as an affectionate family await the period of a father or brother's return from prison; and it is when people are in this state of feverish expectancy with regard to the appearance of a beloved form that they are especially liable to be deceived.

9. There remained for the confederacy one more artifice to prepare the disciples' minds for a ready belief in any pretender who might present himself to them, and that was to station some of their party at the sepulchre when the body was abstracted, to start the report that Jesus had actually risen from the dead, and was gone into Galilee to the place where he had appointed to meet them. In Luke and John we are told of two angels, or men clothed in white garments to have that appearance, being posted at the sepulchre on the morning of the resurrection to give the necessary information to inquiring disciples. In Mark it is said that when two female disciples came early to the sepulchre "they saw that the stone was rolled away, for it was very great. And entering into the sepulchre, they saw a young man sitting on the right side, clothed in a long white garment; and they were affrighted. And he said unto them, Be not affrighted: ye seek Jesus of Nazareth, which was crucified: he is risen: he is not here: behold the place where they laid him. But go your way, tell his disciples and Peter that he goeth before you into Galilee: there shall ye see him, as he said unto you" (xvi. 4–7).

In Matthew's account the rolling away of the stone is magnified into a "great earthquake," and the white-robed young man becomes an "angel of the Lord," but the message delivered is nearly the same. From the circumstance of the two women coming to anoint Jesus with spices it has been inferred that they could have had no expectation of his rising again, but the mark of respect that they were anxious to show the Master's body in the sepulchre no more implies a disbelief in his resurrection than the anointing at Bethany. From the others disbelieving the report of the women, it has been argued that they were naturally incredulous, and had no thought of seeing Jesus return to life. They certainly expected him to reappear according to his promise, but naturally disbelieved the report of the women, partly because it was somewhat unseasonable. He was to have lain in the sepulchre three days, and it was now only a day and a half since his burial. The women themselves were perhaps not considered reliable witnesses. Mary Magdalene appears to have been at one time accounted a demoniac (Luke xvi. 9), and the disciples might think that what this poor woman reported originated in her own feverish and disordered mind, and was unworthy of consideration. It would seem, too, very unlikely that she should have the high honour of a first interview with their risen Lord; and as the twelve disciples were jealous of their rank, other chance interviews were discredited by those not present (John xx. 25). During the last supper Jesus had told the disciples that after he was risen he would meet them at a certain mountain in Galilee. Those who were to rule over the twelve tribes of Israel expected their risen Lord to meet there in a stately and formal manner, and did not suppose that he would be witnessed by any one until the whole party were regularly assembled according to his appointment.

10. We have thus seen that the disciples were fully prepared and confidently looking for their revived Master before any one in that character made his appearance. They probably did not at first expect to meet him until they had arrived at the mountain in Galilee; but when they found that the sepulchre was empty, heard that he was risen, and that he had been seen alive in the neighbourhood, their minds would not fail to become excited, and their eyes would have been ready to anticipate his appearance in the form of every stranger who approached them. When, therefore, a personator of Jesus did actually present himself, a few weak circumstantial evidences that he was armed with sufficed to convince them of his identity. On one occasion he fell in with two disciples casually as they journeyed to Emmaus, and exhibited considerable skill and address in drawing from them a recognition. He did not rush before them and exhibit at once all his " infallible proofs," and so risk the chance of a complete failure, but began by sounding them and preparing their minds for belief, and then proceeded cautiously to display his signs of identity one after another till they should be persuaded that they were in the presence of their risen Lord. Even if they had not after all been induced to recognize him in this way, the game would only have been suspended, and he might have quietly withdrawn to renew his pretensions and seek better fortune elsewhere. The two disciples going to Emmaus seem to have been convinced at length that their travelling companion was no other than Jesus, by his peculiar manner of breaking and blessing bread. At the last supper. Jesus had probably told the twelve that as soon as he should rise and reappear he would again

break bread with them, and the personator, by
performing this ceremony in his manner, evidently
meant that it should serve as a sort of masonic
sign to accredit him as the risen Christ. If they
had had no expectation of the reappearance of
Jesus the stranger's manner of blessing bread and
expounding Scripture would have merely served
to remind them of him, but as they believed that
he would rise again after the third day and had
just heard a report that he was risen, they only
required to see a few such points of formal
resemblance to imagine that he stood in their
presence.

11. As soon as the supposed Jesus was recognized by the two brethren who went to Emmaus,
we are told that he "vanished out of their sight."
From this vague statement in reference to his
abrupt departure, it is commonly believed that
he suddenly became invisible and disappeared in
the manner of a ghost or wizard. But the probability is that he did not want them to acquire too
much familiarity with him, as they might have done
under a prolonged interview, and contrived to
engage them in prayer or divert their attention in
some other way, and then quickly withdrew
unobserved so as to leave them in a cloud of profound wonder and amazement. Again, in the
evening of that day, when other disciples were
met together with closed doors conversing on their
Lord's reappearance, we are told that he suddenly
" stood in the midst of them " (Luke xxiv. 36;
John xx. 19), and they were "terrified and affrighted,
and supposed that they had seen a spirit." They
were probably assembled on this occasion at the
same house of the confederacy where they had
eaten the Passover feast, and where they afterwards, on the day of Pentecost, witnessed the
miracle of the fiery tongues. The personator of

Jesus with some of his colleagues might be concealed in another room, so as to overhear their conversation and learn the current of their thoughts, and then, at a favourable moment while they were praying, he would only have to rush in among them by a sudden *coup de théâtre* and exhibit his pierced hands and feet, and the amazed disciples would have been fully convinced of his identity.

12. But the very fact of his exhibiting crucifixion wounds as a proof of his being the genuine Jesus, and giving prominence to this proof, and relying on it as above all others complete, must seem to every intelligent and impartial judgment the most damning evidence of his imposture. For if the crucified Jesus had actually risen from the dead, his wounds, which were the cause of his death, must certainly have been healed, so that he would have come forth from the tomb perfectly whole. This would have been just as necessary in his case as if he had been decapitated or drawn and quartered; a man could no more live with a deep spear wound in his pericardium than with his throat cut. What would be thought of John the Baptist rising from the dead without the reunion of his divided vertebræ, and going about exhibiting to his astonished disciples the broad gaping passage of the headsman's axe as the crowning proof of his identity? There was an important difference between the wounds of the genuine Jesus and those of the pretender; the former were deep and serious enough to cause death, while the latter were only *stigmata*, such as several saints imprinted on themselves, and such as the monk Jetzer at Berne received from the Dominican confederacy. A true man would never exhibit wounds or any other artificial marks that can be easily imitated as the main proof of his identity. Marks of genuineness

to be worth anything should be natural and entirely beyond the reach of human simulation, and the disciples, from not having this consideration before them, were as blind as the old patriarch who mistook Jacob's kidskin sleeve for the hairy arm of his son Esau. When a person now and then comes forward professing to be the lost heir of an estate, any scars or tattooings which he may exhibit for the purpose of identification are invariably regarded by shrewd magistrates with the greatest distrust. Yet it is precisely on evidence of this kind exhibited nearly two thousand years ago that we are now expected to believe in the supernatural origin of Christianity.

13. The mountain in Galilee where the personator of Jesus met the disciples (Matt. xxviii. 16) was probably the same mountain where three of them, with Jesus himself, had not long before seen objective visions of " Moses and Elias " (xvii. 1–9). It does not seem that he exhibited crucifixion wounds, or came in actual contact with them on this occasion, but the evidence relied on was his appearing exactly at the place where Jesus had promised that he would appear. When the disciples, full of faith, undertook their journey into Galilee, as they approached the mountain where the Master had appointed to meet them, their expectation would have been wrought up to the highest pitch ; they would have been all on tip-toe to catch a first glimpse of their risen Lord, and no sooner had a human form become visible on the mountain than all would have been ready to exclaim, "There he is ! " If the personator had been habited in a white garment the evidence of his being what he professed to be would have seemed to most of them conclusive, and they were probably cautioned, like Mary Magdelene, to keep at a little distance, or might be prevented by superstitious fear from

approaching near enough to have a good observation of his features.

14. Notwithstanding all the artifices resorted to by the personator of Jesus to force a recognition from the disciples, and exceedingly credulous as they must have been, they could not help entertaining some feeling of distrust in reference to his identity. Their slowness to believe that they were actually in the presence of their late Master forms a difficulty which is admitted by most orthodox commentators. It is remarkable that on his first appearance they all failed to observe in him any striking likeness of Jesus, and but for the mannerisms which he thrust upon their notice would have passed him by as an ordinary stranger. When he first appeared to Mary Magdalene, she, we are told, supposed him to be the gardener, and addressed him as such (John xx. 15). When he fell in with the two disciples on their journey to Emmaus and entered into familiar conversation with them they failed to notice anything either in his features or the tone of his voice to remind them of their Master, which is only to be accounted for by the statement of Mark, that he appeared unto them "in another form" (xvi. 12). Even when he met the party of disciples according to appointment at the mountain in Galilee, and they were in every way prepared for his recognition, we are told that "some doubted" (Matt. xxviii. 17). If the disciples had been but little acquainted with Jesus or had not seen and associated with him for a considerable time before his death, they might have had an imperfect remembrance of his features, which might also have altered by sickness and prolonged suffering. But this was by no means the case; for as the orthodox Dr. Wardlaw says, "They had long intimate familiar acquaintance with their Master previous to his death, and up to the time of

his death. They had associated with him constantly
for three years. They knew him in every feature
of his countenance and every member of his frame ;
in every attitude, every gesture, every look, every
tone of voice, in every particular by which it is
conceivable that personal identity can be ascer-
tained; and having thus known him, there was no
interval of subsequent separation to weaken the im-
pressions or obscure their reminiscences of him.
Suppose our most intimate friend to die, to die
not by a lingering and wasting process of dissolution, but by a sudden death in his full strength,
without tedious emaciation or aught that could
induce any alteration of his ordinary appearance ;
suppose him to continue dead from Friday afternoon
till Sunday morning, and then to appear to us, not in
vision, but really and corporally his bonâ fide self,
is it possible, think you, that in so short a time we
could so have forgotten him as to be even in the
slightest degree at a loss to recognize him and to
be sure of his identity ? " (" On Miracles,"
ch. iv., sec. iv).

15. Certainly not. We would undertake to say
that there is not a Sadducee in the country but
would in such a case recognize his resuscitated
friend the moment he saw him, and the disciples
would have been equally ready to recognize their
late Master, if he had only appeared to them in
reality. It would not have been necessary for him
in such case to exhibit wounds, or have recourse to
any other artifice to draw from them a recognition.
It must be borne in mind, too, that they had none
of our antecedent unbelief to restrain them,
because they had seen other reputed risen men,
and a resurrection was not deemed in those days
an impossible, or very extraordinary occurrence.
When Lazarus, who pretended to be dead and
buried, came forth out of the cave artfully wrapped

about in burial clothes, the people who had known him, and who had been invited to witness his apparently miraculous rising, as well as those who came to see him afterwards, appear to have had no doubt or misgiving as to his being the genuine Lazarus of Bethany. It is worthy of especial observation that when the resurrection of Lazarus took place *many witnesses were invited* who were satisfied every one of that man's identity, and only wanted proof of his *death*. In the case of Jesus the opposite side of an imperfect miracle was exhibited; for his death had been made a kind of public spectacle, but *his rising was secret*, and when at length a living person professing to be him did appear stealthily to a few chosen witnesses, it was not without considerable difficulty that they were got to believe in his *identity*.

16. What, after all, is the amount of evidence adduced in support of this great "Foundation Miracle" of orthodox Christianity? Was this "the sealing and signing of the New Covenant," the "ratification of the New Law" witnessed by the whole Jewish nation? Was the entire population of Jerusalem called forth to bear testimony to it? Did it take place in the presence of all those spectators who had recently witnessed the Crucifixion? The bare unvarnished fact is, that this momentous sealing and signing of the nation's new covenant, as it is called, was not witnessed by a solitary Israelite! Indeed the Resurrection itself, the rising of the body from the sepulchre, as represented by Christian painters, was not witnessed by a single individual. A party of Pagan soldiers are reported to have seen the stone rolled away from the sepulchre by an "angel," or man dressed in white. Some of the disciples saw a white-robed stranger at the sepulchre who told them that Jesus was risen from the dead. Another stranger after-

wards appeared to the credulous disciples, and pretended with much art that he was the risen Jesus. But where is the connecting link of this marvellous evidence ? Where is the actual resurrection ? It seems to have been much such a miracle as the transmutation which now takes place occasionally under the box of a conjuror; the people who stand by as spectators are permitted to see the dead thing which goes in and the live thing which comes out, and having these few intimations and suggestions of a miracle given them, are expected to imagine and believe the rest.

17. The evidence that we have of the resurrection of Jesus is not even so complete and satisfactory as that which is offered for the modern confidential miracle producing a new religion—the resurrection of the Book of Mormon. The four witnesses of the Mormon Covenant testify that "they saw the angel descend, they heard his voice, they saw the plates in his hand, they saw the engravings upon them as the angel turned them over leaf after leaf, at the the same time they heard the voice of the Lord out of the heavens." Pratt, the Mormon apologist, compares the testimony of these four witnesses with that of the disciples who saw the risen Jesus. He declares that of all the disciples who are said to have seen Jesus after his resurrection only four—Matthew, John, Paul, and Peter—have handed down to our day their written testimony. "Therefore," he says, "when this generation can establish the writings of these four apostles to be genuine, uncorrupted, and translated correctly, they will have the testimony of as many witnesses to establish the resurrection of Christ as there was in the first place to establish the divine authenticity of the Book of Mormon ; but until then the witnesses of the Book of Mormon will not only be equal in number but superior in certainty to

those which this generation have of Christ's resurrection. Why is it, then, that men will believe four witnesses who lived eighteen centuries ago, and reject the same number of witnesses that have lived in their own day, who testify of things with equally as much certainty, having both heard and seen? It is because it has become popular through tradition to believe what their fathers believed, without at all inquiring into the strength of the evidence on which their faith is founded" ("Authenticity," p. 51).

18. The apologist of Mormonism can hardly be said to have made the best of his case : he has not placed the evidences of his own religion and those of Christianity quite in juxtaposition with each other. He ought to have placed the testimony of Matthew, John, Paul, and Peter, who are said to have seen Jesus *after* his resurrection, beside that of the many simple and sincere Mormon disciples who were permitted to see their sacred book after it was disinterred and partly translated. In the evidence of Christ's resurrection there is not to be found any counterpart to that of the highly favoured witnesses who profess to have seen the Book of Mormon delivered from the hands of the angel. If the Nazarene confederacy had done as much to authenticate their foundation miracle as has since been done by the Mormon confederacy : if the stealthy Joseph, Nicodemus, and two more of their colleagues had handed down their written testimony to the effect that they were present at the Resurrection, that they saw the angel descend on the sepulchre, saw him roll away the stone, and saw the dead body of Jesus suddenly revive and rise up out of the sepulchre, the evidences of Christianity would then, and only then, fully compare with the evidences of Mormonism.

19. The Ascension of Jesus is generally believed

s 2

to have been a much more public and indisputable
miracle than the Resurrection, and painters have
made an imposing spectacle of it by representing
him soaring sublimely into the cloud regions while
a number of witnesses stand below with wondering upturned eyes as people are now accustomed
to gaze on a balloon. But we are as convinced
that they have very much magnified the marvel as
that certain Catholic artists have gone beyond the
sober reality in their representations of the "Apparition of the Blessed Virgin at La Salette." Had
there only been a photographer present to fix
correctly the phenomena presented to human
observation he would not have handed down to
posterity such an imposing scene. The narrative
of the Ascension is so brief and vague that we are
not informed whether it took place by night or by
day, or how many of the disciples were present to
witness it. It had probably just as little publicity
as the Transfiguration vision, which in some respects
it appears to have resembled. The disciples being
sufficiently persuaded that their Master was risen
from the dead, would as a matter of course believe
in his ascension whenever the impersonator should
discontinue his visits or withdraw from the
neighbourhood. According to Luke's account he
made a final parting with them on Mount Olivet,
and perhaps retired from view on the other side of
the mount with the avowed purpose of ascending
into heaven. While they stood gazing into the
skies, "two men in white apparel," who might
have been "Moses and Elias," or the "angels"
who had recently been posted at the sepulchre,
suddenly approached and persuaded them to cease
gazing, as Jesus had flown away beyond their
sight, but would at some future time so come from
heaven and visit them again (Acts i. 9–12).

20. It would be interesting to know something

of the intercourse which Joseph of Arimathea and
his colleagues maintained with the leading disciples
of Jesus during the few years immediately following his death. But we have no other account
of this important and critical period in the church's
history besides that which Luke has furnished in
the early chapters of what he calls "The Acts of
the Apostles," but which might have been more
correctly called " The Acts of Paul," of whom alone
the writer appears to have had any clear and detailed
information. It is evident that Jesus and Paul
were during the lifetime of the former complete
strangers to each other. Jesus travelled from
place to place communing with various classes of
people, instructing and exhorting them to prepare
for the kingdom of heaven, but he never deemed it
worth while to spend an hour of his ministry with
the young disciple of Gamaliel, as he surely would
have done, if he had intended with prophetic
foresight to call him to the apostleship and make
him the chief revelator of the church. As there is
not the least hint thrown out in his discourses that
he intended after his death to convert by a special
miracle one of the unbelieving Pharisees, of whom
he had said "no sign shall be given them," nor any
warning to the twelve that their new brother would
be commissioned to preach new doctrines and abase
the Law to bring in the Gentiles, so neither does
Paul in his Epistles utter a single word to make it
seem probable that he ever had communion with the
original Jesus. Not only does he never profess to
have attended the public ministry of Jesus, but he
seems to have had no good second-hand knowledge of
that ministry, such as we obtain through the writings
of the Evangelists. He does not quote a syllable
from either of the Gospels, and we may reasonably
infer that he had never seen them nor heard any
complete narrative like them. When charged by

those Christians who relied on the testimony of eye-
witnesses with preaching a false gospel, he does not
endeavour to set himself right with them by seeking
authentic information. He seems to have conferred
once or twice with the leading disciples of Jesus, but
would neither learn anything from them nor yield to
their higher authority. He says expressly, "the
gospel which was preached of me was not after men.
For I neither received it of man, neither was I
taught it but by the revelation of Jesus Christ"
(Gal. i. 11-12). He declares in the same chapter
that immediately after his conversion, instead of
going up to Jerusalem and learning of the other
apostles, he went away into Arabia, where he probably
meditated in solitary places and had mystic visions
and trances (2 Cor. xii. 2).

21. The Nazarenes, who were looking for a
spiritual restoration of the kingdom of Israel,
naturally regarded Paul and his Gentile followers
as a body of heretics, but this sect, by reason of
their lighter obligations, rapidly gained ground of
their opponents, and became at length the stronger
community. The Paulinists grew in time to have
the same relationship to the primitive Christians
that the Sabines are said to have had to the
primitive Romans—they conquered their better
established rival tribe, imposed their principal laws
and customs on them, jointly occupied their
dominion, and assumed their name (Newman's
"Regal Rome," p. 57). And just as patriotic Roman
historians laboured to disguise their old feuds and
divisions, and give a vexatious conquest the
appearance of a friendly arrangement and con-
cession, so there arose in the Christian Church a
reconciliation party, who, in order to obliterate
their dissensions, and facilitate the amalgamation
of the Judaic Christians with the Paulinists,
endeavoured to represent that from the very first

they had lived and laboured together in concord. The Second Epistle of Peter, which recognizes Paul as a "beloved brother," and defends the "things hard to be understood" in his writings, is admitted by such orthodox critics as Neander to be a spurious production of the second century, written for the express purpose of reconciling the followers of Paul with those who adhered to the doctrine of Jesus. The author of the Acts of the Apostles has evidently a similar object in view; he is intent on making Paulinism seem a supernatural outgrowth of the church's original tree, and not a heretical graft, as it had been commonly regarded, and on this account the early portion of his narrative, including the story of Paul's conversion, is believed by many expositors to be mythical.

22. There can be little doubt that this early chronicler of the Church takes the full licence of the age in inventing speeches, but the marvellous stories which he records are quite likely to have some basis of fact. It is wholly incredible that the Roman government would permit the chief priest to employ Saul of Tarsus, as a grand inquisitor, and send him through the different provinces as far as Damascus, arresting followers of Jesus everywhere, both men and women, and committing them to prison (Acts viii. 3; ix. 2). But the confederacy that arrested and brought Jesus to trial, as if they had been agents of the chief priests, could easily, under the same cover, subject his disciples to a mock persecution. It is not unlikely that Saul, who was known to be hostile to the Christians, should have been lured into an expedition against them by pretended officers of the chief priests with the view to effect his conversion. The guides who accompanied him on his journey might have been disguised Nazarenes,

who had concerted to take him into a sort of
ambush, where one of their party was stationed, to
frighten him from his purpose by impersonating
the risen Jesus, they themselves helping to
accomplish this object by falling to the earth on
meeting the apparition and feigning to be greatly
alarmed. Such a pious stratagem might reasonably
be expected from the crafty miracle-mongers who
got up the Transfiguration scene and planned the
Crucifixion and Resurrection of Jesus. It was
fear that drove the disciple of Gamaliel into the
church, and not sympathy with its doctrines, but
he was too opinionated and self-assertive to be
kept long in leading strings; he looked to his own
subjective visions for guidance, and became just the
independent Christian preacher that a Hellenized
Jew of Cilicia might be expected to become from
such a sudden and irregular process of conversion.

23. As the Jews in Paul's estimation were vessels
of honour favoured with divine revelation above the
rest of mankind, so a certain small fraction of Jews
—the followers of Jesus—were at length favoured
in like manner above the rest of their countrymen.
It was their good fortune to see performed in
obscure places a number of miracles and listen
to revealed doctrines respecting which the bulk
of their nation, both in Judea and beyond its con-
fines, were kept in profound ignorance. Through
seeing, hearing, and believing they became, as it
were, a new chosen people—the select of the select—
while the few who were present and doubted, and
the many more who were absent and knew not that
anything unusual was transpiring in the country,
became thereby marked out as a reprobate people—
vessels made unto dishonour and doomed to everlasting perdition. It was hard that the great mass
of Jewish people should be thus condemned for
disbelieving miracles they had not seen, especially

that of the alleged Resurrection of Jesus. The
Nazarene prophet having had a public death, it
was probably expected that his predicted rising
would be public; and, since people were then frequently imposed upon by objective visions and
other dramatic illusions, the secrecy of his reported
rising could not fail to fill many reflective minds
with suspicion and doubt. It was not only the
Sadducees who treated the report as absolutely
incredible; their opponents, the Pharisees, were
equally constrained to reject it, and Paul among
the Pharisees was as confident and earnest as any
in declaring his unbelief. But the risen Jesus,
while carefully avoiding the chief priests and
rulers, presently appeared to Paul in an over-
powering vision, and absolutely compelled him to
believe. Had he been endowed with humility and
a genuine love of justice, had he felt assured from
the bottom of his heart that God was no respecter
of persons, he would now have earnestly prayed
that the same convincing evidence that had
been vouchsafed to him might be presented to
the rest of his countrymen. And remembering
how he had scornfully rejected the miracle testimony
of Stephen and the twelve, he would have felt a
little modest diffidence in delivering his own report
and expected that what he now said of the supernatural would be received with equal incredulity.
Having, however, unlimited assurance, and believing
that he had been singled out from all other Jews as
an object of divine favour and regard, he was not
the man to be troubled with such reflections. He
had now, in addition to the conceit of superiority
which was common to most Pharisees, acquired the
arrogant dictatorial spirit of a Pope. He advanced
his high pretensions and asserted himself as a
" chosen vessel " somewhat to this effect,—" When
Stephen and the rest had visions of the risen Jesus,

what they saw was nothing to me; it was not to be supposed that I should take their word, but now that I have had such visions, you are all bound to accept my word, although it were contradicted by an angel from heaven, or without doubt you will perish everlastingly."

24. The wide credit which was given to the supernatural claims of Christianity in the first century resembles in many respects the more rapid success which is now obtained by here and there a fortunate Roman Catholic miracle. The original witnesses of an apparition of the Virgin are invariably simple-minded and credulous people so deficient in the critical faculty that they may be easily imposed upon by any well-contrived dramatic illusion. Having a good honest reputation and no apparent motive for palming on the world a fiction of that kind, their testimony is considered worthy of credit by some of the shrewder neighbours, who, had they been present at the scene of the miracle, would have found reasons to doubt its reality. As the story continues to spread and to get embellished the circle of believers daily increases and at the same time rises in intelligence; for just as a river grows in volume and strength and first carries down only sticks and straws before it, and next small logs and branches, but after awhile big trunks of trees, so the current of faith gets stronger and more persuasive as it increases in magnitude; and there are many educated and thoughtful people who would not have gone with the first ten, nor even with the first thousand, but are constrained at length to go with the million. And such superior converts, when they meet with objectors, are generally able to furnish very substantial arguments in support of their faith. They contend that there is no antecedent improbability attached to the apparition, and

insist strongly on the simple honest character of the witnesses. Had it originated from mere human contrivance they express their firm conviction that the whole plot must have been speedily detected and exposed. They proceed to judge the miracle by its moral effects, they point to the host of pilgrims which it has brought together from distant parts, and to the manifest religious revival which it has produced throughout the district, and contend that it seems to them quite inconceivable how all these beneficial results should have been generated by a miserable imposture.

25. There cannot be a doubt that the great success which Christianity obtained in the course of three centuries . among the more credulous populations of the Roman empire was largely due to the obscurity of its origin. Had Jesus been a man of resplendent genius towering high in wisdom and virtue above all other teachers of that age, he would have been so much visited by intelligent writers from various parts of the world, and so correctly reported, that it would have been impossible to start any extraordinary fiction about him and get it believed. His influence in his lifetime would have been much greater, but, after his death, he could not have been invested with a halo of myths and magnified more and more by superstitious reverence till he should be worshipped at length as the highest Divinity. It was no small advantage to the early Christian propagandists that when they went from city to city declaring how their founder excited the enmity of the Jewish rulers by his wonderful works, and then suffered, and died, and rose again, no one had hitherto heard of his existence. Thus, however much their story might be doubted or disbelieved by thoughtful people, it continually gained ground because, from want of information, it could not be readily contradicted.

Some of the dispersed Jews occasionally disputed with these ardent missionaries, and affirmed that they calumniated the chief priests and rulers, but to very little purpose, as they had not been present in Jerusalem at the time of the Crucifixion to say what then actually occurred. Even if any inquirer had written to the city a few years after that event to learn something about it from disinterested eye-witnesses there could not have been thrown upon it much light. For the Nazarenes were not in their origin such a sect as the Quakers or the Methodists, having everything about them open and above-board; they were a secret society working by miracle and mystery, and as little understood by the people of Jerusalem as by the rest of the world. If the wire-pulling arrangements of the confederacy had been unravelled to some extent; if its stratagems had been betrayed, and those who personated Moses, Elias, and Jesus in objective visions clearly identified, the whole illusory movement which imposed on the credulous would have completely broken down; it was only in consequence of well-maintained secrecy that it had a permanent and immense success.

CHAPTER X.

THE FRUITS OF CHRISTIANITY.

Mr. Froude's view of early Christianity as a reforming influence. 3. The results of its proselytism as shown by Merivale and Milman. 6. Effect of its doomsday illusions. 7. Character of Origen considered. 9. Untruthfulness followed by injustice. 10. Other religious systems not without salutary moral force. 11. Julian's projected reforms. 12. Archdeacon Farrar's exaggeration of Christian benefits. 14. Failure of Christianity to reclaim the rude and lawless. 15. Reform must begin with good family life. 16. The radical error of Christian communism or club life. 19. Aggressive and revolutionary communism. 20. Modern Christian Socialists. 23. The supposed tyranny of Capitalism. 24. Extremes of wealth and poverty considered. 26. The alleged evils of competition. 28. Its authoritative regulation in the public interest. 29. Its unjust restriction by selfish combinations and rings. 30. Violence of Trade-unions. 31. Christian ministers pander to lawlessness. 32. Hard bargaining and forced bargains. 33. Promotion by merit discouraged. 34. Employers and employed, who should be well mated, kept at discord. 35. A gleaner's combination. 36. Chinese banded beggars. 37. Distinguished prelates bid for popular support, and are strife-makers rather than peace-makers.

MR. FROUDE, like many German writers, has endeavoured to exalt Christianity to the highest place among the religions of the world, not on the ground of its supernatural claims, but by reason of what he considers its sovereign efficacy in correcting the vices of Paganism. He says in one of his instructive essays,—"Religion as a rule of life neither is nor can be a record of events which once occurred on a corner of this planet. It is the expression and statement of our duties to one another and of our relations to the Sovereign Power that called us into existence. And these duties and these relations are not conditions which once were or which will be hereafter. They are conditions of our present being as much as what we call the laws of nature. For the laws of bodily health we are not depended on the observations of Galen or the history of the plague at Athens. We learn from present experience as Galen himself learnt, and we refer to the records of the past only as a single chapter in the vast volume of our instructions. The evidence of the truth of religion is not the testimony of this or that person who saw or thought he saw long ago something which seemed to him an indication of a supernatural presence. The evidence is the power which lies in religion to cope with moral disease and bind the brutal appetites and intellectual perversities of man, and to lift him out of grossness and self-indulgence into higher and nobler desires. This was what Christianity effected as no creed or system of philosophy ever did before or has done since, and Christianity was thus, as Goethe declares, beyond comparison the grandest work that was ever accomplished by humanity. It is a height, he says, which having once risen to it, mankind can never again descend ; and thus of all studies the most interesting to us is that of the conditions under which so extraordinary a force developed itself" (" Origen and Celsus").

2. He proceeds to examine these conditions with the help of old Christian and Pagan writings— those of Origen, Celsus, and Lucian. In reproducing from Origen's quotations the argument of Celsus in a clear connected form, he tries to be impartial, but still sees with Origen's eyes, and throughout the investigation gives unmistakable

proof of being under a strong bias. Professing to exhibit the moral forces which were at work throughout the Roman empire in the third century, he skilfully embellishes the character and aims of the Christian propagandists, while he blackens the Pagan teachers, and altogether ignores the Jews. The message of the disciples of Christianity, he tells us, "was a message never before heard on earth. It was to invite their fellow-men to lead new lives, to put away sin, to separate themselves from the abominations of the world, to care nothing for wealth, and to be content with poverty, to aim only at overcoming each for himself his own sensuality and selfishness ; to welcome pain, want, disease, and everything which the world most shrank from, if it would assist him in self-conquest; and to expect no reward, at least in this life, save the peace which would arise from the consciousness that he was doing what God had commanded."

3. This is an attempt to make it appear that the early Christians preached virtue for its own sake, that they were pure, disinterested, simple-minded reformers, caring only for the cultivation of character and the inward satisfaction and peace of mind derived from leading a good life. No representation can well be further from the truth. For the promulgators of Christianity to win over the rabble of every city by such a lofty message as this would really have been more marvellous than all the miracles believed by the orthodox. There were undoubtedly some few Christians of superior character who rebuked to good purpose the licentiousness of their times, just as there were some virtuous Pagan teachers, such as Seneca, Epictetus, and Marcus Aurelius; but the majority of the ignorant and credulous people who became converts were not influenced at all by ethical discourses and a thirst for righteousness; they were

simply idle fortune-seekers desirous of going to some far-off blissful region where everything would be provided for their enjoyment without labour and care. By coming into fellowship and submitting to the Church's disciplinary regulations they could not fail to be morally benefited to some extent, but this was not at all the object which they mainly had in view. What they really cared for was to escape the threatened torments of Hell and attain the promised felicity of Heaven with as little trouble and procrastination as possible, and they had no more solicitude for virtue and the reformation of their evil habits than the penitent thief. Merivale, speaking of the conversion of the Franks, says:—"The old religion appealed to the imagination, and it was on the imagination and not on the moral sense that the early influence of Christianity among them showed itself. They went on in their former fierce irregular ways; they gave up nothing of their love of carousal, bloodshed, and violence . . . . The Franks had given up their worship of nature as a thing of purity and beauty for a worship in which they still did not get beyond material conceptions, while, as their manners degenerated from their early simplicity and vigour, these conceptions grew dark and distorted, and represented that the world was swayed by hateful and magical forces. Christianity was degraded into a scheme of sorcery and enchantment; Christian faith consisted in a superstitious regard for relics and a credulous acceptance of the grossest miracles; Christian practice in outward acts of confession and penance, and of expiatory prodigality engaged in during the intervals of crime" ("Early Catholicism in Western Europe").

4. Milman, writing of the earlier proselytism of the third and fourth centuries, says:—"While then the religion of the world underwent a total change,

while the church rose on the ruins of the temple, and the pontifical establishment of Paganism became gradually extinct, or suffered violent suppression, the moral revolution was far more slow and far less complete. With a large portion of mankind it must be admitted that the religion itself was Paganism, under another form, with different appellations ; with another part it was the religion passively received without any change in the moral sentiments or habits; with a third, and perhaps the more considerable part, there was a transfer of the passions and the intellectual activity to a new cause. They were completely identified with Christianity, and to a certain degree actuated by its principles, but they did not apprehend the beautiful harmony which subsists between its doctrines and its moral perfection. Its dogmatic purity was the sole engrossing subject; the unity of doctrine superseded and obscured all other considerations. . . . . . Everywhere there was exaggeration of one of the constituent elements of Christianity, that exaggeration which is the inevitable consequence of a strong impulse on the human mind. Wherever men feel strongly they act violently. The more speculative Christians, therefore, who were more inclined in the deep and somewhat selfish solicitude for their own salvation to isolate themselves from the infected mass of mankind, pressed into the extreme of asceticism. The more practical, who were earnest in the desire of disseminating the blessings of religion throughout society, scrupled little to press into their service whatever might advance their cause. With both extremes the dogmatical part of the religion predominated. The monkish believer imposed the same severity upon the aberrations of the mind as upon the appetites of the body; and, in general, those who are severe to themselves are both dis-

T

posed and think themselves entitled to enforce the same severity on others. The other, as his sphere became extended, was satisfied with an adhesion to the Christian creed instead of that total change of life demanded of the early Christian and watched over with such jealous vigilance by the mutual superintendence of a small society. [The great requirement at first was faith, and the renunciation of property and industrial pursuits rather than a reformation of character.] In proportion to the admitted importance of the creed men became more sternly and exclusively wedded to their opinions. Thus an antagonistic principle of exclusiveness co-existed with the most comprehensive ambition. While they swept in converts indiscriminately from the palace and the public street, while the emperor and the lowest of the populace were alike admitted on little more than the open profession of allegiance, they were satisfied if the allegiance in this respect was blind and complete" ("History of Christianity," p. 402).

5. The historian says a little further on :—"The ferocious and ignorant populace of the large cities, which found a new aliment in Christian faction for their mutinous and sanguinary outbursts of turbulence, had almost been better left to sleep on in the passive and undestructive quiet of Pagan indifference." What were the Christian teachers doing to reform and elevate these degraded masses who had been swept pell-mell into the proselytizing net of the church? Some were wandering in solitary places, spending much time in fasting and prayer, and submitting to severe mortifications of the flesh, so as to acquire the reputation of saints. Others were establishing monasteries, imposing on the neighbouring people with fictitious relics and miracles, carrying on a lucrative trade by pretending to deliver souls from purgatory, and

offering a safe asylum to murderers and other fugitive criminals who had broken the laws of their country. The bishops and the rest of the established clergy were, with a few bright exceptions, wholly indifferent to the intellectual and moral improvement of the rude populations over whom they exercised a spiritual authority. They were constantly insisting on the text, "He that believeth and is baptized shall be saved, but he that believeth not shall be damned" (Mark xvi. 16). So long as a man had been sprinkled with baptismal water and had faith in the magical virtue of the blood of Jesus to cleanse his soul from impurity, it mattered very little in their estimation what his character might be, or whether he sinned little or much. What they were most solicitous about was to prevent intelligent people from entertaining a distrust of the efficacy of sacerdotal charms; they continually warned those who lived virtuously not to rely on their own good conduct for salvation, and thus fall at length into everlasting perdition.

6. The early Christians undoubtedly did something towards checking sensualism by propagating the mistaken belief which they shared with the Essenes and some other Jews as to the near approaching end of the world. There were not wanting in that age enlightened religious teachers to denounce the voluptuousness and profligacy which existed around them and demonstrate the higher happiness which every idle pleasure-seeker might obtain by leading a virtuous life. And they had their thoughtful disciples, they each attracted by such discourses an intelligent and truth-loving audience. But a certain portion of the people, although not quite brutalized, were too ignorant and too weak-minded to appreciate the reflections of a wise teacher; the ablest reasoning was thrown away upon them; they could only be

influenced at all by working on their hopes and
fears in some such way as is done by a modern
ranting Revivalist. The Christian missionaries
drew simple-minded believers of this sort from
their vicious indulgences (and even from innocent
pleasures) by exhorting them to flee from the wrath
to come, and they based their prophetic warning,
not merely on the shortness and uncertainty of
individual life, but on the impending doom of the
world. The preaching of this illusory belief produced at some places a veritable panic : " fear came
upon every soul," hundreds of excited converts
were listening from hour to hour for the archangel's
trumpet blast, ever fancying that they saw in the
heavens signs of the coming Christ, and beholding
the sun set with little expectation that it would
ever rise again. Under the influence of such
solemn anticipations pleasure was of course not to
be thought of ; the right thing to do was to engage
in fasting, prayer, and penance, and have a continual preparation for eternity. Even among
sturdy Pagan unbelievers the sight of this Christian
asceticism might have a sobering effect; it was a
constant reminder of the shortness of carnal
pleasures, something like the skull which the old
Egyptians were accustomed to place at their feasts
for the purpose of checking intemperance. But it
cannot be said that such fanatical excitement
contributed in any degree to the cultivation of a
high morality ; and some men are likely to have
been thoroughly disgusted at the severe mortifications of the Christian saints, and to have been
rather driven thereby into the opposite extreme of
self-indulgence.

7. Mr. Froude, in reviewing the important discussion between Origen and Celsus, says :—" On the
moral and spiritual side Origen was as completely
victorious as Celsus was irresistible on the intellec-

tual. Celsus insisted that Christianity was identical in character with a thousand other superstitions. Origen was able to insist on the extraordinary difference, that neither the philosophy of the schools nor the mysteries, the festivals, the rituals of the heathen gods availed to check the impurity of society, or to alleviate the miseries of mankind, and that vice and wretchedness disappeared in every house into which the Gospel found an entrance. This was true : and it was a truth which outweighed a millionfold the skilfullest cavils of the intellect. A new life had come into the world ; it was growing like the grain of mustard-seed by its own vital force, and the earth was growing green under its shadow. Such an argument was unanswerable. No other creed could be pointed to from which any stream was flowing of moral regeneration" (Ibid).

8. As to Origen's having a great moral superiority over his antagonist in the argument, it is hard to see where that superiority lies unless there is moral excellence to be found in boasting, exaggeration, and untruthfulness. Bishop Horsley and others have shown that this distinguished man—the most learned Christian of his time—was extravagantly unveracious as a controversialist. He did not hesitate to resort to any sophistry or misrepresentation that seemed likely to serve his purpose or give him an apparent advantage in arguing on behalf of Christianity. In his discussion with Celsus he makes things appear or disappear for the improvement of his case in the manner of a conjuror ; he refers to monstrous fables as if they were facts, and when he finds it hard to give a reasonable explanation of any Scripture difficulty, instantly converts the narrative into an allegory. That such an unscrupulous writer should decry Paganism, magnify his own religion, and make it

appear that all the vices and evils that beset
mankind were being charmed away before the
benignant light of the Gospel, is not at all to be
wondered at, but it surprises us greatly that an able
historical inquirer of the nineteenth century should
admire his moral qualities and consider him entitled
to belief.

9. The Christians were not only untruthful in
their persistent efforts to impose their faith on the
whole world, but extremely unjust. It was their
policy to allure first the credulous multitude by
persuasion and craft, and then, having once secured
a majority on their side, to intimidate with their
denunciations the intelligent and sceptical, and bend
them at length to outward conformity by brute
force. They did not mind the arguments that were
directed against them by a few learned philosophers
so long as they were able to convince the rude
populace. While a hundred sensible people were
reading and appreciating the "True Story" of Celsus,
a thousand of their illiterate neighbours were being
persuaded to accept the irrational belief which it
controverted. The masses of ignorance were thus
made at length to over-ride and conquer intelligence;
two hundred years after Origen wrote his lame and
crooked apology the clergy found a short and easy
method of refuting Celsus by committing his book
to the flames, and had he been living at that period
he would have been pretty sure himself to share
the same fate. Now that they had grown powerful
with continued proselytism, and had at their
command the resources of the Roman empire, it
was no longer necessary for them to argue this and
that point with unbelievers, or creep into obscure
places with their marvels to escape criticism; they
resolved to drive criticism clean out of the world.
All the treatises which had been written against
the claims of their religion in the whole preceding

period of free discussion were hunted up as far as possible and rigorously suppressed, and every independent thinker, whether Jew or Gentile, who ventured to differ from the dominant creed was compelled to maintain a discreet silence.

10. Mr. Froude asserts that when Christianity was being propagated throughout the Roman empire in the time of Origen "no other creed could be pointed to from which was flowing any stream of moral regeneration." Could people then be morally regenerated only by making themselves eunuchs for the kingdom of heaven's sake, fanatically urging their friends and neighbours to seek the glory of martyrdom, and carrying on a work of conversion by having recourse to unblushing falsehoods and pious frauds? The Stoics and Neo-Platonists of that period were moral reformers, and much was unquestionably done towards reclaiming the heathen by the mild proselytism of the Jews. The morality of the purest primitive Christians was in no respect superior to that of the Essenes. Nay, the latter community were a more peaceable, tolerant, and truthful sect; they were a people who minded their business better, and did not set out with the ambitious design of imposing their spiritual yoke on the whole world. It has been said that the Jews made such slow advances with their own missionary enterprises, that if the conversion of the Roman empire had been left entirely to them it would not have been by this time accomplished. Their progress in reclaiming their heathen neighbours was undoubtedly slow, as from the nature of the case it must have been, but it was sound progress. They had learnt wisdom from experience; in the old Maccabean times their zealous ancestors had repeatedly taken up arms to proselytize by force and make a clean sweep of idolatry, but only to end at length in complete failure. Images had been often

broken and altars overthrown to cleanse their country swiftly from the infection of heathenism, but as there was no internal reform, as the minds of the people were still corrupt, a restoration of the old superstitious customs was as a matter of course soon effected. And even when the old idolatry was rooted out many hasty attempts which were made to convert strangers into true Israelites ended in their half conversion, and a compromise of Jewish doctrine and worship with that of the Gentiles. From all these untoward results the dispersed Jewish teachers had learnt to proceed cautiously with their proselytizing efforts and trust wholly to slow educational reform; and Christian missionaries contending with heathenism in India and elsewhere have now found it discreet to follow their example in this respect, but only after the lapse of many centuries.

11. Much has been said of the mighty and unparalleled reformation which the followers of Jesus accomplished, a few centuries after his death, throughout the Roman empire; but it was after all only a mixing and blending of faiths; the Christians were in the end quite as much converted to Paganism as the Pagans were converted to Christianity. The greater part of the so-called conversion was not a moral work at all, but a forcible suppression of the old forms of worship by military power: the most successful missionaries were the fierce soldiers of Constantine, Theodosius, and Charlemagne, who drove timid crowds at the sword's point to renounce their ancient idols and bow to the new images or saints. And the intolerant propagandists who thus carried on a long revolutionary war with the Pagans for religious supremacy, when they became at length victorious, were found to be divided among themselves and equally ready to assail one another. Even before the death of Constantine a sanguinary

struggle broke out between the great rival sects—Athanasians and Arians—and the one which was eventually successful and made its views prevail was that which had gone furthest in idolatry. It was the spirit of intolerance which had been introduced, and the terrible conflicts which raged between the sects, that drove Julian, an enlightened moral philosopher, to abandon Christianity in disgust, and entertain a belief that the various populations of the empire would get on far more peacefully and prosperously together under the teaching of a reformed Paganism. A grand design was formed by him which he did not live to carry out. "In every province," says Milman, "a supreme pontiff was to be appointed charged with a superintendence of the conduct of the inferior priesthood, and armed with authority to suspend or depose those who should be guilty of any indecent irregularity. The whole priesthood were to be sober, chaste, temperate in all things. They were to abstain not merely from loose society; but in a spirit diametrically opposite to the old religion, were rarely to be seen at public festivals, never where women mingled in them. In private houses they were only to be present at the moderate banquets of the virtuous; they were never to be seen drinking in taverns or exercising any base or sordid trade. The priesthood were to stand aloof from society and only mingle with it to infuse their own grave decency and unimpeachable moral tone. . . . A tax was to be levied in every province for the maintenance of the poor, and distributed by the priesthood. Hospitals for the sick and for indigent strangers of every creed were to be formed in convenient places" ("History of Christianity," p. 468).

12. Archdeacon Farrar, in casting about for additional evidences in support of his faith, has been tempted to go quite as far in conjuring with

history as St. Paul went in conjuring with
Scripture. He says :—"The effects, then, of the
work of Christ are even to the unbeliever indisputable and historical. It expelled cruelty; it curbed
passion; it branded suicide; it punished and repressed an execrable infanticide; it drove the
shameless impurities of heathendom into a
congenial darkness. There was hardly a class
whose wrongs it did not remedy. It rescued the
gladiator; it freed the slave; it protected the
captive; it nursed the sick; it sheltered the orphan;
it elevated the woman; it shrouded as with a halo
of sacred innocence the tender years of the child.
In every region of life its ameliorating influence
was felt" ("Life of Christ").

13. After ascribing in this eloquent strain every
step of human improvement and every social and
moral reform called forth in the great circle of
Roman civilization to the revolutionary religion
which proclaimed that the end of the world was at
hand, he argues that there can be no doubt whatever as to its having a Divine origin. He evidently believes this himself; but in magnifying
the virtues of Christianity to the utmost he is
unconsciously practising something much like
imposture, and a multitude of sympathetic readers
will be imposed upon by the magic of his words.
"It expelled cruelty," says he, as though there
were no cruelty in its fierce sectarian wars and
massacres, and Jew and heretic persecutions, and
witch-burnings. "It curbed passion," like every
system of asceticism, in one direction, but inflamed
it to madness in another. "It branded suicide,"
in the case of people who were simply weary of
life; but exalted and sanctified it where fanatics
provoked persecution and rushed upon death to
gain in haste the joys of paradise. "It punished
and repressed infanticide," yet this practice is not

expressly prohibited in the New Testament as it is in the Koran, and to this day it is more frequent in Christian than in Mohammedan countries. "It drove the shameless impurities of heathendom into a congenial darkness," but it did not reform them away, and they still flourish under covert in all the great cities whose temples are dedicated to its saints. "There was hardly a class whose wrongs it did not remedy," and there was hardly a people outside its own pale on whom it did not inflict some wrong. "It rescued the gladiator," only to make him a bull-fighter, a prize-fighter, or a duellist. Pagan reformers did as much to suppress sanguinary sport. Apollonius of Tyana, for instance, "spoke against the cruel gladiatorial shows; and when the Athenians, who were celebrating such games, invited him to the public assembly, he replied that he could not tread on a spot stained by the shedding of so much human blood" (Neander's "History"). "It freed the slave," so far as its anarchical teaching abolished mastership and established communistic brotherhoods; but beyond such small select circles, in the whole wide Christian world it took no decided steps to mitigate the cruelties of slavery nor to remove from mankind the horrors of war. Its modern fanatical anti-slavery crusades and universal emancipation movements have led to terrible conflicts, excited furious race-hatred, and aggravated human misery a hundredfold. It has acquired more distinction from protecting the fugitive criminal than the war captive, and the Western woman owes her elevation not so much to any religious teaching imported from Asia, as to the love of social freedom inherent in the European race.

14. The Christian nations at the present day are distinguished by superior energy and intelli-

gence rather than by a higher morality. They are beyond question the most quarrelsome, the most aggressive and warlike communities in the whole civilized world. In no Mohammedan or heathen countries will be found such rank vices of drunkenness, prostitution, gambling, roguery, and prodigality as flourish in the lands which boast of being evangelized. Christianity, a mere hortatory system, has never known how to deal effectively with rude barbarous people who are accustomed to live without law. Jesus selected for his disciples a few simple honest peasants who could be influenced by preaching and by working on their superstitious fears. He did nothing towards reclaiming the brigands of Palestine and the criminal population of the towns, since he relied on persuasion alone, and they required systematic industrial training and government. So when the religion derived from him was extensively propagated and whole districts became professedly Christian, it was only a small portion of the baptized believers who were men of pure and innocent lives. As 'Milman testifies, not the slightest moral improvement was effected in the conduct of the majority; they continued in their old lawless brutal ways, pretty much as if they had been baptized swine. The same checkered moral conditions may be witnessed at the present day throughout the whole of Christendom. Bodies of decent orderly people whom words will influence regularly assemble in all the churches, while the brute masses who cannot be attracted and impressed by such means are left to take their own course. The population of every Christian country, that is, its believing population, consists of multitudes of sinners interspersed with small groups of sympathetic saints. And the former cannot be regenerated by the latter, because they need for their moral elevation what the Gospel has failed to prescribe—a system of reformatory government. The missionaries who go forth into remote regions to reclaim savage races preach to these rude people as though they were intelligent men instead of governing them as if they were children. They treat them very kindly, but the simple people are not regularly protected, subjected to discipline, and restrained for their good, therefore, as soon as they come in contact with traders and the vices of civilization, they begin to wither and perish, as before the invasion of a deadly epidemic, and the efforts to reclaim them are found to have been labour expended in vain.

15. The great work of uplifting savage and brutalized humanity at the present day, is the reclamation of the degraded masses to be found in all the great cities of Christendom. Every civilized nation may be considered a confederation of kindred families—domestic communities speaking the same language and subject to the same law—and if each of these families were well cared for and properly governed, very little more would be wanted in the way of government. A good householder brings his children up virtuously, carefully trains them in industrious and provident habits, starts them fairly in some profession which befits their capacity, and they may be trusted to do well and not become in any way a source of trouble to their country. A bad householder, on the other hand, presents an evil example to his children, and gives them scarcely any training at all; they are under no domestic law, they run about as wild and free to do what they please as the offspring of Kaffirs and Hottentots. They could neither do much harm nor catch harm in a wilderness, but in the midst of a great city, with no other prospect of living than that of beggary or crime, they are

sure to suffer greatly as well as prove a constant
annoyance. It is for such victims of parental
neglect that prisons and workhouses have to be
erected in every province, and an army of police
employed to keep constant watch on them, and as
far as possible check their aggressions. The
better course for a government, however, is to
prevent this evil development by insisting on a
proper discharge of parental duty throughout the
nation, and making people more responsible for
their children's misdeeds. The bad householder,
who is hatching trouble for his country, should
not only be disallowed any voice in the management
of public affairs, but should be deprived of his own
domestic rule, and his neglected children, with the
view to their proper training, should be made
directly subject to the nation's higher paternal
authority.

16. Primitive Christianity, instead of seeking to
improve family government in the interest of social
order, rather sought to effect its entire abolition
and to encourage parental neglect. There was to
be no more wholesome restraint, no more toiling
and storing up wealth, but children and parents
were to forget alike their obligations to each other,
and herd together in a free mendicant community.
Even at the present day the misery of a slum
population is ascribed not to vices acquired from
want of early training, but to the greed of their
industrious and provident neighbours who have
been reared in good homes. And it is the latter,
and not the former, who are called upon to set
about in humble penitence and alter their manner
of life. It was the belief of the early Christians
that some people had too little of the good things
which are requisite to make life enjoyable in
consequence of others having too much, and
that justice demanded an equalization of human

possessions. If the world which we inhabit were a great monastery, or if the food, clothing, and shelter which we need were placed gratuitously within the reach of us all, their notion would not be incorrect or unreasonable. Those who, like the old medicant friars and the first followers of Jesus, are accustomed to rely wholly on alms for their support, may well expect to receive evenly, since no one among them contributes more than another towards procuring the means of subsistence. It is not surprising that an unequal distribution of largess among poor people should excite a feeling of jealousy in their breasts and give rise to more grumbling than gratitude. But wealth is not ordinarily distributed as a free gift any more than learning : it has to be diligently sought for, earned by wise calculation and persevering effort, so that he who gets most usually deserves most. It is, moreover, advantageous for the whole community that those who have the ability to acquire and conserve wealth in excess of their individual needs should keep what they win under their own management and direction, rather than pass it gratuitously into less capable hands.

17. In the case of an ordinary working family consisting of seven members it would not be equitable and conducive to their general welfare to divide the property which they own into seven shares, or to allow the simple improvident children the same free access which the parents have to the cupboard and the purse. Under such an arrangement it is quite certain that these youthful members would be got to do very little work, and the family capital, instead of increasing, would be fast dissipated. Similar results on a much larger scale would be brought about by any attempt to equalize the property of a nation. As many working people are mere children in. mental development, accustomed

to live from hand to mouth, and incapable of making
any provision for the future, an equalized share of
the national capital placed in their hands, so far
from permanently bettering their position, would
only cause them to live idly till the whole was spent.
Christian Socialists do not see the need of improving
the moral habits of a large portion of the community;
they are continually assuring us that to remedy the
dreadful poverty that exists there must be a more
even distribution of wealth. It is quite clear,
however, that such distribution would lead to great
waste and idleness, and thus bring about eventually
still worse poverty. Where people are both
intemperate and improvident, destitution will come
and cannot be charmed away. But it is certain that
the more a country advances in prosperity and
accumulates capital the better wages will its
industrial population receive, and it can only
continue prosperous so long as its wealth is under
the control of the comparatively few who are both
wise managers and good storekeepers. Those who
have capital which they cannot turn to good account
themselves have generally sense enough to put it in
the hands of others who are likely to use it well
and make it productive, just as a gun might be
lent to a good marksman and not to those who
would be sure to waste the ammunition, and besides
commit serious mischief.

18. In the eyes of the early Christians one
person was as fitted to be entrusted with wealth as
another; they recognized no difference of business
capacity among men, denounced all industrial
and providential undertakings as worldly, and
expected true believers to live from hand to mouth
in a state of holy poverty, which fitted them for
the joys of Heaven. The great error of these
enthusiasts was their attempt to dissolve family
life, from which civilization had sprung, and introduce

in its stead a social system like that of the Essenes, based on club life, or communism. It is only a few persons 'of' kindred disposition and good moral character that have ever been able to form a successful communistic association. It would be possible in almost any neighbourhood to select a number of good amiable people who, while satisfied with the present constitution of society and not asking for revolutionary changes, might be relied upon to get on as well as the Shakers and the Moravians if circumstances arose which rendered it expedient for them to adopt the same mode of living. They would doubtless take cheerfully to communistic ways and study each other's welfare admirably, just as courteous strangers do when they happen to be thrown together for a time in a railway carriage or on board a passenger ship. Instead of being ever on the watch to get some petty selfish advantage, or obtain more than their proper share of the provisions and accommodation afforded, they would strive rather for the honour of rendering the greatest amount of service, and promoting in the most effective manner, the common welfare. But though such people, by segregating and living apart in this way, might be very happy and exhibit a picture of great harmony, it can hardly be considered right and commendable that they should do so purposely and altogether turn their backs on the unregenerate world. The Shakers, and those who shut themselves up in monasteries, would be much better employed in guiding congregations, teaching schools, or going about as temperance lecturers to reclaim some of their more degraded countrymen. People who lead virtuous lives and are capable of doing something in the way of elevating the masses, may reasonably be expected to confer together occasionally and compare notes for their mutual enlightenment; but they cannot be constantly herding together as a religious club for the sake of congenial society without incurring blame for a great waste of working talent and neglect of the duty which they owe to the general community.

19. The various Christian brotherhoods established from time to time have always been harmless and peaceable; they have presented to the world a pattern of the strict religious life which they have felt bound to follow, without expecting their rules to be adopted by all sorts and conditions of people. From being of kindred sentiment and accustomed to self-control they have found it possible to associate as friends and hold their property in common, and when any outsider of good character is desirous to join them, they will receive him as a probationer and help him to conform to their ways. If, after a sufficient trial, he fails to submit to their discipline, or is not satisfied with their mode of life, he has only to part company with them and return quietly to his former social conditions. But unfortunately there have always been levelling sects and teachers who have held the social regulations of the primitive church to be of universal obligation, and have endeavoured to force the equalization of property on the whole Christian community. One of the first of these revolutionary sects was that of the Circumcellions, who during the reign of the emperor Constantine raised an insurrection in Africa, and plundered without compunction all possessors of property, that they might so relieve the wants of the poor. It was not without much difficulty, and after terrible murders and ravages had been committed, that they were finally suppressed. Many sects with similar aims sprung up at the period of the Reformation, such as the Hussites in Bohemia, the followers of John Ball a

England, and the Anabaptists, who, under the lead of Muntzer and Bocold, created great disorders both in Germany and in Holland. The communistic ideas which were propagated in this way by fanatical preachers contributed in no small degree to produce the English Civil War, as in the following century, when disseminated by equally fanatical writers, they helped to provoke in quick succession the American and the French Revolutions.

20. Authoritative Socialists at the present day uphold family life, and seek to promote greater concord upon earth by inducing the various orders of the social hierarchy to recognize their relationship in a kindly spirit, and mutually fulfil their obligations towards each other. The Democratic or Christian Socialists have very different aims; they think of producing harmony by abolishing all class distinctions and bringing people to a common level. In their eyes a nation, instead of being a great familyhood, ought to be a great brotherhood or universal club, the members of which are all free and equal. This is the revolutionary doctrine persistently preached in our time from hundreds of pulpits and advocated with much fervour in such journals as the *Christian Million* and the *Christian Socialist*. In recommending the communization of land and other such measures, they appeal not only to the practice of the Apostolic Church, but to earlier Jewish customs, and might just as reasonably, on the same ground, support the Mormon revival of polygamy. The Rev. Stewart Headlam recently protested against the London School Board omitting from its practical Scripture lessons the chapter in Leviticus which sets forth that the land shall be restored to its original possessors in the year of Jubilee. The *Christian Million* has the following paragraph on the same subject. " Why was Leviticus xxv., the account of the Mosaic

Jubilee, excluded from the Bible lessons of some
of our elementary schools? The chapter is truly
democratic in the highest and best sense of the
word, and it stands in strange contrast to some
modern 'jubilees.' Surely with the land question
pressing for a political solution, with 'usury'
as the known and perceived cause of our worst
social evils and dangers, we should be careful
to instruct our children in what God taught on
these subjects."

21. The following argument is advanced by
the *Christian Socialist* in behalf of a community of
goods. Its doctrine is a very hard one for the gifted
and noble worker, but encouraging for the criminal
class, since it makes robbery a justifiable act, and so
annuls individual responsibility, that an assassin
might contend that the foul deed with which he is
charged was really performed by God and
humanity:—"When a full-grown man goes to his
place 'to work for himself,' he goes indebted to a
series of social institutions for what he is. He is
not his own; he is bought with a great human
price. Follow any man as a producer, and see how
the divine and the social mix themselves inevitably
with his labour. Observe a man making a table,
for example; he shapes the pieces of wood, puts
them together, and says, 'the table is mine.' But
you notice that he did not make the wood, the tools,
the skill, the time, or any of the things essential to
the production of the table. Nor did the idea of
the table originate with him, but shaped itself in the
course of living. He may say he bought the wood
and the tools, but his purchase of the wood is a
fiction. It is a divine creation, and no one has a
right to charge for it. What he paid for when he
got the wood was only the human labour expended
in bringing it to his hand. If he paid for anything
else in the name of the price of wood, the payment

was improper. Through the wood, the time, the
light, and other divine forces necessary to the
production, God is a joint owner with him in the
table. Then through the tools and the skill
humanity is another joint owner. The tools
represent ages of experience and invention. The
skill is partly an inheritance and partly an acquire-
ment. God and humanity are the real 'creators' of
the table. The man who produced it is only their
agent and trustee. He may justly have the use of
it, but he is not its 'owner.' If there are others
who have no table he owes them the use of the table,
and has no right to any 'interest' for the loan of
it. Ownership cannot be individual, because production is collective " (vol. vii., No. 68).

22. It would not much matter if those who
advocate these views were content to carry them
out in a small way by themselves, after the manner
of the Shaker and the Moravian communities.
But our Christian Socialists, or a majority of them,
like their precursors the Anabaptists, wish to
impose their regulations on all people, whether they
are approved of or not, and make them everywhere
prevalent by physical force. They think that they
have as good a right to overthrow the existing
constitution of society by violent means as a former
generation of fighting Christians had to suppress
the Pagan institutions of the Roman Empire. In
respect to theological doctrines they are as liberal
and tolerant as Rousseau, and they are altogether
free from the asceticism of the primitive church ;
the one permanent and essential requirement of
Christianity in their eyes is, that every man shall
exalt Christ and be a good Communist. And if he
continues unorthodox in this matter, and persists
in holding private property, he must be coerced,
not by the faggot and stake, but by the guillotine,
and his possessions divided among the people. This

is the Gospel that Marat preached so successfully a hundred years ago, the Gospel that invariably finds favour with a slum population, and disposes the more lawless among them to distribute property to some extent by the pillage of shops and warehouses. It is true that our popular pulpit Socialists do not directly incite distressed people to engage in open riot, but they are always predicting an outbreak and wondering that it does not take place, and when it does occur are always ready to excuse it and accord it their sympathy. They do scarcely anything in the way of ameliorating the condition of the poor by promoting moral reform and a better system of industrial education, while there is nothing wanted on their part to minister to ignorant discontent, foster a spirit of anarchy, and light up the flames of a fanatical and destructive revolution.

23. The outcry which these modern preachers make against the tyranny of Capitalism is just as unreasonable as the old Puritan excitement against the devilish iniquity of witchcraft. Capitalism may be truly said to originate in the family; it begins with the starting help which children derive from the parents by whom they are reared. We are frequently told that all wealth is produced by labour—a proposition which is not true in reference to that which comes directly from the hand of nature—but admitting it to be so produced, how does labour get its operative force? A child would never be able to run on errands, weed a garden, mind cows and sheep, and do other little services which it is ordered to do unless it is first clothed and fed. The first employers of labour that we have any record of in the pages of history were those who, like the old patriarchs, regularly employed their own children. And in every civilized country thousands of young people at the present day are

well trained to industry and qualified to earn a living in some profession or other under parental authority. When they grow up and can act for themselves there is one of three industrial courses open before them—they may be their own masters and work independently ; they may co-operate with men of equal ability and share their joint earnings ; or they may take a subordinate position under a person of more experience and superior business capacity, on his offering them a fixed remuneration. For many thousands of hard-working men without much calculation, especially such as marry early and live from hand to mouth, the position of a wage-earner is decidedly the most profitable, or they would not cheerfully sacrifice for it their independence. A wage-earner is not expropriated and robbed, as Karl Marx teaches, nor worsted, as Mr. Ruskin would make it appear ("Munera Pulveris, p. 131"), but benefited by an advantageous industrial alliance. If a capitalist taxes the labour of the men in his employment, it is not to the extent of the increased earnings that he enables them to make ; what they get from him more than counterbalances what he gets from them, or they would very soon dissolve the connection. It sometimes happens that the gain resulting from an industrial enterprise is taken wholly by the humble wage earners, and the profit earner, who is supposed to fleece them unmercifully, has to submit to a dead loss. We never hear of the converse of this : there is no such thing as a capitalist clearing a handsome sum out of the work which he undertakes and the men in his employment getting nothing. If there were any truth in the stupid theory of capitalists being necessarily oppressors, sensible working people would be seen migrating to some part of the world where there are none to be found, but they really take the opposite course, knowing that the highest remuneration for labour is always to be obtained where there are the greatest accumulators of wealth.

24. Christian Socialists complain of the extremes of wealth and poverty which exist side by side in every civilized country ; this is not, however, as they represent, caused by wealth squeezing poverty, but by its having attracted poverty. If the rich and poor, who live near together, dwelt apart from each other, and had no intercourse, the inequality in their conditions would only be increased. Take the pauper population, the lame, halt, and blind, who are cared for and kept alive by charity in a rich country, and transfer them to a poor country where no superfluities exist for their maintenance, and the greater portion of them would speedily perish. It is said that our constitution of society tends to make the rich richer and the poor poorer. In reality it does nothing of the kind ; it permits all classes to better their condition if they are disposed to do so, and the different rates of progress which are made only arise from people being by nature differently endowed. The sturdy rustics, who race for small prizes at a village fair, generally stand in line and start together from a common goal, but on getting fairly off the evenness in their rank is not long maintained ; some are seen to forge ahead while others lag behind, and the farther they go the more are the front and rear men drawn apart from each other. Very similar is the order of progress in the great march of civilization ; people are not like gifted either physically or morally ; some individuals get on faster than others in ameliorating their condition, and it is the same with communities, and the unevenness thus established between them naturally increases with time. Among the Zulus and other primitive races the difference in rank and intelligence is compara-

tively slight, the king and his state officers are elevated but very little above the rest of the people. But in each succeeding generation the superior and inferior classes become somewhat more divided and distinguishable. Only let such rude peoples continue to flourish and attain a high civilization, and their occupations will become diversified, their possessions will vary till they have eventually as many social grades rising one above another as there are terraces on the Great Pyramid.

25. The improvement of their material condition which is effected by energetic and thoughtful people may in some instances prove detrimental to their sluggish neighbours, who are unwilling to exert themselves and make any corresponding progress. Thus when European settlers reclaim a distant wilderness they benefit themselves and the world at large, but the savage native inhabitants, who refuse to profit by the agricultural lessons presented to them, find in awhile their hunting-ground reduced so that they gradually retire and their numbers decrease. A like melancholy picture of displacement and decadence may be seen in the midst of civilized communities, where an ignorant, prejudiced, and dilatory class of people fail to readily adapt themselves to new circumstances and advance with the times. Every step of human progress necessarily disturbs old arrangements, and is therefore likely to inconvenience and throw out of gear some of the more laggard portion of the community. The improvements effected in spinning and weaving in the early part of the present century deprived many textile workers of their customary employment and incited them to carry on a ruthless war against machinery, just as savages fight against the introduction of fences and agriculture. At a more recent period the rapid construction of railways took away the

employment of thousands who were dependent on the old mode of conveyance, and, where they could not take readily to some new occupation, distressed them greatly and even shortened their lives. These various sufferers from collision with the wheels of progress are often simple inoffensive people entitled to a great deal of pity and charity, and they should be helped as far as possible to get on their legs again and recover themselves, but it cannot be made out that they are actually wronged by the changes which have proved adverse to their conservative interests so as to have any claim to judicial compensation.

26. Much is said by the preachers of Christian Socialism on the economic disadvantages and other evils resulting from *Competition*. But though human rivalries may be beneficially restrained and modified to some extent, they cannot be entirely got rid of without a sacrifice of liberty to which the world will not willingly submit. Single men are constantly competing one against the other for wives, and single women are striving in like manner for husbands, and how can we manage by legislative or any other means to put an end to the strife? A great deal of jealousy, mortification, and agonizing distress comes from it: murder is sometimes committed as one of its results, and it not unfrequently leads to madness, suicide, and premature death. Yet we cannot get opposing suitors to renounce their freedom of choice, and submit to be paired authoritatively: all that may be hoped for is to train them to compete sensibly, to respect the claims of their rivals, and to bear disappointment without overmuch grief. Competition stimulates people, as nothing else would, to make the best of themselves and afford pleasure and satisfaction to others. Lovers would be slovenly if they had no rivals, students would be idle, servants neglectful.

masters overbearing, and tradesmen would impose on their customers rather than study to oblige. In primitive colonial communities, as well as in small towns and in remote country villages, great extortion is often practised by a trader or professional man who has the field to himself and is able to command a monopoly. If no restraining authority exists to prevent people so circumstanced from taking undue advantage of their neighbours' needs, it is only by a rival stepping in that they will ever be brought to revise their tariff and content themselves with moderate charges. Hence in all communities that have suffered more or less from monopolist impositions it is common to hear the saying "Competition is good for the public," and no adage commands a more general acceptance.

27. In most of our large towns, however, quite an opposite state of things exists at the present day; people have hardly had any experience of the evils of monopoly, while competition is so keen in some trades that profits are not only rendered moderate, but reduced so low as to be hardly sufficient to support life. The only true remedy for the suffering in such case is to lessen the industrial pressure, to diminish the competition by well-distributed migration and emigration; but the Kingsley school, instead of directing their efforts wisely in this way, have raised a howl against the operation of economic laws and the universal striving to buy cheaply, that is, to get things at the market rates. They might just as reasonably stand by and denounce the cruelty of the law of gravitation when a number of rash youths, without calculating correctly their strength and their prospects, have plunged beyond their depth into a rough rolling sea. Where grown-up people have not sense enough to place themselves wisely on the earth's surface for obtaining the means of

subsistence they ought to be dealt with as children. Many years ago there were a number of Christian saints in Syria who perched regularly on the tops of pillars, and the neighbouring people held them in great veneration, and were very assiduous in ministering to their wants. At the present day such anchorites, instead of being well waited on, would probably be told in an unceremonious manner to come down and work. Yet even now we have thousands of shiftless men as well as women who persist in settling where they are not in the least wanted, and have scarcely any better prospect of earning an honest living than if they were located on pillar tops. Carlyle has said that working horses are always valuable, while working men in this confused world are often so little in request that they become a burden on society, and suggest the desirability of persuading them to go and hang themselves. This is because horses are wisely distributed; if they were permitted to crowd to certain places without direction according to their humour, and remain there for an indefinite period whether wanted or not, so far from being valued more than men in the same plight, we should soon see them shot down as a nuisance.

28. If workpeople and others are only rightly distributed, so that there is no excessive competition or industrial congestion, they ought to experience no distress. This happy condition of things may be witnessed in certain well-governed localities. Some years ago an agricultural parish in a central part of England belonged entirely to one benevolent gentleman, who constantly studied the welfare of his dependent people. He settled all disputes that arose among them and maintained a good school for their children at his own expense. He had one grocer's shop, or general store, in the village conducted by an honest tradesman, who, on

the condition of his selling good articles at the market price, was protected from competition. Carpenter, smith, tailor, and what few other artizans the village contained, were under precisely the same regulations; they had no fear of rivals stepping in, but were bound to render fair and efficient service, and both they and the agricultural population were seen to prosper and get on harmoniously together. Competition might very well be regulated in the same way by the municipal authorities of a town, and the number of traders and artisans protected from hurtful pressure on the condition of their properly discharging their duty. The Government has done much of late years to secure elementary schools from hurtful rivalry, and at the same time to increase their efficiency by regular inspection. Competition between railways has been authoritatively limited and regulated with no less beneficial results. Hundreds of lines are projected by scheming adventurers where they are not really wanted and there is not the slightest prospect of their being remunerative. But any such line will serve the purpose of the schemers if it can only allure investors for its construction, or be worked in such a way as to annoy some other company and force it to buy up the annoyance. Government, therefore, although sometimes imposed upon, generally refuses to sanction such ill-concerted enterprises: it agrees to protect the really useful companies from injurious competition on the condition that the public shall receive from them liberal treatment and fairly share their advantages.

29. But because Government, or an impartial magistrate, can thus regulate competition advantageously in the interest of the general public, it affords no warrant for any body of selfish traders or workers attempting to regulate it in their own interest. While the municipal authorities of a town

might be deemed competent to decide whether any more shops of a certain class are needed for the accommodation of the inhabitants, such decision would not be safely left to the shopkeepers themselves, since they would aim at limiting their number as much as possible, to create a monopoly and enhance the price of their goods. In short, they would want to check competition for the purpose of raising things to an artificial value so as to cheat the public, having precisely the same end in view as those who give deficient weight and measure or practise adulteration. Four hundred years ago such a system of fraudulent restriction was actually carried on in England by a number of affiliated societies called Trade Guilds, till the public would no longer endure their unjust monopolies, and they were suppressed by legislative enactment. "The decline of the guilds," says Wade, "like that of most other oppressions, resulted from an endeavour to exercise a power incompatible with the general welfare. Their object was to promote the interest of their own monopolies by the sacrifice of the interests of the community. This was conspicuous in the selfish and contracted policy with which they opposed the admission of apprentices, against which several statutes in the reigns of Henry VII. and Henry VIII. were specially directed" ("History of the Working Classes," chap. xii).

30. Carlyle has rightly said that there were some good moral features in the old Trade Guilds, but that the Trades Unions which have succeeded them "are avowedly for increase of wages alone; of thievery, knavery, botchery, meeting in the work done." In short these societies are an attempt on the part of banded working people to revive the guilds in a more aggravated form. They not only combine to keep up the rate of wages, but, to make this end more attainable, widen their conspiracy

against the public by urging their masters to further combine and keep up the rate of profits. A body of discontented colliers, when told that the state of trade will not admit of any increase in their wages, demand that the price of coals shall be raised a shilling a ton, and the employers in several instances have actually been driven to take concerted action and carry out their behest. The ironmasters have in like manner been dictated to by their workmen and forced to raise the price of iron goods, and the same artificial enhancement has been brought about by the action of unionism in many other industries, to the disadvantage of the public. Men in combination have also gone so far as to insist on their masters discharging all non-unionist hands from their employment and in limiting the number of their apprentices. In short, they have been seeking in various ways to force on their employers a narrow protectionist policy and practically revive the old industrial monopolies of the middle ages. Moreover, they despise law, and do not hesitate to take advantage of their employers and the public by resorting to intimidation and violence. Mr. Voysey, a warm-hearted friend of the working class, says in one of his discourses, "No sensible or just person will find any fault with labourers who, dissatisfied with their wages, demand an increase from their employers. They have a perfect right to do this, and also a perfect right to combine together voluntarily to refuse to work except at their own terms. No one, I say, can justly find fault with this in a country which professes to be free. But when these men, having refused to do the work offered, venture to prevent other men from accepting it who are willing and glad to take it on the terms offered, then surely they are wholly in the wrong, violating all the traditions and laws of freedom; yes, violating that very freedom under whose protection they live, and setting up a tyranny not to be endured for a moment in a land like ours" ("Theistic Sermons," vol. xiii., No. 9).

31. There may be some few Christian ministers who would endorse these just views, but the majority of such have not the moral courage to publicly avow them from the pulpit. When a strike occurs and numbers of poor men are being maltreated and mobbed away from their employment by ruffianly picketers, a certain portion of the clergy will meekly look on and not venture to express an opinion. They will refer to the text, "Man, who made me a judge or a divider over you"? (Luke xii. 14), and say, as the Rev. Harry Jones did at a recent Church Congress, "after this high and suggestive example, the Church has no business to offer, and no call to accept the office of judge in the settlement of money disputes." Those, however, who form the Christian Socialist party—such as Cardinal Manning, Canon Scott Holland, and Canon Wilberforce—boldly take up a position by the side of labour agitators, and pander in like manner to an outbreak of mob violence in order to acquire popularity. They justify strikes which are rendered successful by a resort to picketing and intimidation, and contend that only in this way can the industrial population cope with the tyranny of capitalism. They assure us that poor working men are too feeble to stand alone and bargain with their employers individually; it is necessary that they should combine for that purpose so that they may obtain better terms.

32. These Christian prelates look upon what is commonly called hard bargaining as a very great iniquity, although arranged by mutual consent, and yet will approve of a bargain which men force on their employers by violence. It may be very reprehensible, as we all know, for one man to aim

at profiting commercially by another's distress, if it be very urgent and exceptional distress. When a neighbour's house is on fire or his life is in imminent danger, we must not think of offering him help on hard terms, as Jacob did to Esau, but proceed promptly to his succour without any thought of compensation. We are under no such obligation, however, to assist all who happen to be in straitened circumstances. Ordinary poverty, if it fails to obtain help from private friends, meets with no favour or consideration in the world's market, and it is not to be expected that it should. Certain small and needy hop-planters in my neighbourhood are often forced to sell their growths at a disadvantage, while those who can afford to wait will obtain a better price. A shopkeeper, if hard pressed by creditors, may be compelled to dispose of a portion of his stock at a considerable sacrifice. And working people, who from some cause or other happen to be in a destitute condition, are often glad to snatch at any poor employment that offers, and earn low wages which at other times they would have been sure to refuse. Such people are not unfairly dealt with : all who sell their goods or their labour very cheaply, under the force of circumstances, will be seen to sell very dearly when once there comes a turn of fortune and they find themselves standing on a vantage ground.

33. A poor man can make his own bargains as an individual quite as effectively as his rich neighbour ; in all the little commercial transactions of life he will be found quite able to take care of himself, if he is not shrewd enough to take advantage of others. When he goes to make shop purchases he needs no union secretary behind him to insure his getting satisfactory terms. Nor does he find it desirable to force down prices by combination pressure after the manner of the Parisian mobs in 1793. The

x

shopkeeper will be reluctant to impose on him or in any way disoblige him, lest he should transfer his custom elsewhere. When he hires a lodging or a house there is no pressing necessity for him to join a tenant's league for the purpose of reducing his rent, as the Campaigners have done in Ireland. For if he is too high rented or not justly dealt with in any way, a more liberal landlord will receive him with open arms, as honest tenants are always in request. Nor is there any better reason for his having associated support in dealing with those who undertake to requite him periodically for his industry. An employer, who understands his own interest, will always be disposed to conciliate a good workman by granting any reasonable request rather than treat him in a way that will be likely to result in the loss of his services. There is unquestionably more justice done to workpeople when dealt with individually than when treated collectively, because in the former case character is properly taken account of, whereas good men and bad are confounded when they act under combination. Many thousands of people are engaged independently in various offices throughout the country—as surveyors, inspectors, managers, clerks, secretaries, teachers, travellers, servants, labourers, &c.—and they are not, for want of unionism, squeezed and oppressed. If discontented they can soon leave, and if they give satisfaction it will be profitable to offer them some inducement to cling to their posts; it is a general rule in such cases to increase their remuneration from time to time in proportion to the increased value of their services. This rule of graduated and correlative advancement is followed by the Government in all its civil departments, and a more just system of compensating people for their labour could not possibly be devised. In the army it is also carried

out even down to the lowest ranks; a deserving
soldier always has before him a prospect of increased emolument, and under such a regulation
men are encouraged to do their best and steadily
advance in efficiency. But the jealous spirit of
unionism discourages improving efforts, it recognizes no industrial superiority, and aims at keeping
all men on the same communistic level; there
must be no such thing as individual promotion, but
a uniform rise for the combined mass, wholly irrespective of merit.

34. Under the ordinary non-unionist engagements
good masters generally become associated with
good men, and bad masters with bad men, so that
character on both sides obtains the recognition
which it ought to receive. But it is the disposition
of unionism to hinder this true assortment of
associated workers, to ignore distinctions of
character, and to lump people together in classes
as though they were all morally alike. It is
desirable that employers should have a frequent
intercourse with their men individually in order to
keep up a good understanding with them, and
where differences of opinion exist among a large
body of men, in no other way is it possible to
ascertain the strength of a formulated demand.
This, however, is just what the agitators endeavour
to prevent by all possible means; they are constantly
fomenting a spirit of ignorant distrust and stubborn
unfriendliness; it is their aim to keep men and
masters apart in two hostile camps glaring fiercely
at each other, and having scarcely any exchange of
views but through an occasional treaty which
themselves shall be privileged to negotiate. It is
pretty generally admitted outside trade-union
circles, that people who are associated as employers
and employed ought as far as posible to maintain
friendly relations and study to promote each other's

x 2

welfare. But if they are selfish in their dispositions and fail to discharge their duty towards each other reciprocally, war is not likely to improve their relations ; they will not be coerced into doing what is right or become more amiable and agreeable when smarting under deliberately inflicted injuries. If they cannot be reconciled, their only proper course is to separate and form re-engagements with the view to securing greater harmony. The man who displeases one employer may suit another admirably ; when Smith and Jones fail to agree, Smith and Brown may get on satisfactorily together, and Jones may have no serious quarrel when he becomes associated with Robinson. It is the aim of unionism, however, to prevent such wise separation and readjustment in the interest of peace ; an employer is not allowed to part with a man who displeases him, but is compelled to discharge one who is friendly and devoted to his interest ; masters and men, instead of working together amicably, must be as ill-mated as possible, so as to be kept in perpetual discord.

35. We all know that injured people have sometimes rightly combined to defeat a strong oppressor, just as a flock of small birds will mob away a predatory hawk, but the various trade combinations which have been established are themselves notoriously engines of oppression. A large proportion of those who join the organizations would much rather be free men, but are compelled to join under a remorseless system of persecution. And having been made recruits by a unionist press-gang, they are forced against their will to make weekly contributions to a military chest and engage any day at brief notice in an industrial war which may involve them in the greatest misery. We are told that trade combinations are necessary before all things for the purpose of checking competition.

But why should competition be forcibly restrained to favour any particular section of the community? What right have we to prevent our fellow-men from competing with us in a free open field of industry, and so arrogate to ourselves exclusive privileges? Those who do not scruple to act in this way can have hardly any better notion of equity than a tribe of lawless savages. The first industrial combination that happened to come under my notice was that of a party of rustic gleaners, who both intellectually and morally were not much superior to Hottentots. Poor cottagers glean after harvest in different parts of the country under different regulations; four families were on this occasion permitted to glean together in a wheat stubble, but on being left to themselves three of them combined for the improvement of their position, and mobbed the other out of the field. No combination on the part of skilled artisans or any other class, relying on physical force or a resort to open war for the attainment of their ends, can have any better claim to respect.

36. Where a civilized government exists and law and order are regularly maintained, not only is a combination on the part of any class wholly unnecessary for the purpose of securing justice for that class in the great struggle of life, but it will be found to contribute in an unmistakable manner to the promotion of injustice. Both at Perak and Labuan it has been found necessary to break up the Chinese secret societies, which, so long as they held together, baffled the police, shielded offenders, and rendered altogether powerless and ineffective the magisterial authority. In some parts of China beggars are said to band themselves together on unionist principles for the purpose of unfairly increasing their gains. A group of them will persistently blockade the door of a shop so as to prevent any more customers from

entering, till the poor annoyed shopkeeper is induced to come forth and negotiate for the resumption of commercial freedom by paying a sufficient ransom. They are also accustomed to surround a person whom they meet in a lone place, and so worry and prevent him from making further progress till he reluctantly accedes to their demands. It might be argued that such stratagems are necessary in the great struggle for existence, and enable the poor to get more liberal treatment• from their prosperous neighbours than they would do by soliciting alms individually. It is clear, however, that when beggars make separate appeals for relief there is a much greater probability of their all being treated fairly according to their deserts. Their combination stratagems, which are only a modified system of highway robbery, are likely to harden people's hearts against them. And if it could be shown that in the long run they got increased alms by their method of extortion, they could not be permanently benefited or socially elevated by proceedings which must necessarily tend to their demoralization.

37. It has always been considered the duty of a civilized government to maintain order among the whole of its subject population, and not allow one citizen to molest, assault, or make war upon another. This is generally well accomplished so far as individuals and small parties are concerned, but where a multitude conspire to gain their ends by a resort to violence they are less easily laid hold of and judicially curbed. In Greece, at a comparatively recent period, brigands were able to set the laws at defiance from having a considerable amount of political influence and being well supported by popular sympathy. It is from similar causes that the land-leaguers of Ireland have managed to carry on a system of disguised robbery in that country and treat the authority of the magistrates with contempt. And

in our own country bands of ruffianly picketers have taken upon themselves almost as much liberty of action as foreign invaders would have done, and have laughed at the opposing efforts of the police. It is not surprising that such lawless combinations should receive as a *quid pro quo* the support of politicians any more than that ordinary criminals should secure special pleaders to advocate their cause. But here, as well as in Ireland and in Greece, the confederated law-breakers have received the heartiest encouragement from Christian ministers who have taken up the *rôle* of the revolutionary agitator with the view to acquire popularity. There may be some excuse for priests acting as partisan advocates where they are entirely dependent on one section or class of the community for support. But an established national clergy, who are placed in an independent position, ought to be as strictly impartial as government magistrates, and, in any dispute arising between class and class, should rebuke wrong on either side and endeavour to bring about reconciliation and peace. This is done, it must be admitted, by some ministers who are specially endowed with good sense, but those who engage in Communistic agitation are at present a growing party, and they are constantly reminding us that Christianity, whatever it may accomplish in the way of purity and charity, is not a religion of justice, nor one well fitted to impart moral strength to the poor and permanently ameliorate their condition.

38. Christian Socialists are for the most part very benevolent, and very sympathetic towards human suffering, yet their mistaken meddling in behalf of their impoverished countrymen often tends to aggravate their woes. There is perhaps not a more noble and generous feeling in the human breast than that of chivalry—the spirit which urges us to

protect the poor, the weak, and the vanquished from oppression, and, if those imbued with it were at the same time always wise and discriminating, they would be true ministers of justice and confer on society an unmixed good. But unfortunately—as Cervantes has taught us in " Don Quixote "— people who are warm-hearted and very chivalrous are not always proportionately wise. In their eagerness to redress wrong they are very apt to let their generous feelings carry away their judgment, and so fall into all sorts of indiscretions. When chivalry degenerates into what is called knight-errantry, it commits the egregious mistake of over-looking the moral grounds of every quarrel and invariably ranging itself on what is supposed to be the weaker side. People in humble circumstances may be very gentle, innocent, and unselfish, and those who lord it over them may be proud, covetous, and tyrannical, yet this is by no means so generally the case as the knight-errant is prone to imagine. On the contrary, those who hold a ruling position in the world, such as teachers, managers, proprietors, organizers of industry, and others, are presumably, by the very fact of their having such a position, more virtuous and wise than their subordinates. Human beings who cannot get on well independently, and find it needful to submit to the direction of others, are not in general the most far-sighted and reflective. They have to be looked after, instructed, told of their faults, kept to their duty, and only the little unpleasantness of being reproved occasionally or not permitted to have their own way, is liable to be regarded by the hot-tempered as a grievance. The amount of service required of them, and the amount of remuneration offered for it will always afford to some, if not for all, a permanent ground for discontent. Disputes between employers and employed are therefore, from the

nature of their relationship, pretty sure to occur
everywhere, and the former are sometimes guilty
of manifest injustice and deserve the greater blame.
But if they were not on the whole more reasonable
and conciliatory than the combinations whom
agitators influence, and more desirous of avoiding
injurious conflicts, the position which they hold
could not possibly be maintained long, and great
organized industries would soon fall to pieces.

39. Our frequent labour troubles, like many other
social evils, may be said to originate largely from
the bad home training or parental neglect which
numbers of the young generation experience. At
nearly every school complaints will be heard of the
great difficulty of managing and contenting a
certain portion of the children who have been
reared in utter lawlessness. Those who form our
violent combinations of strikers and leaguers at the
present day are only unruly boys grown up to be
turbulent men, and transferring the hostility which
they once entertained against the school teacher to
the employer, the magistrate, and the police. Their
aim is to be free from restraint, to counterwork
the efforts of all who are in a position of authority,
to thwart and circumvent them in such a crafty
manner as to render the maintenance of order
nearly impossible. In the proceedings of moon-
lighters in the west of Ireland, in the unionist
atrocities perpetrated in some of our large manu-
facturing towns, and in the destructive riots that
have occurred on certain railways, we may see the
budding ruffianism of bands of schoolboys fully
developed. The adult combinators have the same
intimidation of witnesses which they practised in
their youth, the same tyrannical pressure to force
the better disposed to enter their ranks, the same
barbarity, only carried to greater lengths, in their
mode of inflicting punishment; and the idea that

they are driven to such courses by genuine oppression, however well it may serve political purposes, is one of the greatest delusions ever propagated.. So perverted has the public judgment become in these days of perpetual agitation and demagogy, that what is deemed most culpable from a moral point of view in the conduct of an individual is not only excused, but considered commendable on the part of a multitude.

"The wrong a bad man does with shame a mob will do with
  pride.
Thus English working men arrange extorting combinations,
And Irish leagues their land disputes by outrage force decide,
  And shield their incapacity and shirk their obligations.

"And priests will favour in a mob what in a man they blame;
  The haughty, proud, imperious lord is now no longer dreaded.
The loftiest kings are looked upon as bears and lions tame,
  And courtiers only cringe and bow to tyrants many-headed.

THE NEW KORAN:

A BOOK OF INSTRUCTION FOR RELIGIOUS REFORMERS,

in Scriptural Style and Arrangement.

POST 8VO., PP. 672. 5S.

" 'The New Koran' is exactly the opposite of the 'Book of Mormon.' Its narratives are short and varied, interesting and life-like, and there is not a page or a paragraph without its useful lessons. It is as readable as ' Robinson Crusoe,' and as instructive as Theodore Parker's Sermons. And its lessons are generally of the most valuable description, and put in the most intelligible and taking forms. In religion, in morals, and in politics you have the genuine inspiration of the spirit of wisdom and benevolence. And it is fitted for people of various ages and all stations. Young and old, rich and poor, rulers and subjects, may read it with equal pleasure and equal profit."—*Barker's Review.*

" The writer is intelligent, clever, and conscientious—aye, much more conscientious than many a professor of a ceremonial faith. His aims are excellent in the direction of peacemaking and toleration, and his labours merit recognition, however much we may differ in matters of faith. He speaks through the mouthpiece of one Jaido Morata, who is a preacher to all nations travelling over the habitable globe, calling all religionists to a sense of brotherly feeling, denouncing their vices and follies, and exhorting them to pursue the paths of rectitude. The work is eminently readable, is far from being pedantic or dogmatic, and displays an amount of keen reflection that proves the writer to be an astute thinker and profound observer of the actions and thoughts of Jews, Christians, and Mohammedans. He exhibits a knowledge of Jewish matters and peculiarities that is truly surprising."—*Jewish World.*

" 'The New Koran,' it should be stated, is not altogether a new book. It was originally published some years since, but at that time experienced the usual fate of books recommended solely by their merit. Its emergence from neglect is highly creditable to the discernment of the few who have not suffered it to be forgotten; and we very sincerely trust that it

S

diffusion will not be retarded by what a liberal mind ought to regard as the eminent merit of sturdy independence of all the reigning schools of thought. It is a rare pleasure to encounter an author capable of thinking so resolutely for himself. Though independent he is so far from unsocial that one of the principal objects of the republication of the work is stated to be the encouragement of religious reformers to collective action more or less after the pattern exhibited by Jaido Morata. Without entering on so large a subject here, we may affirm that whenever a congregation of the description contemplated does assemble, it will find 'The New Koran' much better adapted for employment in its services than the old one. Objective, dramatic, impressive, aphoristic, pregnant with thought, and transparent in expression, it has every requisite for public recitation, while far more than a 'forty parson power' of homilising would be needed to exhaust its manifold suggestiveness."—Dr. Richard Garnett, in the *Examiner*.

MONARCHY DEFENDED :

A Treatise for Revolutionary Times.

CLOTH 8VO., PP. XV.–230. 2s. 6d.

"His arguments in favour of hereditary constitutional monarchy, as contrasted with various forms of republicanism, have been repeatedly urged and have certainly weight. A form of government cannot be pronounced good or bad in the abstract, as in the way of debating societies, but must be considered in relation to the people governed and their circumstances. . . . . . Mr. Vickers remarks that a city community is apt to be more democratic than a rural community, not so much from its possession of higher intelligence as from its lower organization, which allows men to be independent of their neighbours, and so indirectly encourages many to live by actual crime. Hereditary monarchy has, he argues, as much to say for itself as any elective arrangement, which in many cases is a notorious failure, and leads merely to the advancement of the noisy and forward, who are often very ignorant and incompetent."—*Spectator*.

" Those who desire a really able *résumé* of the arguments in favour of a constitutional monarchy and at the same time the completest answer to those who bid us look to the Republics of other countries—notably that of America—cannot do better than procure Mr. Vickers's book. . . . . The chapters in which incompetence, economy, wars, and progress are respectively considered and contrasted under the Monarchical and the Republican *régimes* are specially worthy of study."—*Northampton Herald.*

" His defence of monarchy is a very able one. . . . . We admire throughout his calm and powerful argumentative style and felicity of language. His book, too, gives evidence of great and varied historical research, and of clear and matured thought. He evidently knows the labouring classes, and especially the agricultural labourers, well; and although he does not flatter them he writes of them as a well-wisher and a true friend. His book is eminently a thought-provoking one, and deserves to be widely read."—*Mark Lane Express.*

THE HISTORY OF HEROD:

Another look at a man emerging from twenty centuries of calumny.

CLOTH 8vo., PP. XXVII.–360. 6s.

" The puzzle which he has set himself, and which he has certainly executed with some skill, is to detect and exhibit the real Herod—the patriotic statesman, philosophic thinker, illuminated theologian, liberal critic, ecclesiastical reformer, amiable kinsman, and generally good and great man—whose noble countenance is veiled behind the scowls and grimaces of the accepted caricature."—*Saturday Review.*

" Although the writer adds no new matter to the story told by Josephus, and although he takes the part of an advocate rather than that of a judge, yet his reading of the text is so fair, and the consequent inferences are so reasonable, that he may justly be held to have earned for his client the favourable verdict of posterity. . . . . . None but an able soldier, a consummate diplomatist, and a just statesman, could have acquired, as Herod undoubtedly did, the confidence of the successive rulers of the Roman world, and the respect of his subjects, as evinced by the tranquillity of his kingdom during the greater part of a long reign and the anarchy which followed his death. . . . . . Our thanks are due to Mr. Vickers for having produced an exceedingly lively and well-written account of the epoch."— *Westminster Review.*

"To all impressed with the justice of the ancient aphorism ' Audi alteram partem,' we would commend the perusal of this really remarkable volume."—*Knowledge.*

"There can be no doubt that one will be better able to judge intelligently not only of Herod as a man and a ruler, but also of the Jewish nation from the time of the return from Babylon to its final overthrow by the Romans, after reading this book. In the case of a ruler whose reputation has come to us only through the word of bitter enemies it is but fair to cross-examine the witnesses."—*The Unitarian* (Chicago).